THE INVENTION OF
ANCIENT ISRAEL

THE INVENTION
OF ANCIENT
ISRAEL

The silencing of Palestinian history

Keith W. Whitelam

London and New York

First published 1996
by Routledge
11 New Fetter Lane, London EC4P 4EE

Simultaneously published in the USA and Canada
by Routledge
29 West 35th Street, New York, NY 10001

First published in paperback 1997

Reprinted 2001 (twice), 2003

Routledge is an imprint of the Taylor & Francis Group

© 1996 Keith W. Whitelam

Typeset in Garamond by
Ponting–Green Publishing Services, Chesham, Bucks
Printed and bound in Great Britain by
St Edmundsbury Press Ltd, Bury St Edmunds, Suffolk

British Library Cataloguing in Publication Data
A catalogue record for this book is available from
the British Library

Library of Congress Cataloguing in Publication Data
A catalogue record for this book is available from
the Library of Congress

ISBN 0-415-10758-X (hbk)
ISBN 0-415-10759-8 (pbk)

CONTENTS

ACKNOWLEDGEMENTS

This work has been a long time in the making, which is only fitting given the historical perspective which it adopts. I began work on it in late 1984 when the manuscript of *The Emergence of Early Israel in Historical Perspective* was finished and have continued whenever time has been available. I am particularly grateful to the University of Stirling for two invaluable periods of leave in 1989 and 1993, and to my colleagues in the Department of Religious Studies who had to take over my teaching and administrative duties. It was only during the last period of sabbatical leave that the work took on its present shape, changing from an attempt to produce a history of ancient Palestine to an exploration of how such an enterprise was hindered by political, social, and religious influences.

This book is indebted to so many people, directly and indirectly, that I could not possibly name them all. Robert Coote has continued to provide invaluable support, constructive criticism, and advice. He, along with Polly, Margaret, and Marion Coote, have frequently provided a vital home from home on my visits to the annual SBL meeting or to conduct research in the Bay Area. Marvin Chaney, Bob's colleague at San Francisco Theological Seminary, has been a valuable sounding board for ideas.

The direction of my research was stimulated and sustained some fifteen years ago by the lively atmosphere generated by the members of the SBL/ASOR seminar on the sociology of the Israelite monarchy. I am indebted to Norman Gottwald for the original invitation to participate and for his openness and help in subsequent years. I was welcomed and befriended by Frank Frick, Jim Flanagan, and Tom Overholt who made those first visits to the USA such a pleasant experience and who have remained valued friends. I owe an equal debt to many colleagues in Britain: Philip Davies, David Clines,

ACKNOWLEDGEMENTS

Robert Carroll, Alistair Hunter, and Lester Grabbe have been very supportive over many years. David Gunn, who inhabits both worlds, has provided valuable encouragement and comment on this project and the early direction of my research.

My colleagues at Stirling, Richard King, Ian Reader, Mary Maaga, Jennifer Haswell, John Drane, and Murray MacBeath have provided constructive comments and suggestions on early drafts of the opening chapters. Richard King and Mary Maaga not only offered critiques but loaned me books and articles which have helped in the production of the manuscript.

The greatest debt, of course, is owed to my family. Stephen, Paul, and Hannah have had to live with the project for a long time. This book could not have been written without the love, support, and help of Susie. It is fittingly dedicated to her.

INTRODUCTION:
THE SILENCING OF
PALESTINIAN HISTORY

This book began as part of a grandiose scheme to produce a two-volume history of ancient Palestine dealing with the material realities, the ideologies, and religions of the region. Its concern with the broad themes of history – settlement, demography, and economy – was conceived to be an antidote to the standard histories of ancient Israel based upon the biblical traditions which have dominated biblical studies since the nineteenth century. It became apparent, however, as I searched for archaeological and anthropological data in order to produce the first volume, that this grandiose scheme was doomed to failure. The first problem, of course, is that such an attempt to write a history of Palestine, as an alternative to the standard histories of Israel which have dominated nineteenth- and twentieth-century biblical studies, runs the risk of being misunderstood as arrogant because it appears to imply the ability to control a vast range of material which is beyond the competence of most individuals and certainly beyond my abilities. It was such a grand scheme that first tempted me when I began work on this book. However, the failure and metamorphosis of the project was due not just to an inability to become acquainted with or competent in, let alone to dream of mastering or controlling, the vast amounts of data necessary for such a task. It stems from a more fundamental problem: the recognition that any such project has to confront and overcome the vast obstacle of what might be termed 'the discourse of biblical studies', a part of the complex network of scholarly work which Said identified as 'Orientalist discourse'. The history of ancient Palestine has been ignored and silenced by biblical studies because its object of interest has been an ancient Israel conceived and presented as the taproot of Western civilization.

This work, then, is not another history of ancient Israel nor is it a

1

history of ancient Palestine. It is concerned with the histories of both but it cannot be described as a history of either. They are of central concern and figure largely in the following pages, but the eventual outcome, however much I might have liked, cannot be described as a history of ancient Palestine. The words of Oliver Cromwell to the Rump Parliament during the debate on reconstruction after the execution of King Charles I have often occurred to me while struggling with the methodological and practical difficulties of the task I set myself: 'I can tell you, sirs, what I would not have but I cannot what I would.' Cromwell's audience was, of course, all male. This work is aimed at trying to articulate a view of history which includes the whole of humanity and is not simply the domain of a few powerful or influential males. In exposing the cultural and political obstacles to the task, it is an attempt to pave the way for the realization of, to paraphrase Prakash (1990: 401), one more of the 'excluded histories'.[1]

It is an attempt to articulate an idea: the idea that ancient Palestinian history is a separate subject in its own right and needs to be freed from the grasp of biblical studies. It is appropriate to refer to it as an idea since it is not as yet a practical reality. For too long Palestinian history has been a (minor) subset of biblical studies dominated by the biblically inspired histories and archaeologies of ancient Israel. In effect, Palestinian history, particularly for the thirteenth century BCE to the second century CE, has not existed except as the backdrop to the histories of Israel and Judah or of second Temple Judaism. It has been subsumed within the social, political and, above all, religious developments of ancient Israel. The search for ancient Israel, in which I include for shorthand purposes second Temple Judaism, has consumed phenomenal intellectual and material resources in our universities, faculties of theology, divinity schools, theological colleges, seminaries, and departments of archae-ology, particularly in the USA, Europe, and Israel. A quick glance through the prospectuses and catalogues of these institutions will reveal numerous courses on the history and archaeology of ancient Israel conducted in the context of the study of the Hebrew Bible from Jewish and Christian perspectives. This is just as true in 'secular' universities with departments of Religious Studies rather than fac-ulties of theology. Interestingly, and revealingly, I have been able to discover very few courses on the history of ancient Israel in de-partments of History or Ancient History. It seems that ancient

Israelite history is the domain of Religion or Theology and not of History.

Where, then, do we find courses on the history of ancient Palestine? Certainly, there is an increasing number of courses on Palestinian archaeology in departments of Archaeology, particularly in the USA. They have emerged from the often bitter debate over the existence of 'Syro–Palestinian' archaeology as opposed to 'biblical archaeology' inspired by W.G. Dever.[2] But the history of ancient Palestine, it seems, does not fall under the domain of either Theology or History in our institutions of higher education. In effect, as an academic subject it appears not to exist: it has been silenced and excluded by the dominant discourse of biblical studies. The marginal nature of ancient Palestinian history can be illustrated by reference to the excellent bibliography of the major histories of Israel and Judah which appears at the beginning of Hayes and Miller (1977: xxv–xxix): in a list of some sixty–five authors and works dating from the eighteenth century to the late twentieth century CE, there are only two titles which deal with the history of Syria and Palestine (Olmstead 1931; Paton 1901) rather than the history of Israel, Judah, or the Jewish/Hebrew people. It is this domination by theology, its political and cultural implications, which we must pursue in order to understand how Western scholarship has invented ancient Israel and silenced Palestinian history.[3]

In contrast to this marginal nature or non-existence of ancient Palestinian history, we might compare the pursuit of and invention of 'ancient Israel'. Biblical studies has been dominated from its inception by a concern for the history of ancient Israel as the key to understanding the Hebrew Bible. It has been of fundamental concern for Christian theology since Christianity is conceived of as a religion based upon revelation within history. Philip Davies (1992) has demonstrated, however, that the 'ancient Israel' of biblical studies is a scholarly construct based upon a misreading of the biblical traditions and divorced from historical reality. The power of scholarly texts, such as our standard treatments of the history of ancient Israel, is aptly illustrated by Said's (1985: 94) critique of Orientalism:

> A text purporting to contain knowledge about something actual, and arising out of circumstances similar to the ones I have just described, is not easily dismissed. Expertise is attributed to it. The authority of academics, institutions, and governments can accrue to it, surrounding it with still greater

prestige than its practical successes warrant. Most importantly such texts can *create* not only knowledge but also the very reality they appear to describe. In time such knowledge and reality produce a tradition, or what Michel Foucault calls a discourse, whose material presence or weight, not the originality of a given author, is really responsible for the texts produced out of it.

(Said 1985: 94)

This is equally as applicable to biblical studies as to Orientalism. There exists, then, what we might term a discourse of biblical studies which is a powerful, interlocking network of ideas and assertions believed by its practitioners to be the reasonable results of objective scholarship while masking the realities of an exercise of power. We are faced with the paradox of the invention of 'ancient Israel', as pointed out by Davies, an entity that has been given substance and power as a scholarly construct, while Palestinian history lacks substance or even existence in terms of our academic institutions. Attempts to challenge this powerful narrative are likely to be dismissed as politically or ideologically motivated and therefore unreasonable.

Why this should be so is tied very closely, I believe, to the social and political context out of which modern biblical studies has emerged. The implications of this for the study of ancient Israel and for the silencing of Palestinian history are explored in chapter 1. The exploration of the political arena in which biblical studies has been forged is little understood, much less acknowledged: it is an engagement which is only just beginning. The central theme of this study is an attempt to articulate the implications for historical research of the profound changes which biblical studies has experienced over the last two decades or more. The powerful convergence of literary studies of biblical texts allied to more explicit social scientific approaches to the construction of Israelite history has led to what many perceive as a major paradigm shift in the study of the Hebrew Bible – a shift which is more apparent than real in terms of the representation of ancient Israelite history or the realization of ancient Palestinian history. It is usual, in discussing this perceived shift, to concentrate upon the study of narrative in the Hebrew Bible and its implications for biblical studies. Thus literary studies in all its aspects has become for many, to use David Gunn's (1987: 65) term, the 'new orthodoxy'. Biblical scholars have been slower to appreciate the equally profound implications of these paradigm moves for historical studies. The election of Norman Gottwald as the President of SBL in 1992 was more than a symbolic event. It marked an acceptance of the so-called 'sociological approach' as an important element in defining the new orthodoxy.[4] What has begun to emerge in recent years, in a variety of different places, is a conception of a wider Palestinian history as a separate subject in its own right increasingly divorced from biblical studies as such.[5] This means that Israelite history and second Temple Judaism, the domain of biblical studies until very recently, form part of this Palestinian history, whereas Israelite history, under the influence of biblical studies, has dominated the Palestinian landscape to such an extent that it has silenced virtually all other aspects of the history of the region from the Late Bronze Age to the Roman period. There are, of course, times when we might say, with Braudel, that ancient Israel or, more particularly, second Temple Judaism, bursts into sight and dominates the landscape, the only way it has been conceived of for much of the history of biblical studies, but at other times plays a minor role, is hidden, or even non-existent. Viewed from the longer perspective, the history of ancient Israel is a moment in the vast expanse of Palestinian history.[6] It is appropriate for historians to focus upon these short spans of time or particular societies, of course. However, it is also necessary to stand back in order to provide a different perspective from which to view the larger picture. The study of ancient Israel has become so all-consuming that it has all too often come to represent the whole picture rather than an important detail on the canvas. It is important, then, to try to redress the balance by focusing on that period of time which has been the domain of biblical studies and which has been dominated by ancient Israelite history in order to show how it might be understood from the perspective of Palestinian history.

It is for this reason that I have decided to concentrate on two crucial periods, the periods of the so-called 'emergence' or 'origins' of Israel in Palestine during the Late Bronze–Iron Age transition and the subsequent period of the founding of an Israelite state in the Iron Age. The analysis could be carried further to include what is variably referred to as the Exilic or second Temple periods or, in terms of a wide-ranging history of Palestine, would need to move both backwards and forwards. However, the periods of the 'emergence' and the creation of a state have for a long time been a focus of biblical scholarship in its search for ancient Israel. They have become defining moments in the history of the region for the discourse of biblical studies. If these periods can be freed from the constraints and limitations of the constructions of the past imposed by this discourse, then all other (prior and subsequent) periods in the history of Palestine will be easier to free from a past claimed and dominated by Israel. The analysis of chapters 2, 3, 4, and 5 takes the form of a commentary on many standard and representative works which have shaped and been shaped by the discourse of biblical studies. It attempts to illustrate how a network of recurrent ideas and assumptions has functioned to provide a perception of the past which has resisted virtually all attempts to imagine alternative constructions of that past. I have deliberately chosen to use a large number of quotations, many of them from works familiar to those in the field, in order to illustrate the discourse of biblical studies in its own words, rather than simply my distorted reporting of what many influential figures have had to say.

Yet little attention has been paid to the factors which have led to the present situation. Current scholarly attention is focused more on trying to work out the practical implications of the shifts: the academic contest for methods and approaches in reading the Hebrew Bible or writing ancient Israelite history. It will be obvious to many readers that there is a growing number of attempts to realize a history of ancient Palestine in the works of G.W. Ahlström (1993), E. Knauf (1988; 1989), N.P. Lemche (1988; 1991), T.L. Thompson (1992a), H. Weippert (1988), and many others. It might be argued that these works and Ahlström's (1993) massive study on the history of ancient Palestine, in particular, negate my claim that Palestinian history does not exist as an academic subject. However, his work, like the others, is still dominated by the concerns of biblical studies and presuppositions drawn from the traditions of the Hebrew Bible. This is revealed most clearly in the peculiar arrangement of the book which begins with a chapter on 'Prehistoric time' ranging from the Palaeolithic to the Chalcolithic periods, followed by 'The Early Bronze Age', 'The Middle Bronze Age', 'The Late Bronze Age', but then switches to the 'Twelfth century BCE', 'The increase in settlement during the 13–12th centuries BCE', 'Transjordan in the 12–10th centuries BCE', and 'The Judges' before concentrating on the rise of the state. The switch, of course, to a more narrow focus on the thirteenth to twelfth centuries BCE, away from archaeological periodization, is due to the long-held belief by biblical scholars and archaeologists that this is the period when Israel 'emerged' in Palestine. Thus Ahlström's study, while set in the broader context of Palestinian history, remains involved in the search for early Israel that has been the goal of biblical studies since its inception. Ahlström has been a pioneer in the move towards a concern with Palestinian history, yet his volume is still conceived within the constraints of the discourse of biblical studies. The spate of recent works has helped to prepare the ground and has been particularly influential in bringing about an important change in historical studies, though they often remain on the polemical margins of the discipline when judged in terms of mainstream activities. Furthermore, they have not addressed in any detail the crucial question of the cultural and political factors which have constrained ancient Palestinian history as one of the many 'excluded histories' silenced by Eurocentric or Western constructions of the past.

One of the greatest drawbacks to the realization of a history of ancient Palestine is that even as it is freed from the constraints of biblical studies it remains the preserve of Western scholarship. Said (1985; 1992) has drawn attention to the intimate connections between culture and imperialism both in the development of Orientalism and the narratives of the West. What we lack above all is, to use his phrase, a 'contrapuntal reading' of Palestinian history from a non-Western point of view.[7] The Subaltern project is one of the most striking examples of an attempt to reclaim the past by Indian historians who claim the right to represent themselves and their past in competition with the long-dominant narratives of European and colonial scholarship.[8] The development of a modern Palestinian identity and expression of self-determination has focused upon the recent rather than the ancient past. 'Palestinian history' is concerned only with the last couple of centuries in the struggle with the Zionist movement and the realization of a modern state of Israel. The ancient past belongs to Israel since this is the way it has been presented from the inception of modern biblical studies. Modern Israeli scholarship has been concerned with the history of ancient Israel written largely from a Western and Orientalist perspective as the ancient expression of the modern state and its Jewish population. The growth of Palestinian nationalism has not resulted in an attempt to reclaim the past similar to the movements in India, Africa, or Australia. The problem here is that the notion of a 'Palestinian history' is confined to the modern period, an attempt to articulate accounts of national identity in the face of dispossession and exile.[9] It is as if the ancient past has been abandoned to Israel and the West. The concluding essay in Said's *Blaming the Victims: Spurious Scholarship and the Palestine*

Question, 'A profile of the Palestinian people' (Said *et al.* 1988), opens with the observation that Palestine had been the home to a remarkable civilization 'centuries before the first Hebrew tribes migrated to the area' (1988: 235). The achievements and nature of this civilization are passed over in a few sentences while the period of Israelite migration, a now outdated view as will be seen below, is abandoned to Israel without further comment. The authors then concentrate on the history of Palestine from the Arab and Islamic conquest of the seventh century CE to the present day. It is precisely the period from the Late Bronze Age to the Roman period which needs to be reclaimed and given voice in the history of Palestine. Asad (1993: 1) has drawn attention to the overwhelming importance of Western history in shaping the views of non-Western peoples who have 'felt obliged to read the history of the West (but not each other's histories) and that Westerners in turn do not feel the same need to study non-Western histories'. Although I might argue for an idea, the separation of ancient Palestinian history from the confines and limitations of biblical studies, the task cannot be completed until we can compare the different perspectives of Western and non-Western scholarship. The following views might represent a counterpoint to a dominant discourse that has been conducted within biblical studies but it lacks the perspective and force of a contrapuntal reading from a Palestinian or non-Western perspective. The irony and paradox of this situation is quite evident: the attempt to articulate a Palestinian history as a subject freed from the constraints of biblical studies or related discourses remains a European expression of an ancient excluded past.

The faltering movements towards a more complete history of Palestine – I refrain from referring to a 'new' history as has become fashionable – are bound to take wrong paths as well as hopefully open up new ground.[10] The failures will inevitably be seized upon by those who disagree with such a project as evidence that there are no alternatives to the standard approaches to biblical history. Yet the time is past when we can merely fine-tune the standard approaches and methods of biblical studies. What is required is a fundamental alteration in our approach to the history of the region. I would hope that my own shortcomings and failures as represented in this book will not put off others from exploring the issues which will lead us to a more satisfactory understanding of the history of this region. Biblical studies has remained removed for too long from the critical discourse that has raged within history, anthropology, ethnography, and economics, exposing the ways in which supposed rational results of Western scholarship have been part of a complex network of ideas and associations which are tied to relationships of power. The tools we have to use are imprecise and crude compared with the precision of the cliometricians with their studies of census, voting, or other forms of quantifiable data. Medieval and modern historians enjoy the comparative luxury of vast amounts of quantifiable data which have remained hidden and unused in state archives and registrary offices for decades or even centuries. New archaeological surveys of Palestine are able to provide much better quantifiable data which have added significantly to our knowledge of particular areas and periods of ancient Palestine and contributed to the paradigm shift. But the information we can glean from these surveys is still imprecise when compared to the sources available to our colleagues in medieval and modern history. The historian of ancient Palestine has to be content with understanding history in a broad sweep. This might be an uncomfortable situation for those brought up on standard biblical histories which prefer the certainties of political history with its alluring portrayal of great individuals as the shapers of historical destiny. This form of history still dominates our bookshelves and academic departments despite the work of Braudel, McNeill and the Annalistes. The cult of the individual which dominates all forms of modern politics in the USA, Britain, Europe, and elsewhere with the use of the power of television, video and satellite only confirms the prejudice that it is great men, and a few women, who shape the destiny of humanity. Any attempt to investigate the underlying currents which have helped shape the preconceptions of these individuals or help to explain their success in 'persuading' the populace to support them is dismissed as crude materialism or an unsophisticated Marxist reading of history. However, like many others in biblical studies, I have become dissatisfied with these theological and political histories that have dominated our discipline for so long. The magisterial works of Braudel, full of original insights which help fire the imagination, have taught me that there are so many facets of history that our political and theological histories do not address.[11] It was the excitement of this perspective which first allured me in the grandiose design of trying to produce a history of ancient Palestine. It only gradually became apparent that the difficulties inherent in the project needed to be related to the wider political and social context of twentieth-century scholarship.

The history of Palestine – we might say ancient history in general

– is dominated by demographic growth and decline along with the expansion and contraction of economy and trade. Unless we are able to understand these twin poles of ancient society, population and economy, or the factors which affect them, then we are unable to understand its history. Much of the data which pertain to these areas of study are still in unpublished form, hampering the realization of the project. However, it is the network of connections in which these scholarly investigations are set which is the greatest hindrance. In the past many of these themes have been ignored, particularly in biblical histories, not just because sufficient data have been lacking but, more crucially, because they have been thought to be unimportant. The cultural and political factors that have dominated biblical studies discourse on ancient Israel have denied the development of a strategy for investigating such issues. Ironically, much of the archaeological work, the regional surveys and site excavations, which have contributed to the paradigm shift are coloured by the overwhelming search for ancient Israel, the material reality which, it is presumed, will help to illuminate the Hebrew Bible. It is necessary to define a clear and precise conception of Palestinian history and then devise strategies for the investigation of this ancient past which are not dominated and controlled by scholars who are, implicitly or explicitly, in search of ancient Israel alone.

This work represents only the beginnings of an attempt to articulate an idea: its realization as a history of ancient Palestine must await others more knowledgeable and competent than myself. The conceptualization has been more important for me than the realization. It has been difficult to uncover or document sufficiently the subtle political and ideological influences which have shaped historical research in biblical studies. No doubt many will be happy to announce the failure of yet another 'sociological' history – when, in fact, as Braudel (1980: 64–82) was constantly pointing out, there is only history. This is not a history of Palestine but a commentary on how such a project has been obstructed by the discourse of biblical studies. It is the unshakeable belief that Palestinian history and with it the history of ancient Israel has to be approached in a radically different way from that of our standard histories which has been the driving force to continue. I can only hope that the kinds of questions I have posed, if not the explanations, and the connections between the political realm and biblical studies as an academic subject which have slowly begun to emerge will be of interest to others in the field.

1

PARTIAL TEXTS AND FRACTURED HISTORIES

PARTIAL TEXTS

The conceptualization and representation of the past is fraught with difficulty, not simply because of the ambiguities and paucity of data but because the construction of history, written or oral, past or present, is a political act. The long-running debate on the possibilities of writing a history of early Israel, focusing recently on various attempts to discover its origins or emergence, has tended, naturally enough, to concentrate upon the difficulties of interpreting the evidence, such as it is, including the crucial question of what it is that counts as evidence. However, this often fierce debate has profound political implications which have rarely surfaced. The reason for the heat of the recent debate is to do precisely with the political, cultural, and religious implications of the construction of ancient Israel. These are, invariably, hidden elements in the discussions and, like most fundamental domain assumptions, very rarely appear upon the surface. The problem of the history of ancient Palestine remains unspoken, masked in the dominant discourse of biblical studies which is concerned principally with the search for ancient Israel as the locus for understanding the traditions of the Hebrew Bible and ultimately as the taproot of European and Western civilization.

It is possible to offer two instructive examples of the ways in which the structure of this discourse can be fractured, allowing these issues to surface. The first is taken from a discussion which took place on IOUDAIOS, an electronic discussion group devoted to the second Temple period. Philip Davies' *In Search of 'Ancient Israel'* provoked a wide-ranging discussion of whether or not the biblical traditions represent a view of the past which accords with reality. One respondent, taking issue with the increasing vociferousness of the more sceptical approaches, complained that 'his history was being taken away from him'. Clearly, perceptions of the past are political and have important ramifications for the modern world because personal or social identity is either confirmed by or denied by these representations (Tonkin 1992: 6). This can be illustrated further by the reactions of the indigenous populations of Australia and the Americas to the celebrations of the bicentenary of the European settlement of Australia and the quincentennial celebrations of Christopher Columbus's discovery of the 'New World' and subsequent European settlement. The objections have been to 'official' Eurocentric histories and representations of the past which all too often deny the history of the indigenous populations of these continents.[1] The accounts of dominant, usually literary, cultures frequently silence versions of peripheral groups in society who are thereby denied a voice in history. The growing challenges to the positivistic histories of nineteenth- and twentieth-century so-called 'scientific' biblical studies are rejected as revisionist, or by some other pejorative label such as Marxist or materialist, because they undermine the search for what Burke Long terms 'a master story', an authoritative account of Israel's past, the broad parameters of which seemed reasonably assured until very recently.[2] The question which needs to be explored concerns the cultural and political factors which inform this search and the narration of a 'master story' about ancient Israel within modern biblical studies.

The second example is taken from a comparative review of Finkelstein (1988) and Coote and Whitelam (1987) by Christopher Eden (1989: 289–92) in which he focused upon the fundamental question of the ways in which 'the strong matrix of personal religious belief, political attitude, and scholarly education, and historical experience and ideology of the wider community is always present, whether overtly or more implicitly, in historical work generally but more extrusively in biblical history (and archaeology), and in the reviews of such histories' (1989: 291).[3] In a generally positive treatment of both works, he adds a negative appraisal for the present day of the implications of Finkelstein's study and a positive appraisal of the implications of Coote and Whitelam's work. Eden's complaint against Finkelstein is that:

> Finkelstein ... emphasizes the isolation and exclusivity of the Israelites from other communities, and their freedom from external forces. These attitudes are compounded by a

disquieting historical and ethnic insensitivity that views Palestinian settlement and agricultural production in the recent past as 'determined almost exclusively by the natural conditions of the country' (p. 130), a view that ignores the specific conditions of Ottoman land tenure and taxation while dismissing the Arab population as incapable of reacting to these conditions. Such an attitude forecasts a dismal and violent future for the region.

(Eden 1989: 292)

Finkelstein (1991: 51) replies that this ignores the entire discipline of his survey which was based on a study of Arab land use and subsistence economy in the nineteenth and early twentieth centuries. Finkelstein, ironically, in rejecting Eden's criticisms as outrageous and politically biased, misses the crucial point about the way in which political attitudes, however unconsciously, shape all historical research. Eden then concludes:

The immediate question raised here is not the use of biblical history to validate modern political stances, but rather the smuggling into 'objective' historical inquiry of values configured by modern experience and expectation. Such values can never be eliminated, but surely can, and must, be understood as part of historical discourse, a part moreover that usually directly shapes the nature of questions asked and of answers presented; the reader can ignore the presence of these values only at risk of a partial text.

(Eden 1989: 292)

Clearly an important element in our attempts to understand 'ancient Israel' and other historical entities, though usually unspoken, is the politics of history, the way in which political attitudes and views define the agenda and strongly influence the outcome of the historian's search – an agenda and search which often presents us with, to use Eden's phrase, 'a partial text'. In the case of biblical studies it has focused upon and, to a large extent, invented an entity, 'ancient Israel', while ignoring the reality of Palestinian history as a whole. The task ahead can be set out in the words of Said (1993: 380): 'the job facing the cultural intellectual is therefore not to accept the politics of identity as given, but to show how all representations are constructed, for what purpose, by whom, and with what components.'

None of this should come as any great surprise if one is acquainted with the use of history through antiquity to the present day. Neil Silberman (1982; 1989) provides a series of telling examples of the interrelationships of history, archaeology, and politics in the modern Middle East. He describes how European nation states from the Industrial Revolution onwards constructed national histories to justify and idealize their positions in the world. This is particularly true of Great Britain where 'the past was taking on a more focused, modern significance – as a source of political symbols and ideals. In the myths, chronicles, and surviving monuments of the ancient Britons and the later Anglo-Saxons, antiquarians and politicians found vivid illustrations of the people's unique "national character" that explained and justified Great Britain's unique position in the world' (Silberman 1989: 2). These nations, and Britain in particular, appropriated the past of classical and biblical antiquity. This mirrored the increasing interests of Western powers in the eastern Mediterranean and the Middle East. The origins of modern archaeology, from the time of Napoleon's intervention in Egypt, are a tale of international intrigue in which the biblical past, and the archaeological treasures of the region, were appropriated by Western powers in their struggles for political advantage and the legitimization of their own imperial ambitions. The way in which the development of academic disciplines such as Orientalism, history, and anthropology were used in these struggles by Western powers is persuasively argued by Asad (1973), Said (1985; 1993), and many others.

One of the ironies of this situation, which has been pointed out by many commentators, is that colonial discourse has also shaped the nationalist discourses which have grown up in opposition to colonial control. Nationalist historiographies and histories have taken over many of the assumptions of the colonial histories that they were designed to reject. Thus Inden (1986: 402) goes so far as to say that despite India's formal acquisition of political independence, it has still not regained the power to know its own past and present apart from this discourse. Prakash (1990: 388) illustrates how Indian nationalism in rejecting British colonial versions of the past nevertheless accepted the patterns set down by British scholarship so that the accepted periodization of Indian history into Hindu, Muslim, and British periods later became the ancient, medieval, and modern eras, while the caste system was accepted as a social and not a political category, along with the existence of a Sanskrit Indian civilization. The origins of the modern nation state were traced to ancient India in the same way that Orientalists had traced Europe's origins in the texts of ancient India. However, van der Veer (1993: 23) in assessing the work of Said argues that the claim that the production of knowledge about the Orient is an exclusively Western affair neglects ways so-called Orientals not only shape their own world but also Orientalist views: 'It would be a serious mistake to deny agency to the colonized in an effort to show the force of colonial discourse.' He adds (1993: 25) that 'it is a crucial aspect of the post-colonial predicament that Orientalist understandings of Indian society are perpetuated both by Western scholarship and by Indian political movements.'

As Prakash (1990: 390) has pointed out, the focus of nationalist historiography and history has always been the nation: 'therefore we need to recognize that it is one of the ways in which the third world writes its own history.' Silberman (1990) documents the ways in which newly formed nation states in the region increasingly realized the importance of appropriating their own pasts as symbols of legitimacy or rejections of imperial control. The continuing dispute over the possession or repossession of the Elgin Marbles and other Greek archaeological treasures demonstrates the importance of a nation state reclaiming its past to illuminate and justify its own present. Furthermore it has led to a struggle with the British government which has united all sides of the political spectrum in Greece from conservative to socialist politicians (Silberman 1990: 8). The current conflict in the Balkans provides further evidence of the point with an increasingly dangerous dispute over the newly pro-claimed province of Macedonia in the former Yugoslavia, whose appropriation of the name lays claim to a past thereby denying an important element of national identity in northern Greece. However, although we have important national conceptions of history from the various modern states in the Middle East which provide that vital counterpoint to Western conceptions and representations of the history of the region, what is conspicuous by its absence is a truly Palestinian history of the past, i.e. written from a Palestinian per-spective. Naturally enough, the Palestinian perspective has focused on the modern period and the struggle for national identity and a separate state.[4] The ancient past, it seems, has been abandoned to the West and modern Israel.

Appropriations of the past as part of the politics of the present, which Silberman documents, could be illustrated for most parts of the globe. One further example, which is of particular interest to this study, is the way in which archaeology and biblical history have become of such importance in the modern state of Israel. It is this combination which has been such a powerful factor in silencing Palestinian history. The new Israeli nationalist historiography, like other recent nationalist historiographies, in searching for the origins of the nation in the past has continued the assumptions and concerns of European colonial scholarship. Trigger (1984) has discussed the variation in different countries in the kinds of archaeological problem which are seen as worthy of investigation and the types of explanation regarded as acceptable interpretations of evidence. The nation state plays a very important role in defining the parameters of scholarship. He points out in his discussion of 'nationalist archaeology' that: 'In modern Israel, archaeology plays an important role in affirming the links between an intrusive population and its own ancient past and by doing so asserts the right of that population to the land' (1984: 358).[5]

The most striking example of the national present discovered in the ancient past is Yadin's excavation of Masada and the political appropriation of the site to symbolize the newly founded state faced with overwhelming odds against its survival in a hostile environment. Yadin expressed its significance in the following terms:

> Its scientific importance was known to be great. But more than that, Masada represents for all of us in Israel and for many elsewhere, archaeologists and laymen, a symbol of courage, a monument of our great national figures, heroes who chose death over a life of physical and moral serfdom.
>
> (Yadin 1966: 13)

The political significance of Masada is encapsulated in its choice as the location for the annual swearing-in ceremony for Israeli troops and expressed through the nationalist slogan, derived from Lamdan's poem, that 'Never again shall Masada fall'.[6] The subsequent debate on Yadin's interpretation of some of the finds or his reading of the Josephus account illustrates how political and religious attitudes shape the investigation and the outcome. Zerubavel (1994) has shown, in a fine study, how Masada has developed from a relatively obscure incident in the past, ignored in the Talmud and medieval Jewish literature, to represent the paradigm of national identity. She shows that, despite a critical discussion of Josephus's account of the siege and fall of Masada, Israeli popular culture does not doubt the historicity of the account. Yet it emerged as a focus of scholarly interest only in the nineteenth century in association with the Zionist movement, representing an important symbolic event for new settlers. The fall of Masada to the Romans marked the end of the Jewish revolt against imperial control and for Zionists embodied the spirit of heroism and love of freedom which had been lost in the period of exile (Zerubavel 1994: 75). Zerubavel traces how this 'commemorative narrative' was constructed by a selective reading of the Josephus account which emphasized some aspects and ignored others.[7] This process was enhanced by the development of a pilgrimage to the site in the pre-state period by youth movements and the Zionist underground which culminated after 1948 with its selection as the site for the swearing-in ceremony for the Israeli Defence Forces. She concludes that 'Yadin's interpretation of the excavation as a patriotic mission was not unlike other instances where archaeology was mobilized to promote nationalist ideology' (1994: 84). Particularly noteworthy is the way in which Yadin linked Masada to the present:

We will not exaggerate by saying that *thanks to the heroism of the Masada fighters* – like other links in the nation's chain of heroism – *we stand here today*, the soldiers of a young-ancient people, surrounded by the ruins of the camps of those who destroyed us. We stand here, no longer helpless in the face of our enemy's strength, no longer fighting a desperate war, but solid and confident, knowing that our fate is in our hands, in our spiritual strength, the spirit of Israel 'the grandfather revived ... We, the descendants of these heroes, stand here today and rebuild the ruins of our people.'

(cited by Zerubavel 1994: 84)

Yadin's linking of the ancient past and the political present (notice his phrase 'a young-ancient people'), and the reference to links in the nation's chain of heroism, is an important rhetorical technique in biblical studies discourse which has played a crucial role in the silencing of Palestinian history. Zerubavel (1994: 88) cites the famous dictum of A.B. Yehoshua as encapsulating this continuum between past and present: 'Masada is no longer the historic mountain near the Dead Sea but a mobile mountain which we carry on our back anywhere we go.' It is this continuum which is crucial to any claim to possess the land, a claim which effectively silences any Palestinian claim to the past and therefore to the land.[8]

European scholarship prior to 1948, and later, was concerned with tracing the roots of the nation state in biblical antiquity. This has been reinforced since the founding of the modern state of Israel by an Israeli scholarship which has been in search of its own roots in ancient Israel, as the Masada project illustrates. This search for ancient Israel has dominated the agenda of historical and archaeological scholarship, effectively silencing any attempt to provide a history of the region in general. The important work of Finkelstein (1988), on what he terms 'Israelite Settlement', provides a further illustration of the point. His archaeological investigations and surveys have been concentrated upon the central hill country of Palestine in order to delineate the nature of 'Israelite settlement' during the Late Bronze–Iron Age transition. It is, in essence, however unwittingly, the search for a national identity which, like other nationalist archaeologies, helps to 'bolster the pride and morale of nations or ethnic groups' (Trigger 1984: 360). The original work was particularly restrictive in the area of its investigation: Finkelstein (1988: 22–3) argued that the 'large Canaanite mounds' were of little value in understanding the processes at work in 'Israelite Settlement'.[9] The search for ancient Israel is concentrated upon the disputed West Bank, 'Judaea–Samaria' of many modern Israelis. The lowlands, understood to be Canaan, are of little interest in this quest for ancient Israel. Once again, the concern with 'ancient Israel' overshadows questions about the wider history of ancient Palestine to such an extent that the broader reality is silenced or at most merely subsidiary to the search for the national entity 'Israel' in the Late Bronze–Iron Age transition.

Most modern nation states have invested considerable resources in the pursuit of the past: official versions of a nation's past confirm important aspects of national identity while denying a voice to alternative claims. Israel, like other modern nation states, has invested tremendous financial and scholarly resources in the search for its own past. However, it is important to bear in mind that research on the history of Israel has been shaped in the context of the formation and consolidation of the European nation state and its transference to the Middle East, particularly with the creation of the modern state of Israel and the spread of competing nationalisms throughout the region.[10] The silence on such matters in the introductions to our standard presentations of the history of Israel provides ample testimony to the nature of our partial texts. There is little or no acknowledgement of this context except for the interesting observation in the opening to Noth's *The History of Israel* that:

It is true, of course, that from the womb of 'Judaism' there has emerged in most recent times a new historical entity named 'Israel' which has sought its *homeland again* in the ancient land of Israel under the auspices of the Zionist movement and has established a new State of 'Israel'. In spite of the historical connections which undoubtedly exist, this new 'Israel' is separated from the Israel of old not only by the long period of almost 2000 years but also by a long history full of vicissitudes and it has come into being in the midst of entirely different historical conditions. It would therefore be improper to extend our historical enquiry from the end of the 'Israel' of old to the 'Israel' of the present day.

(Noth 1960: 7; emphasis added)

Noth sees a continuum between the past and the present which links the modern state of Israel to his investigation of ancient Israelite history.[11] Although he claims that it is improper to extend his discussion to the present, he fails to acknowledge that it is the very existence of the nation state in the present that shapes so much of what passes for historical research in this field. It is the domain assumption of a direct connection between ancient Israel and the modern state – encapsulated in his belief of a return to its 'homeland' in the 'ancient land of Israel' – that predetermines the search. The choice of the term 'homeland' is not insignificant in the context of the promise contained within the Balfour Declaration of 'a natural home for the Jewish people' in Palestine. It is also the overwhelming concern of this quest for 'ancient Israel', as the roots and legitimation of the present state, that dominates all historical discussions and silences the search for a general history of the region.

Nationalism, having emerged in the eighteenth century, has triumphed as the dominant political force in the nineteenth and twentieth centuries (Taylor 1985: 125). The nation state, with its great statesmen, civil service, state archives, and educational system, has cast a shadow over modern biblical studies from its inception. The very conception of history, derived from von Ranke, which has underpinned modern biblical historiography, has its origins in the context of Bismarck's struggle for German unity. The search for the origins and consolidation of the nation state, including the actions of great statesmen, has been of central concern from the nineteenth century through the works of Alt, Albright, Noth, and Bright to the present day. Said (1993: 50–1) argues for a similar influence on

19

Enlightenment concepts of history as distinct from the natural sciences:

> It is not a vulgarization of history to remark that a major reason why such a view of human culture became current in Europe and America in several different forms during the two centuries between 1745 and 1945 was the striking rise of nationalism during the same period. The interrelationships between scholarship (or literature, for that matter) and the institutions of nationalism have not been as seriously studied as they should, but it is nevertheless evident that when most European thinkers celebrated humanity or culture they were principally celebrating ideas and values they ascribed to their own national culture, or to Europe as distinct from the Orient, Africa, and even the Americas.
>
> (Said 1993: 51)

He goes on to argue that disciplines such as the classics, historiography, anthropology, and sociology, like Orientalism, were Eurocentric and that as national and international competition increased between the European powers in the nineteenth century so 'too did the level of intensity in competition between one national scholarly interpretative tradition and another'.[12]

The seminal work by Sasson (1981) illustrates how American and German biblical scholarship has been influenced by the political context in which it was conceived, imposing very strong models on the past:

> Because biblical scholarship is pursued internationally, the models dominant in reconstructing the formative periods of Israel's history differ markedly. This is the case as much because they were originally designed to explain radically contrasting conditions which obtained in western nations during the 19th and 20th century as because these models themselves were based on competing and diverse elaborations.
>
> (Sasson 1981: 8)[13]

He goes on to add that the model of a national history of ancient Israel was based upon similar attempts for ancient Greece and Rome. This study of antiquity 'took on a self-authenticating momentum' (1981: 4). Frick (1985: 26–8) also highlights the importance of this context for understanding many of the concerns of modern biblical scholarship: almost all the sources in the biblical narratives bear the mark of the state and were written under state sponsorship. Furthermore, most twentieth-century biblical scholars come from the developed states of Western Europe, Israel, or North America, and so consciously or unconsciously give the state pre-eminence. This is an area of research, identified more than a decade ago by Sasson, which has not received the attention that it deserves. Fortunately the recent dissertation by Kray (1991) has provided invaluable information on the context of German biblical scholarship from Wellhausen to von Rad during the formative century from 1870 to 1971. The historical context of the work of Wellhausen is more than symbolic: Smend (1982: 8) points out that 'his active career, begun with doctoral graduation in 1870, spanned almost precisely the period of the German state founded by Bismark; he died on 7 January 1918, the year in which the state foundered'. The way in which the state was viewed in nineteenth-century German historiography has informed the study of the ancient Israelite state and its formation through to the present day. The belief that the nation state was the greatest manifestation of advanced culture has been reinforced in the perception of the development of the modern state of Israel. These factors have combined in intricate ways to shape and dominate the study of ancient Israelite history, producing a model that has denied validity to any other attempts to understand or produce a history of ancient Palestine.

The dominant model for the presentation of Israelite history has been, and continues to be, that of a unified national entity in search of national territory struggling to maintain its national identity and land through the crises of history. It is a concept of the past which mirrors the presentation of the present. Zionism, with its roots in nineteenth-century European nationalist movements, has invariably presented its 'historic mission' in terms of a return to an empty, desert wasteland awaiting European technology in order to make it habitable and prosperous. As Shohat (1992: 124) notes, the modern state has been continually portrayed as an integral part of the 'civilized world' and 'the only democracy in the Middle East'. The way in which the model of the European nation state has dominated historical and archaeological research can be seen in some of the most important studies in recent years. As has been mentioned, Finkelstein's study (1988) of 'Israelite Settlement' is an interpretation of archaeological data from the Late Bronze to early Iron Ages which assumes the unity and identity of Israel, in effect an incipient nation state, in the Palestinian highlands. The notions of ethnicity and nationality continue to be extremely influential within biblical studies and have shaped many of our standard textbooks on the history of ancient Israel.

Thus the development and concerns of biblical studies, particularly in terms of its historical investigations, need to be understood within the larger political and cultural context. The discourse of biblical studies needs to be set within the wider discussion of Orientalist discourse. Said (1993) has exposed the interconnections between culture and imperialism in the West. What he has to say about great literature is equally applicable to the role and position of historical narrative:

> A great deal of recent criticism has concentrated on narrative fiction, yet very little attention has been paid to its position in the history and world of empire. Readers of this book will quickly discover that narrative is crucial to my argument here, my basic point being that stories are at the heart of what explorers and novelists say about strange regions of the world; they also become the method colonized people use to assert their own identity and the existence of their own history. The main battle in imperialism is over land, of course; but when it came to who owned the land, who had the right to settle and work on it, who kept it going, who won it back, and who now plans its future – these issues were reflected, contested, and even for a time decided in narrative. As one critic has suggested, nations themselves *are* narrations. The power to narrate, or to block other narratives from forming and emerging is very important to culture and imperialism, and constitutes one of the main connections between them.
>
> (Said 1993: xiii)

This echoes Homi Bhabha's (1990: 1) assertion that 'nations, like narratives, lose their origins in the myths of time and only fully realize their horizons in the mind's eye'. Both draw upon Benedict Anderson's (1991: 6) definition of the nation as 'an imagined political community'. It is not just that the modern nation is an imagined community. This imagination has been projected back into the past to provide the legitimation and justification of the present.[14] It has led to the construction of an imagined past which has monopolized the discourse of biblical studies, an imagined past which has come to dominate and deny Palestinian history. The history of the vast majority of the population of the region has not been told because it did not fit the concerns and interests of Western-inspired scholarship.[15]

It is not easy to make these connections between biblical scholarship and the political context in which it is conducted and by which it is inevitably shaped. For the most part, they are implicit rather than explicit. The connections will be denied by many, decrying any such analysis as politically motivated, as part of the modern fad of deconstruction and revisionism in history, or as an outrageous attack upon the objectivity of biblical scholarship. Biblical studies has remained aloof, a kind of academic ghetto, from many of the contemporary movements which have swept through academia questioning and undermining its claim to disinterested objectivity. The study of the social and political context in which it has been undertaken, which inevitably compromises its critical distance, is in its infancy. The gradual exposure of the interrelationship of the discipline of biblical studies with politics will provide a better understanding of the forces which have helped to shape the imagination of a past that has monopolized the history of the region.

The examples cited above provide ample evidence of the construction of the past as a political act and that the construction of Israel's past in particular carries important political consequences which cannot be ignored. Eden alerts us to this crucial matrix of politics, religion, ideology, and society in understanding modern scholarship. But equally we only have a partial text if we ignore this matrix when trying to understand ancient representations of Israel's past. It is at this point that the unspoken or unacknowledged political and religious attitudes of modern scholarship conspire to obscure the ancient politics of the past. We need to explore why this is the case and what the consequences of making this process explicit might be.[16]

IMAGINING ANCIENT ISRAEL AND THE POLITICS OF THE PAST

The picture of Israel's past as presented in much of the Hebrew Bible is a fiction, a fabrication like most pictures of the past constructed by ancient (and, we might add, modern) societies.[17] The oft-cited dictum that any construction of the past is informed by the present is as applicable to representations of the past which have come down to us from antiquity as it is to the works of modern historians.[18] A primary question which has to be borne in mind is, 'What function does this particular representation of the past fulfil and what other possible representations of the past is it denying?'

The politics of history in the presentation of Israel's past has not been a major issue because most biblical scholars have agreed on the basic parameters of the enterprise, traditionally investing a great deal of faith and trust in the historicity of biblical sources along with a trust in the objectivity of the modern scholar.[19] Although there has been a very significant shift in perceptions in the last decade concerning the problems of constructing Israelite history, the dominant view remains that the biblical traditions provide the basis, the primary source, for the historian of Israel. Whatever the gains and insights of those who study the artful construction of biblical narratives, von Rad's pronouncement that the 'Old Testament is a history book' remains a basic instinct of many in the discipline who research the history of Israel or teach various courses in our faculties of Theology and Divinity, theological colleges, seminaries, or even departments of Religious Studies. This has been coupled with a model of historical research which further reinforces the conviction that we are dealing with trustworthy transmitters of tradition and that modern scholars are heirs to this important thread of objectivity. The forensic model of historical research provides the forum in which ancient and modern approaches intersect to reassure the reader that the account of Israel's past is objective and trustworthy.

Halpern's study (1988) offers an interesting case as the most explicit attempt to address this key issue of objectivity and trustworthiness in the biblical traditions. In an attempt to defend ancient Israelite historians against their modern critics whom he sees as presenting these ancient scribes as being 'illogical, dull, or dishonest' (1988: xvii), he chooses as a guiding principle the view that some of the biblical authors 'wrote works recognizably historical – had authentic antiquarian intentions. They meant to furnish fair and accurate representations of Israelite antiquity' (1988: 3).[20] Narrative economy of an account he takes to be one of the pointers which indicates that we are dealing with historiography rather than fiction. In order to counter the inevitable criticism that narrative economy can hardly be an adequate criterion for such a judgement, he adds that in itself it is not sufficient: the historiographic intention of the author is revealed through a comparison of the account with its sources (1988: 61). Unfortunately, as he recognizes, the sources are no longer extant so he has to resort to 'the probable nature of the sources'. A detailed study of the Ehud narrative (Judges 3) is used to illustrate how the historian working with the story made 'painstaking' (his word) use of other sources such as the layout of the palace, as known to Israelite audiences, the stations of the courtiers, or the topography of the Jordan Valley. He acknowledges that this reliance on sources does not certify that the account is accurate but none the less it means that 'the historian grounds his reconstruction as far as possible in the reality of Israelite life. His interest lies in recreating events experienced by real people in real time. The Ehud narrative, so bare, so terse, is as close as the ancient world comes to modern historical narrative. What must one add or subtract to convert it into history? hardly a word' (1988: 67). It is not clear what he means by history or how far he believes it corresponds to some objective reality in the past or is history in the sense that the author believed it to have taken place. He continues the discussion with a detailed study of the Deborah narrative, in which he discovers clear evidence in Judges 4 and 5 of a historian working with a written source. He is able to conclude (1988: 82) that 'virtually no detail in Judges 4 is without an identifiable source; nearly all of them come from the poem, and from the historian's reconstruction of the event, based on a painstaking analysis of the poem. This case offers an exceptional opportunity to dissect the construction of a Biblical historical account.' A further guiding principle of Halpern's is that 'historical knowledge is based upon evidence in just the way that deliberations of the jury are' (1988: 13).

This forensic model of historiography is widespread and probably the dominant view of the way in which historians work.[21] It underlies the methodological introduction to Ramsey's (1982: 3–23) review of scholarly constructions of Israelite history in which he equates the work of the lawyer and the historian. Fogel illustrates how *The Harvard Guide to American History* provides a classic account of this type of methodology in which the assessment of 'witnesses' is an essential element:

> Like treason in the Constitution, a historical fact ideally should rest 'on the testimony of two witnesses to some overt act, or confession in open court'.
>
> (cited by Fogel 1983: 14)

Or again:

> A judge and jury, indeed, would go mad if they had to decide cases on evidence which will often seem more than satisfactory

to the historian. But there is no escape; the historian, if he is to interpret at all, will try and convict on evidence which a court would throw out as circumstantial or hearsay. The victims of the historical process have to seek their compensation in the fact that history provides them with a far more flexible appellate procedure. The historian's sentences are in a continuous condition of review; few of his verdicts are ever final.

(cited by Fogel 1983: 14–15)

Notice throughout the language of the law court: judge, jury, evidence, testimony, witnesses, confession, compensation, and so on. The emphasis is upon justice and impartiality so that the reader is continually reassured that their trust can be placed in the historian and his or her account of the past. No mention is made of the politics of history, of past or present accounts, because this process is designed to sift out the truth by cross-examination of the various witnesses. Questions about the political and social context of our histories or their sources become unnecessary within such a model because it confirms the impartiality of the modern historian and emphasizes that their ancient counterparts are trustworthy transmitters of tradition because untrustworthy witnesses are identified and their testimony is counted out of court.[22] Yet recent celebrated cases in English courts ought to give pause for thought before we accept wholeheartedly the impartiality of the process being described. The discourse of biblical studies cloaks the cultural and political factors which shape it by divorcing the production of knowledge from the context in which it is produced.

Halpern presents us with Israelite historians who differ little in their working attitudes or practices from the way in which their modern counterparts are thought to prosecute their profession. Ancient Israelite historians are commonly constructed in the image of their modern counterparts, in the image of civil servants and state archivists of our modern nation states, but in such a way that we are led to believe that the initial impulse stems from the genius of ancient Israel so that modern Western biblical historians become their direct descendants.[23] Halpern might be correct in his assumption that modern historians and their Israelite counterparts are not far removed in the ways in which they go about their tasks, but not because they work in terms of this forensic model. Rather, it is the politics of history that draws them together, because their representations are invariably in terms of their own present and are in competition with other possible representations of the past. Thucydides and Herodotus are often held aloft as the founders of modern historiography: their basic methodology has only had to be refined and honed by modern historians. Yet Momigliano (1990: 41–4) points out that the past for Thucydides was of little interest in itself, its significance lay in the fact that it was the prelude to the present. The forensic model is concerned first and foremost with the problem of whether or not any particular account of the past is trustworthy. In order to answer such a question we need to know how and why the past was produced in ancient societies. Does the picture presented by Halpern represent a realistic account of how the past was produced in Israel or the ancient world? What was the social location of Israelite historians or producers of the past? When did they work? How? Where? Where were their sources? What was the audience? How were their presentations of the past delivered? Were they in oral or written form – or a written form which was read aloud? What effects do the levels of literacy in Palestine – whether universal or functional literacy, or a literacy of the elite – have upon our understanding of the production of this past?[24]

There are further major obstacles imposed by our contemporary context which have hindered the investigation of the politics of history in the production of the Israelite past. One of these is the current and, some would argue, dominant mode of viewing the past as something alien, something to be transcended or to be thrown off (cf. Paterson 1991: 3–4). Here we might point to Bellah's (1976) well-known analysis of the 'crisis of modernity': a growing dissatisfaction in Western society with Enlightenment rationalism, a decline in traditional church structures, and a growth in New Religious Movements (NRMs). Western societies have experienced over the past thirty to forty years what has been termed the 'privatization' of religion: one of the major features of the decline in traditional church structures and the growth of NRMs has been an emphasis upon the personal and individual. The context in which our most recent histories of Israel have been shaped and read in the West is one in which the individual has triumphed. It is a context which articulates well with and encourages the common view of history as the acts of great men, unique individuals, or the realm of discrete and unique events. In such a context, the individual is attested as autonomous and self-made rather than the product of some determinative historical process (see Paterson 1991: 3–4). The triumph of the individual is represented by Margaret Thatcher's celebrated statement that 'there is no such thing as society only individuals'.[25]

The problem of understanding the production and use of the past in antiquity has been compounded further by what John McPhee termed the discovery of 'deep time'.[26] The works of James Hutton, Charles Lyell, and Charles Darwin, among others, have left a legacy of the concept of time in geological terms which is so immense as to be almost incomprehensible and, for many, threatening. The discovery of 'deep time' has led to an emphasis upon chronology and time's arrow, a notion which has often implied progress within history and which articulates well with Christian teleologies. It allows for little appreciation of the importance of time's cycle in traditional conceptions of the past which are usually relegated to the 'prehistoric' or the 'mythic'. For many in the late twentieth century the past is, to use the title of Lowenthal's (1985) well-known work, 'a foreign country', remote and removed from contemporary experience. In order to make the past understandable or manageable it is necessary, under the forensic model, to separate the historian from his or her work, the producer from the product, and through the elimination of subjectivity produce an authentic, trustworthy, and verifiable account of the past in terms of time's arrow neatly categorized in terms of chronology and periodization. It is just such a 'master story' which has been produced by nineteenth- and twentieth-century biblical studies, in which only the details and recently the starting point have been at issue, but it is a 'master story' which is clearly informed and shaped by the political context in which it arose. It is also a 'master story' that creates ancient Israel in its own image, the image of Western nation states, and at the same time silences other possible accounts of ancient Palestine's past. The seeming objectivity of these accounts masks the political subjectivity of biblical accounts and, in effect, takes their side in silencing competing pasts.

The past in many so-called 'traditional' societies is not demarcated in such clear terms as separate or different from the present. It is dynamic and immediate in the ways in which it addresses the concerns of the present. In Polynesian history, for instance, 'the past and the present are not so much sequential chapters in a linear plot, as they are organically linked aspects of a continuum' (Berofsky 1987: 128).[27] As is well known, genealogies are constantly revised in many societies to reflect a political and social reality of the present rather than lineage or blood-relations of the past. In the same way, other accounts of the past are remade. The historian, whether literate or oral, is set in a particular social context at a particular moment in time: the account is produced under 'specific social and economic conditions by authors whose attitudes to a perceived potential audience would have affected the way they presented the material' (Tonkin 1992: 38).[28] Yet this is as true for modern societies as it is for ancient, so-called 'traditional' societies.

The way in which differences in the representation of the past between ancient and modern societies are presented is usually in terms of the dichotomy between 'myth' and 'history'. Yet this is a false dichotomy which helps to reinforce the reader's trust in the objective presentation of the modern historian as compared with the subjectivity of myth.[29] We might ask 'Where does myth end and history begin?' In terms of the Hebrew Bible, as is often pointed out, there is no apparent differentiation between Genesis 1–11 and what follows, either to the end of the book or through to the end of 2 Kings. Thus Hughes (1990: 96) concludes in his recent study of biblical chronology that the chronology of Judges and Samuel is a purely fictitious Exilic creation to provide a 1000-year scheme covering Israel's existence in Canaan. As such, it cannot be used to provide a chronology for the history of Israel.

Myth, no less than history, is a perception of the past which is intimately linked to the context in which it is constructed and delivered, and is designed to foster a particular ideology. Samuel and Thompson (1990: 20) argue that 'traditions are as likely to be recycled in transformed contexts as to be invented'.[30] Recent approaches to the way in which tradition is invented or recycled have undermined the fundamental assumption within biblical studies that such traditions, despite a significant temporal separation from the events they describe, necessarily preserve some kind of historical kernel or historical memory which can be extracted from the narrative to provide raw data for the modern historian. These accounts of the past, whether they are termed myth or history, are not the product of collective memory but rather the product of particular groups in society, a point van Seters (1975; 1992: 34) has been keen to emphasize in contrast to standard perceptions of the development of the biblical traditions. What are termed historical memories probably only represent those perceptions of the past which are important for individuals or groups who share a similar social status or background (see Tonkin 1992: 131–2). They have a vital role to play in shaping identity and in denying competing claims to the past. For example, the epic poems 'The Brus' and 'The Acts and Deeds of Sir William Wallace', from the fourteenth and fifteenth centuries respectively, were composed, the latter under royal patronage, at a time when Robert the Bruce and Sir William Wallace were important symbols of national identity. The desire, among the upper classes, to create a 'British identity' in the eighteenth and nineteenth centuries meant that these anti-English poems and figures were conveniently forgotten (Ash 1990). It is an account of the past which has been revived with the rise of modern nationalism, providing an alternative account to 'official' versions of Scotland's history.

Accounts of the past, then, are in competition, explicitly or implicitly. They are written or heard at a particular moment in time, addressed to a known audience which has certain expectations (of which we may be ignorant), and designed to persuade. This last point is important since Tonkin (1992) demonstrates that oral accounts, no less than written ones, are carefully structured and have their own poetics that need to be studied and understood. Recent literary studies have alerted us to the fact that it is no longer possible simply to scan narratives for the few useful facts which provide the basis for an expanded modern account while discarding the rest of the narrative as secondary or unimportant. 'Any such facts are so embedded in the representation that it directs an interpretation of them' (Tonkin 1992: 6). Rather than presenting evidence for some past reality, they offer, like many such accounts from modern and traditional societies, evidence for the politics of the present. The thorny question remains in each case: whose present?[31]

Standard approaches to the book of Judges provide a brief, but useful, illustration of the problems outlined above whereby the construction of Israelite history has been conducted from a contemporary Western perspective. Bright's (1972: 169) approach to the text provides a convenient benchmark of earlier scholarship. He was of the opinion that the book of Judges was the sole source for Israel's earliest phases in Palestine. While noting that the series of 'self-contained episodes' did not allow a continuous history of the period to be written, he none the less followed the broad outline of the book in presenting a period of intermittent conflict, peaceful interludes, and internal and external crises. Most noticeably it provided authentic evidence, in his view, for a covenant league held together by the spiritual power of its religion. The notion of the nation state, or in this case an incipient nation state, provides the controlling assumption which surmounts any obstacles or professed reservations with the text.

When we turn to Miller and Hayes (1986), by way of comparison, as the high point of modern biblical histories, we find that Bright's initial reservations have been taken further. Once again the book of Judges is declared to be 'the only direct source of information for this period of Israelite and Judaean history'. It cannot be used for historical construction because the editorial framework is 'artificial and unconvincing' and the 'matters of detail in the individual stories . . . strain credulity' (1986: 87). However, the accounts of the various 'judges' when stripped of these miraculous elements provide the basis for their description of the pre-monarchic period. In order to achieve this, Miller and Hayes make a move which seeks to retrieve the text or at least what they call the 'component narratives' which have a 'more authentic ring' than the framework (1986: 90). The narratives may not provide a 'basis for a detailed historical sequence of people and events' (1986: 91) but 'they probably do offer a reasonably accurate impression of the general, sociological, political, and religious circumstances that existed among early Israelite tribes' (1986: 91). Miller and Hayes are not unique in this view since it is shared with the vast majority of historians and commentators, including in particular proponents of the so-called 'sociological approach'.[32] The discussion then concentrates on the nature of extended families, clans, tribes, tribal structure, and segmentary society as the constituent parts of pre-monarchic Israel. Yet such an approach is only a slight variation on the earlier argument of Bright (1972: 76) that the Patriarchal narratives provide authentic historical data because they 'fit unquestionably and authentically in the milieu of the second millennium, and not in that of any later period'. Just as this argument for understanding the Genesis material has been progressively abandoned under sustained critique by Thompson (1974), van Seters (1975), and others, so it is the case that such an approach to the Judges material suffers from the very same weaknesses.

The type of information concerning social structures which is salvaged from the text is hardly a pointer to the authenticity of the narrative for the pre-state period. The narrative does not 'fit unquestionably and authentically', to borrow Bright's phrase, into the twelfth or eleventh centuries and nowhere else. Palestine has been a primarily agrarian society with an important pastoral element from at least the Bronze Age to the present century. The component elements of such a society as identified from the text of Judges could fit easily into any period of this vast temporal span. The attempt to salvage the text of Judges for historical reconstruction, either as the guardian of a historical kernel or as the repository of information on the social organization of Israel in the pre-state period, needs to be understood in the context of the search for the nation state and its origins. In fact, the triumph of the European nation state is complete to such an extent that its antecedents are retrojected back into the period prior to the formation of an Israelite state.

The extended scholarly discussion of the redactional history of the book of Judges is well known from Noth's (1981; German original 1943) original analysis half a century ago through its various revisions by Smend (1971), Dietrich (1972), Cross (1973), Nelson (1981), and Mayes (1983), among many others. It is not the details of these analyses which are of immediate concern but the common thread which appears to run through them: it is the image of the historian or redactor working carefully with various sources. Noth's Deuteronomistic Historian is conceived of in terms of the state archivist sorting, arranging, and interpreting extant written material, which he used with the greatest of care (1981: 77). For Noth, the Deuteronomistic History is no fabrication but is an objective presentation of Israel's history based upon authentic sources. It is this objective historian which Halpern is determined to defend against all detractors: a scribe painstakingly comparing and arranging source materials while his modern counterparts work equally carefully to expose these same sources so that they might form the basis of a modern objective history of Israel.

One of the ironies of the ways in which the book of Judges has been used for historical reconstruction is that modern historians have been forced to impose a concept of time's arrow on the text when all commentators accept that the specific structure of the work as a whole is imbued with time's cycle. For the modern historian the use of the text for historical reconstruction requires a denial or, at best, a disregard for the very structure of the work which does so much to frame and convey its sense or understanding of the past. The cyclical view of history is not one which most modern historians are happy with or would accept. Linear time is the essence of history or, as some would put it, 'chronology is the backbone of history'. Yet it is precisely the aesthetic and rhetorical devices which are integral to the work as a whole and to its presentation of the past which recent literary approaches have done much to expose. Webb (1987: 177), in particular, has argued for an understanding of the unity of the book based upon a 'dense network of interlocking motifs' which cut across traditional materials and editorial framework alike. The book of Judges as a unity offers a tantalizing glimpse of one way in which the past was claimed and reshaped.

FRACTURED HISTORIES

The recognition that we are constantly working with partial texts, ancient and modern, and an acceptance that it is important to understand the politics of our ancient and modern accounts of the past have important implications for the directions of historical research. The realization that accounts of the past are invariably the products of a small elite and are in competition with other possible accounts, of which we may have no evidence, ought to lead to greater caution in the use of such accounts to construct Israelite history. Their value for the historian lies in what they reveal of the ideological concerns of their authors, if, and only if, they can be located in time and place. The historian has to work with partial texts, trying to expose the questions which lie behind the text and which have been vital in claiming and shaping the past. The increasing move away from a concern with biblical texts as the repositories of transparent historical data, whether it is the emergence of Israel or the historical David, Josiah, Jeremiah, or Nehemiah, has obvious repercussions for standard approaches to the history of Israel. To continue with this venture, as more and more texts are removed from the historian's grasp, runs the risk of being reduced to writing a 'history of the gaps': not the gaps in our data, a given for any historian, but 'a history of the gaps' analogous to the 'theology of the gaps' which nineteenth-century scholars and clerics tried in vain to construct as they struggled to come to terms with increasing scientific discoveries, which included, of course, the discovery of 'deep time'.

As the social and political context, the modern nation state, which has thus far sustained modern biblical historiography and its critical methods, fractures and is transformed, so we can expect even more radical attacks upon the model it has imposed upon the past. This is likely to mean an increasing divergence between text and artifact rather than the convergence for which many biblical scholars hope. Davies (1992) has outlined the ways in which the consensus within biblical studies has fractured in recent years. He draws out some of the profound implications for biblical studies of new literary studies

of the Hebrew Bible and the revisionist historical work of the mid-
to late 1980s. As noted above, the shifts are not restricted to biblical
studies alone but go way beyond this to include the wider environment of historical studies. It is vital to try to recognize the
cultural and political factors which have shaped biblical studies and
which have combined with ancient presentations of the past to provide the master narrative which forms our standard 'biblical histories' of ancient Israel. Biblical criticism, no less than Orientalism,
arises out of the period of European colonialism and is intricately
linked with it. As Young (1990: 119) has pointed out, the most
significant fact since the Second World War has been the decline of
European colonialism and the subsequent questioning of its history.
Sasson's insight into the cultural and political setting of research into
the history of ancient Israel is particularly noteworthy: 'In the last
quarter of this century, however, altered historiographic perceptions
in post-war Germany and in post-Vietnam America have contributed to fracturing the models which informed the heretofore
dominant reconstructions of Israel's early past' (Sasson 1981: 17). It
is the implications of this fracturing of such models, helping to
expose the political and religious assumptions that have underpinned
the construction of the past in biblical studies, which are central to
this study.

The crisis of confidence which has accompanied the production of
major histories of ancient Israel in recent years helps to illustrate just
how far the consensus has fractured in less than a decade. The self-
doubts which characterized Soggin's (1984) attempt to compose a
'master story', at least doubts about the pre-state period (1984: 19),
were in marked contrast to the overly confident works that had
characterized the late 1950s and the 1960s. This attempt to address
seriously some of the methodological difficulties facing historical
research on early Israel was taken further by Miller and Hayes (1986).
Their volume marked a significant turning point in the writing of
Israelite history from a biblical perspective. The authors acknowledge the problems with biblical texts relating to the pre-monarchic
period, so that they are not willing to venture into historical constructions for these periods. Even when they begin their construction
of the period of David, they acknowledge that this can only be a 'best
guess' (Miller and Hayes 1986: 26), thereby undermining Soggin's
'datum point' (1977: 332), the reign of David, as the starting point of
the historical venture. The candour and clarity in their presentation
of the problems which they have faced and the reasons for the choices

they have made have ensured that Miller–Hayes has become the standard modern presentation of the history of Israel and Judah. It is a work, which the authors acknowledge was conceived as working within accepted parameters, 'firmly anchored in the tradition of Wellhausen–Alt–Noth–Albright' (Hayes 1987: 7). It represents, then, the pinnacle of historical works which stand in the broad tradition of the type of historiography which has dominated biblical studies throughout this century (Hayes 1987: 6–7). Yet, in retrospect, it illustrates all too clearly the ever-increasing problem of ancient Israelite history as a history of the gaps continually forced to abandon its 'sure results' and the firm ground from which the enterprise can begin. Long (1987: 10), in reviewing the volume, has posed the question in its starkest form: 'Should one even try to write a modern critical history of Israel largely on the basis of a single amalgamated, culturally self-serving, and essentially private version of that history?'[33] The reappraisal of biblical narratives, which has continued with increasing vitality and self-confidence, has continued to contribute to the fracturing of the consensus.

The major implication for historical research has been to signal the death of 'biblical history', which is gradually being replaced by the growing recognition of Palestinian history as a subject in its own right.[34] A history of the region increasingly divorced from biblical studies: a broad-based thematic conception of history concerned with the economy, demography, settlement, religions and ideologies of Palestine as a whole. A history of the region concerned with its various micro-environments in which what little we know of Judah and Israel plays an important but by no means dominant or unique role. If the research on early Israel published from the mid- to late 1980s, particularly the studies of Lemche (1985), Ahlström (1986), Coote and Whitelam (1987), and Finkelstein (1988), has taught us anything, it is that the proposals were not radical enough. The various studies are misleading because they reveal nothing of the so-called emergence of Israel, since we are unable to attach ethnic labels to the material culture of the region at this time, but are concerned rather with the settlement and transformation of Palestinian society in general: they too have been misled by the search for the nation state in the guise of Israel imposed by the general context of biblical studies. So in a way our complainant on IOUDAIOS is correct in that some people's history will be removed – not, I believe, an objective history that ever happened but a shaping of the past projected by some 'biblical' writers and perpetuated by modern 'biblical historians', cloaked in the aura of impartiality. Yet it is important to bear in mind that, however self-critical and reflective, the historian not only works with partial texts but inevitably produces a partial text. This, too, is a partial text which tries to come to terms with the modern context in which it arises while trying to free the past realities that are ancient Palestine from the Late Bronze Age to the Roman period from the domination of an imagined past imposed upon it by the discourse of biblical studies.

Thus we return to the profound problem posed by Césaire, echoed by Young (1990), of how to write a 'new' history when all history is European, male, and white.[35] The attempt to provide an alternative conception of the past to that which has emerged from the discourse of biblical studies over the last century or more can only give partial voice to those populations who have been silenced by our modern studies. It is obvious that any counter-history is contingent and partial. What is most important, however, is the exposure of the wide-ranging implications of the search for ancient Israel within nineteenth- and twentieth-century biblical studies. For, as Inden (1986: 445) says of Indian history, a deconstruction of the discourse in which students of India have been inducted is a necessary first step: only after the nature and implications of this discourse have been exposed can Indologists hope to think their way out of it. The problem of Palestinian history has remained unspoken within biblical studies, silenced by the invention of ancient Israel in the image of the European nation state. Only after we have exposed the implications of this invention will Palestinian history be freed from the constraints of biblical studies and the discourse that has shaped it.

2

DENYING SPACE AND TIME TO PALESTINIAN HISTORY

INTRODUCTION

The concepts of space and time are so familiar, yet so crucial, to the historian that they hardly seem worthy of detailed consideration. It is assumed that these matters ought not to detain the historian or the reader for long since they function as givens, providing merely the temporal and geographical limits of the subject matter. Chronology, it is often said, is the backbone of history while the spatial realities are the stage on which such history is played out. However, the consideration of time and space is not such a simple matter for the historian that it can be passed over quickly as a prelude to the more important task of construction. Time and space are social products which, like the construction of the past, are tied to notions of identity and authority. The differing Christian, Hindu, Jewish, or Muslim conceptions of time are ample illustration of its ideological implications. The long-running dispute in the Balkans over the use of the name Macedonia demonstrates how crucial the definition of space is to identity. These twin concepts, then, are crucial to our pursuit of an ancient Palestinian history and to our appreciation of why such a history has rarely been given voice in academic discussions.

Robert Alter (1973: 19), in discussing the importance of the symbolism of Masada, states that there is a 'certain appropriateness' in the link between ancient events and modern politics 'given the peculiarity of Israel's location in history and geography'. Alter does not elaborate on this 'peculiarity' since it seems enough to assert it so that the reader will accept that we are dealing with a very special, if not unique, entity. Herrmann expresses this notion of Israel's uniqueness more explicitly:

This is the stage for the history of ancient Israel. Israel's territory and its potential as a world power were necessarily limited. Its fate was bound up in a network of unavoidable dependant relationships. However, what took place almost in a corner of the world and its history was to have far more influence on world history than might ever have been suspected. Tiny Israel, historically weak and really insignificant, unleashed forces which were stronger than any calculations in world politics. This Israel became a phenomenon pointing beyond itself and raising in paradigmatic fashion the fundamental question of the nature of historical existence. The answer to that question seems to lie beyond any understanding which merely registers causal connections.

(Herrmann 1975: 22)

Herrmann's view that this is 'a corner of the world' exposes his Eurocentrism. Furthermore, the notion that Israel points beyond itself, whatever that might mean, reveals an underlying theological assumption which connects the history of Israel directly with divine action in the mundane realm. Similar phrases, expressing Israel's special place in time and space, can be found in many different academic and popular works suggesting that Herrmann is repeating a widespread belief in Israel's unique relationship to time and space. As we have already seen, the importance of perceptions of the past for shaping identity and the competing nature of such perceptions of the past mean that the concepts of space and time are of vital importance to our undertaking. Both concepts are, like 'the past', ideological constructs to be manipulated, often as part of a hidden discourse, in the construction of social identity while denying competing identities which might lay claim to that same time and space. In the current context, such views cannot be divorced from the contemporary struggle and conflict between the modern state of Israel and the Palestinians of the occupied territories or those in exile. It is for this reason that the use of the term 'Palestine' or the phrase 'Palestinian history' in academic discourse is bound to be contentious. Said (1986: 30) notes that 'there is no neutrality, there can be no neutrality or objectivity about Palestine'. The discourse of biblical studies in reconstructing a past that impinges upon affirmations and denials in the present cannot claim to remain above or outside contemporary political struggles. This becomes apparent when the contrast is drawn between a broad regional history of ancient Palestine in contrast to or, it might be more correct to say, in competition with standard 'biblical histories' of ancient Israel. The discourse of biblical studies has professed to remain aloof from this contemporary political situation while all along denying time and space to any Palestinian claim to the past. It is a discourse which has allocated time, particularly the Late Bronze–Iron Age transition and the Iron Age, as well as geographical space to Israel: other entities such as the Canaanites, the Philistines, or any indigenous groups might inhabit this time and space but it is only on Israel's terms.

THE DENIAL OF PALESTINIAN SPACE

The concept of space in historical terms is no more static than the notion of time which is more usually seen to be at the heart of historical investigation. It has become increasingly recognized that the definition and control of space has formed a crucial role in Europe's construction of its Other, a counterpoint to its own self-definition as rational, powerful, and stable. The discussion of the use of the term 'Palestine' is inevitably an intricate part of the same Orientalist discourse and its construction of the Orient. Biblical studies has not remained aloof from this discourse with its representation of the Orient, including Palestine, as Europe's essential Other. It is possible to trace Orientalist presuppositions through some of the most influential works in biblical studies of the nineteenth and twentieth centuries. The standard 'biblical histories' of Israel invariably begin with a chapter devoted to geography, the definition of space, ostensibly as an objective presentation of geographical information designed to provide the reader with essential background knowledge. The interrelationship between biblical scholarship's search for 'ancient Israel' and the rise of the European nation state and nationalism should alert us to some of the problems of trying to define the spatial dimensions of our subject matter.

The choice of terminology for the region, the meaning with which it is invested, implicitly or explicitly, denies any other perception of the past or present. These are intertwined in such a way that it is the present which has priority in defining and determining the past. The problem for the historian is not simply a question of the description of the physical boundaries of the space, but the naming of that space. It is the choice of nomenclature which carries with it so many implications, so many denials or assertions, that are both crucial and controversial. The long-standing Israeli occupation of the West Bank and Gaza, the Palestinian *intifada*, and the Palestinian struggle for self-determination and a homeland make the choice of this term controversial. The dramatic developments at the beginning of September 1993 with the signing of an accord between Yitzhak Rabin and Yasser Arafat, followed by the gradual and difficult implementation of the Gaza–Jericho First policy, have only served to add further weight and significance to the problematic definition of space.[1] The question of 'Palestine' and 'Palestinian history' *vis-à-vis* 'Israel' and 'Israelite history' cannot be divorced from contemporary claims and counter-claims to the past. The various attempts to define the physical boundaries of Palestine are of less significance than its use as an image in scholarly and popular literature.

Biblical scholarship employs a bewildering array of terms for the region: 'the Holy Land', 'the Land of the Bible', 'Eretz Israel' or 'the land of Israel', 'Israel', 'Judah', 'Canaan', 'Cisjordan', 'Syro–Palestine', 'Palestine', and 'the Levant'. To the casual reader of many standard works on historical geography or studies of the history of the region, these terms may appear to be interchangeable or even neutral. Yet the naming of land implies control of that land: designations such as 'Levant', 'Middle East', or 'Near East' betray a Eurocentric conception of the world. Anderson (1991) has shown how the map played a crucial role in conceptualization and control of European colonial territories. Equally, it is important to examine how the terms 'Eretz Israel', 'the land of Israel', and 'Palestine' have been invested with, or divested of, meaning in Western scholarship. Despite the fact that Western scholarship has continually employed the term 'Palestine', it has been divested of any real meaning in the face of the search for ancient Israel.[2]

The political implications of the terminology chosen to represent this area can be traced through some of the classic works of historical geography which have informed biblical studies over the last century. The classic early treatment of historical geography can be found in George Adam Smith's *The Historical Geography of the Holy Land*, first published in 1894. The subtitle of the work is revealing: 'Especially in Relation to the History of Israel and of the Early Church'. He uses the term 'Palestine' as interchangeable with 'Holy Land' while his preface makes it quite clear that his primary motivation is to illuminate the Bible:

Students of the Bible desire to see a background and feel an atmosphere – to discover from 'the lie of the land' why the

history took certain lines and the prophecy and gospel were
expressed in certain styles – to learn what geography has to
contribute to questions of Biblical criticism – above all, to
discern between what physical nature contributed to the religious development of Israel, and what was the product of
purely moral and spiritual forces.

(Smith 1894: vii)

Thus Palestine has no intrinsic meaning of its own, but provides the
background and atmosphere for understanding the religious developments which are the foundation of Western civilization. Palestine
does not have a history of its own, it is the history of Israel and
thereby the history of the West. Commensurate with this lack of
history is also the absence of inhabitants in the land. Palestine is a
religious curiosity shop, what Smith (1984: viii) calls 'a museum of
Church history ... full of living as well as of ancient specimens of
the subject'. He recounts (1894: x) the ancient ruins of the past
through to the present and notes that after the trail of Napoleon's
march and retreat we find that 'after the long silence and crumbling
of all things native, there are the living churches of to-day, and the
lines of pilgrims coming up to Jerusalem from the four corners of the
world'. The reader is left in no doubt as to the vitality of European
culture in contrast to the decline and devastation which have been
supervised by the indigenous population.

The land seems empty and devoid of interest apart from the
vestiges of ancient monuments that are important for understanding
the development of European civilization. This is reinforced in
Smith's own day by the 'European invasion of Syria' (1894: 19). He
goes on to describe this process throughout Palestine and Syria,
culminating with his view of the significance of the introduction of
the railway:

Not only will it open up the most fertile parts of the country,
and bring back European civilization to where it once was
supreme, on the east of the Jordan; but if ever European arms
return to the country – as, in a contest for Egypt or for the
Holy Places, when they may not return? – this railway running
from the coast across the central battlefield of Palestine will be
of immense strategic value.

(Smith 1894: 20–1)

His view of the place of European civilization reveals that indigenous culture and history are of little interest by comparison. The land is the rightful property of Western powers if they so decide: a superiority defined in terms of military power.

When he goes on to discuss the place of Syria–Palestine in world history, he does so in terms of Opportunity and Influence, which means in terms of religion (1894: 21). Smith's account is a classic Orientalist expression of Europe's Other. In describing the religious development of the Semitic in the 'seclusion' of Arabia, he is able to proclaim that:

> The only talents are those of war and of speech – the latter cultivated to a singular augustness of style by the silence of nature and the long leisure of life. It is the atmosphere in which seers, martyrs, and fanatics are bred. Conceive a race subjected to its influences for thousands of years! To such a race give a creed, and it will be an apostolic and a devoted race.
>
> (Smith 1894: 29)

For Smith, as for so many theologians and biblical specialists since, Israel's genius, the reason its religion rose to prominence while its neighbours fell into the degradations of fertility worship, was the ethical impulse of its belief. Though this has been shown to be a false representation of indigenous religion or those of surrounding cultures, the influence has remained very strong in biblical scholarship, retaining a powerful hold on popular perceptions.[3] One of the important consequences is that it is Israelite culture which represents the pinnacle of achievement while Canaanite fertility religion is surpassed and supplanted. Thus Israelite history supersedes and in effect silences Canaanite, i.e. indigenous Palestinian history. The description of the land is presented in terms of its importance for Western civilization and the origins of its monotheistic faith: European powers were returning to protect the land which had provided the taproot of its own civilization.[4]

Recent standard treatments of the history of Israel illustrate just how influential these ideas have been and how they have been perpetuated and strengthened throughout this century. Martin Noth's (1960) classic *The History of Israel* opens with a section entitled 'The land of Israel'. Noth, like most biblical scholars, states that the history of Israel was conditioned by its geographical setting to such an extent that a knowledge of the geography of the region is one of the preconditions for a proper understanding of its history.

However, in discussing the name of the region, he acknowledges that the phrase 'the land of Israel' is used only once in the Hebrew Bible (1 Samuel 13: 19) and that the 'original name for the land' has not been preserved. He then goes on to argue that:

> as a natural phenomenon it was never a homogeneous, self-contained entity and was never occupied by a homogeneous population, and it was hardly at any time the scene of a political organization which substantially coincided with its actual area. So the expression 'the land of Israel' may serve as a somewhat flexible description of the area within which the Israelite tribes had their settlements.
>
> (Noth 1960: 8)

The history of those inhabitants of Palestine not included in the Israelite tribes is silenced by Noth's concern with Israel. Only homogeneity seems to count. The history of Palestine in general is subsumed by the concern with Israel despite his acknowledgement that it is usual to call the land of Israel 'Palestine'. The effect of this, however, is to divest the term 'Palestine' of any meaning by transforming it into a mere shorthand for the land of Israel. The proper object of study then becomes Israel rather than Palestine or the inhabitants of Palestine. Thus he goes on to state that:

> As real and authentic history, the history of Israel was always profoundly conditioned by the nature of the soil on which it took place. A knowledge of the geography of Palestine is therefore one of the preconditions for a proper understanding of the history of Israel; and an exposition of the history of Israel must be preceded by a brief survey of the basic characteristics of the land itself.
>
> (Noth 1960: 8)

The land that might be termed 'Palestine' has no intrinsic value of its own but becomes the arena for the 'real and authentic history' of Israel.

Noth's following description of the physical features of the region presents a peculiar landscape virtually barren and devoid of human habitation. What population exists is anonymous and notable only for its lack of unity (1960: 10). A seemingly 'objective' description of topography presents an empty land waiting to be populated by Israel, at which point Noth's historical description can begin. Revealingly, these anonymous inhabitants of Palestine are never described as 'Palestinians'. Noth's work is representative of the assumptions and hidden discourse of biblical studies which effectively silences Palestinian history in favour of the search for ancient Israel. It has divested the term 'Palestine' of any meaning and ignored the history of the indigenous population of the region.

Herrmann (1975) begins his account of Israelite history with a chapter entitled 'The scene' in which he claims that:

> Israel's history is inextricably bound up with the land, indeed the lands, in which it took place. Without qualification, that is the case with the people of Israel in the Old Testament. We can see the rudimentary beginnings of Israel on the one hand in northern Syria and neighbouring Mesopotamia, and on the other in northwest Egypt, before Israel found a homeland in Palestine, 'the promised land', possession of which was never undisputed.
>
> (Herrmann 1975: 6)

It is noticeable that Palestine once again becomes shorthand, this time for 'the promised land' which is designated to be Israel's homeland: it is not a Palestinian homeland or the homeland of the indigenous population. As we have already noted, the choice of the term 'homeland' takes on an added significance in light of the use of this term in the Balfour Declaration. Herrmann's treatment, which continues in the line of German biblical historiography inspired by Alt and Noth, again provides a barren and empty landscape: what population is mentioned is largely anonymous. Palestine is introduced to the reader merely as 'the scene of the history of Israel' (1975: 6). It only becomes inhabited and of significance with the fulfilment of the promise which sees Israel's entry onto the stage. He detects an important link between past and present when reviewing the achievements of ancient Israel – a claim of considerable political import given the contemporary struggle for Palestine. He denies that there has been any fundamental climatic change between ancient and modern times, concluding that the bareness of the land and its resistance to agriculture can only be overcome by the most extraordinary effort, 'like that expended by the modern state of Israel'.[5] The continuum between past and present means that this difficult land can only be made to yield up its produce by the extraordinary efforts of Israel. No one else, it seems, possesses this ability. The claim that it is Israel, and Israel alone, which has made the land bloom has long been part of the Zionist justification for Jewish immigration and the founding of a modern state. The Zionist representation of an 'empty land' has been paralleled in biblical scholarship by a construction of the past which ignores the role of the indigenous population in many periods. Once again, it is the uniqueness of Israel that allows it to overcome overwhelming odds: Palestinian history simply does not exist or is of no account by comparison.

American biblical historiography is represented by John Bright's (1972) classic treatment *A History of Israel* which is a culmination of Albright's scholarship and influence upon biblical studies. Despite the fact that Noth's and Bright's histories have long been seen as representing alternative approaches to the history of ancient Israel, particularly for its early periods, it is remarkable how they share fundamental assumptions which have dominated modern biblical studies. Bright, like Noth, represents ancient Israel as part of the ancient Orient, a term whose ideological implications Said has exposed. Yet he does not provide the usual geographical introduction to his volume, preferring to use the term 'Palestine' without any discussion of its possible meanings. Yet once again, although he discusses the history of the region prior to the emergence of Israel, he never refers to its inhabitants as Palestinians. The land might be called Palestine, yet its inhabitants are Amorites, Canaanites, or Israelites.

By contrast, Miller and Hayes (1986), who describe their work as standing within the tradition of Alt–Noth–Albright–Bright provide a chronological and geographical setting for their study of Israelite and Judaean history. They present the Palestinian hill country as the 'center stage' (1986: 30) for this history, acknowledging that Palestine 'was shared by a diversity of people' (1986: 30). The recognition that this region was not the sole reserve of Israelites and Judaeans but was populated by various 'inhabitants of ancient Palestine' (1986: 33) does not extend to their identification as 'Palestinians'. The inhabitants are for the most part anonymous, only taking on an identity when they become Israelite or Judaean. They discuss the various designations for the region in ancient texts which include Retenu, Hurru, Amurru, Canaan, Philistia, and many others, although their description of the region is in terms of its topographical and physical features. It is possible to refer to the 'Palestinian coastline', 'Palestinian agriculture', or the 'Palestinian economy' (1986: 51), but the inhabitants are never described as Palestinians.

The examples chosen here, from biblical reference works or specialist articles on the history of ancient Israel, could be multiplied many times over. The point at issue, however, is more than adequately illustrated by this series of extracts from a number of representative works on ancient Israelite history that have dominated biblical studies. The fact that they refer to the geographical region as Palestine but never refer to its inhabitants as Palestinians is a denial and silencing of Palestinian history. We are continually presented with images of a land in which its inhabitants are anonymous or non-existent. The history of Palestine effectively only begins with the history of Israel and becomes coterminous with it. The reason for this cannot be that the focus of these works is upon the history of Israel or that they can claim that their accounts only begin with the emergence of Israel onto the historical stage, since all refer to periods prior to the existence of Israel or Israelites. All refuse studiously to use the term Palestinians to describe the inhabitants, even though the adjective 'Palestinian' is acceptable to describe inanimate objects such as the physical setting or economy. The refusal to use the same qualifying adjective of the inhabitants of the region is thereby a denial of their existence and history. Thus Palestine can be presented as a small, poor, isolated region – frequent descriptions in biblical studies – which has been transformed and made notable by the unique historical presence of Israel. Biblical studies is, thereby, implicated in an act of dispossession which has its modern political counterpart in the Zionist possession of the land and dispossession of its Palestinian inhabitants. As a people without history – or deprived of that history by the discourse of biblical studies – they become unimportant, irrelevant, and finally non-existent. It is an act of interpretation presented as objective scholarship, carrying the full weight of Western intellectual institutions, which is intricately bound to the dominant understanding of the present in which the modern state of Israel has made an 'empty' and 'barren' land blossom.

This assumption, inherent in the work of some of the most influential figures in biblical studies, particularly German and American biblical historiography, as we have seen, has also maintained a profound hold over biblical archaeology this century. The constitution of the Palestine Exploration Fund at its establishment in 1865 illustrates clearly the widely held assumption that Palestine held little intrinsic interest apart from its connections with the Bible. The PEF's stated aims were 'the accurate and systematic investigation of the archaeology, the topography, the geology and the physical geography, the manners and customs of the Holy Land, for biblical illustration' (cited in Kenyon 1979: 1). Palestine becomes 'the Holy Land', as it was for Smith, and its history and physical features have little intrinsic value in their own right, being important solely as illustrations for understanding the Bible. This is the dominant assumption which informs so much of biblical scholarship in the West such that Palestinian history ceases to exist and the history of the region becomes the history of ancient Israel as depicted in the biblical traditions.

Katherine Kenyon acknowledges that the area is important for our understanding of the origins of civilization and not just for illustrating the Bible. However, it needs to be remembered that 'civilization' is here shorthand for the West, which is heir to the Judaeo–Christian tradition. Although Kenyon's work is ostensibly a study of the archaeological findings of the region, it is clear that her views are dependent upon a prior understanding of the biblical traditions rather than a reading of the archaeological data in its own right. So she is able to state that:

> The period is undoubtedly that in which the national con-
> sciousness of the Israelites is developing greatly. The biblical
> narrative shows how the groups were gradually combining
> together, with tentative efforts at temporal unification under
> the Judges and the stronger spiritual link of a national religion,
> with the high priest at times exercising temporal power. It is
> during these centuries that the groups allied by race, but
> differing in the manner and time of the settlement in Palestine
> ... must have come to combine their ancestral traditions
> together under the influence of the Yahwehistic religion, and
> to believe that all their ancestors took part in the Exodus. The
> nation was thus emerging, but its culture was as yet primitive.
> Its settlements were villages, its art crude, and the objects of
> everyday use homely and utilitarian.
>
> (Kenyon 1979: 230)

It is difficult to see what it is in the archaeological record that would allow for her conclusion that 'the national consciousness of the Israelites' was developing in this period. As will be seen below, the problem of trying to attach ethnic labels to material remains for this period has become a crucial factor in helping to free the history of the region from such long-dominant, unargued assumptions. The reading of the archaeological evidence is determined by Kenyon's prior understanding of the biblical narratives. Her statement is dominated by the terms 'national' and 'nation': it is the nation state which is the representative of (European) civilization. Ancient Israel, as a nation state, or incipient nation state, provides a direct link with Europe as the very essence of civilization. The significance of the region then lies in its importance for understanding the origins of (European) civilization and the biblical traditions which have underpinned the development of a Judaeo–Christian culture in the West. However, it does not extend to an investigation of any intrinsic value attached to the history of the vast majority of the indigenous inhabitants of the region.

The work of William Foxwell Albright, whose influence on all aspects of the discipline remains strong despite current reassessments of many of his conclusions, illustrates how these underlying domain assumptions are often implicit and not always apparent to the reader. His classic treatment *The Archaeology of Palestine* (1949) uses the terms 'Palestine' and 'Palestinian' throughout. Even in his discussion of the Iron Age, designated by many Israeli archaeologists as the 'Israelite period', he consistently refers to the archaeology of Palestine. The history of the region is presented in a sober fashion which seemingly values Palestine in its own right. In his conclusion he is able to state that:

> The role of archaeology in providing data for objective evaluation of the history of Palestine is already so great that no student can now neglect it without intellectual disaster. Although twenty years have elapsed since the study of Palestinian archaeology reached a sufficiently stable phase to warrant use of its data by sober historians, it is still very difficult for the non-specialist to pick his way among the conflicting dates and conclusions of archaeologists.
>
> (Albright 1949: 252–3)

However, the theological presuppositions of Albright's approach are revealed particularly towards the end of his study:

> In one's enthusiasm for archaeology research, one is sometimes tempted to disregard the enduring reason for any special interest in Palestine – nearly all the Hebrew Old Testament is a product of Palestinian soil and Israelite writers, while most of the events which underlie the Greek New Testament took place in the same sacred terrain.
>
> (Albright 1949: 218)

Here we discover the reason for any 'special interest' in the region: it is the locale for the development of the Old and New Testaments. He acknowledges the contribution of surrounding cultures to both these works but adds that they have been 'transmuted' by religious insight into something far surpassing these contributory cultures. He then tries to defend the objectivity of biblical scholarship against the charge of religious bias:

> It is frequently said that the scientific quality of Palestinian archaeology has been seriously impaired by the religious preconceptions of scholars who have excavated in the Holy Land. It is true that some archaeologists have been drawn to Palestine by their interest in the Bible, and that some of them had received their previous training mainly as biblical scholars. The writer has known many such scholars, but he recalls scarcely a single case where their religious views seriously influenced their results. Some of these scholars were radical critics; still others were more conservative critics, like Ernest Sellin; others again were thorough-going conservatives. But their archaeological conclusions were almost uniformly independent of their critical views.
>
> (Albright 1949: 219)

Notice how Palestine now becomes the 'Holy Land'. Furthermore, the seeming objectivity of approach and the pursuit of Palestinian history and archaeology in its own right are exposed in his conclusion, where he tries to account for the importance of Palestine in world history despite its small size and lack of resources:

> Though archaeology can thus clarify the history and geography of ancient Palestine, it cannot explain the basic miracle of Israel's faith, which remains a unique factor in world history. But archaeology can help enormously in making the miracle rationally plausible to an intelligent person whose vision is not shortened by a materialistic world view. It can also show the absurdity of extreme sectarian positions, from the once reputable doctrine of verbal inspiration of Scripture to the weird vagaries of believers in the divinatory properties of numbers, measurements, and alleged biblical ciphers. Against these and other modern forms of ancient magic, archaeology wages an unceasing war, and few things are more irritating to the sober archaeologist than to see religious faith compounded with

magic by exponents of cheap materialism. To one who believes in the historical mission of Palestine, its archaeology possesses a value which raises it far above the level of artifacts with which it must constantly deal, into a region where history and theology share a common faith in the eternal realities of existence.

(Albright 1949: 255–6)

It becomes clear that the history of Palestine is of little intrinsic interest in its own right: 'the historical mission of Palestine' derives from its occupation of the 'sacred space' out of which the Old and New Testaments appear. Albright's theological beliefs, despite denials to the contrary, clearly shape his assessment and construction of Israelite history. This is history, moreover, in which Europe or the West is the real subject, as Asad and others have pointed out of other modern accounts of the past. It is ultimately a pursuit of the roots of Western 'civilization'.

The problems of terminology and methodological approach can be illustrated further from Baly's influential revision of his *The Geography of the Bible* (original 1957; completely revised 1974). He states his aim as twofold: to provide a work for scholars who require 'solid, detailed, and accurate information' in the form of 'a serious geographical and biblical study' (1974: xi) which is at the same time a simple and straightforward presentation for the beginning student and general reader. Baly is well aware of the problems that his venture holds: the problems of the time limit and the theological presuppositions imposed on the study.

> When the study is limited to the biblical period, it is difficult to avoid the suggestion that the history of Palestine began with Abraham and came to an end in A.D. 70, an impression which is already too firmly implanted in the minds of many Western people ... it cannot be denied that the events of the biblical period are those which most concern the ordinary American or British reader, and it seems, therefore a useful place at which to begin, though obviously it is only a beginning.
>
> (Baly 1974: xiii)

Here we can see that the problems of time and space are intricately related. Yet, as with Albright, the presentation of the 'history of Palestine' is informed by theological considerations which override all others, as Baly admits. He refers (1974: xiv) to the complaint that 'theologians are not interested in geology, and geographers do not want theology in a geography book'. His defence is that it is important to understand the culture and climate of the country in order to understand the nature of the environment which has had such a profound influence upon its inhabitants. But related to this is his view that it is equally important to understand the nature of the 'Book' with its claim to the existence of the one God who is both active and effective. The theological claims mean that the history of the region can only be understood in terms of 'biblical history': it is defined by and dominated by the concerns and presentation of the biblical texts. It is not, then, a history or geography of Palestine but a history and geography of 'biblical Israel'. To refer to the history of the period of Abraham is to accept a biblical definition of that history and to deny any other perception of the past. Baly attempts to overcome the problems of definition which are tied to the present and determined by theological presuppositions in his choice of terminology:

> There still remains, however, the problem of names, for as anyone who has dealt with Middle Eastern geography knows to his cost, names tend constantly to take on political significance, and to be the cause of much recrimination. Therefore, it must be said clearly that *no name at all, whether 'Israel' or 'Palestine' or any other, will be used in its modern political sense, unless this is expressly stated.* The name 'Palestine' will be used to mean 'the country of the Bible,' on both sides of the Jordan, in the sense in which it is used in many biblical commentaries. 'Israel' will be kept for the ancient kingdom of Israel, lying to the north of the kingdom of Judah. In speaking of the two regions on either side of the great Central Valley of the Jordan and the Arabah we shall speak of 'Cis-jordan' and 'Trans-jordan'. The whole coastland, stretching from the borders of modern Turkey to Egypt, may be described as the 'Levant Coast'.
>
> (Baly 1974: 5)[6]

The problem here is that the designation 'Palestine' is merely shorthand for 'the country of the Bible'. It is theological assumptions and biblical definitions which ultimately determine any understanding of the region. This is confirmed by the map at the beginning of the book entitled 'Old Testament Palestine' in which the regional designations are all biblical tribal designations: 'Zebulun', 'Manasseh',

'Ephraim', 'Benjamin', etc. The theological claims of the Hebrew Bible have been given priority in determining the designation of the land, thereby silencing any alternative claims to understanding the region and its past.[7]

The problems of different designations for the region and their underlying competing claims to the past and the present become even sharper in modern Israeli scholarship. Yohanan Aharoni's *The Land of the Bible. A Historical Geography* (1962) has been particularly influential in shaping the discipline. Throughout the work, the phrase 'the Land of the Bible' is used interchangeably with 'the Holy Land' and 'Palestine'. At first sight the terms do not appear to be particularly controversial or self-conscious. However, the title of the Hebrew original, *The Land of Israel in Biblical Times*, tends to suggest that, as with Baly, the term 'Palestine' is simply shorthand: it is defined primarily in terms of Israel and the biblical understanding of the past. Part Two of the work, entitled 'Palestine during the ages' contains a separate chapter on 'The Canaanite period' followed by a series of chapters dealing with 'Israelite' and 'Judaean' history. It is noticeable that in chronological terms 'Canaanite' is separate from, is succeeded by, and replaced by 'Israelite' history. This chronological distinction between 'Canaanite' and 'Israelite' periods pervades biblical scholarship and is an important archaeological and historical differentiation in Israeli scholarship in particular. The Israeli convention of designating archaeological periods as 'Canaanite' and 'Israelite' is in contrast to the American and European practice of designating these periods as the Bronze and Iron Ages. However, as we have seen in the work of Albright, despite the differences in archaeological nomenclature, the assumption of much of biblical scholarship is that 'Israelite' culture succeeds, replaces, and surpasses 'Canaanite' culture.

Rainey, one of the leading contemporary authorities on historical geography, and the person who revised the second edition of Aharoni's classic work, has described the importance of the subject in the following terms:

> The abundant research being conducted today in the land of the Bible has its roots in the historical and religious interest inherent in the Judaeo–Christian tradition. According to Halakhic Judaism, one cannot fully express one's faith by living out all the commandments unless one lives on the soil of the 'Land of Israel'. The Christian concern for the geography of

the 'Holy Land' is motivated by the desire to see and in some way relive the experiences of the Scriptures at the places where they occurred. The biblical tradition itself is predicated on a certain amount of geographical knowledge. Israel's constitution as a nation is firmly linked with its occupation of the 'Land of Canaan'. The historical and religious experience of Israel took place in a specific geographical context.

(Rainey 1988: 353)

The political implications of the choice of nomenclature become much clearer in this passage: the possession and naming of the land, both past and present, is of vital importance. The interrelationships of past and present are made explicit in this conception of the nature of Israel and its possession of the land. Israel is conceived here in terms of the nation state, which is inextricably linked to national territory by right of 'occupation'. The rationale for historical geography is given as the historical and religious interests of the Judaeo–Christian tradition. No mention is made of any interest in Palestinian history: it is silenced by the concern for Israel's historical and religious experience 'in a specific geographical context'.

These points can be illustrated further from Aharoni's (1982) other classic work, *The Archaeology of the Land of Israel*. The way in which the search for 'ancient Israel' has obscured and silenced Palestinian history is brought out in Rainey's preface to the second edition:

> Throughout the book we have usually used the term Eretz-Israel or the Land of Israel. By this is meant the total area inhabited by the Israelite people, corresponding most closely to the territory governed by David and Solomon. Aharoni has demonstrated its legitimacy as a geographical entity throughout most of the biblical period. Although it is something of an anachronism for the prehistoric and Canaanite eras, the reader will find it no less than the commonly accepted Palestine. Eretz-Israel is perhaps the only nonpolitical term in use today, except perhaps for Canaan, which does not represent precisely the territory dealt with in the Israelite period.
>
> (Rainey 1982: xiii)

The appeal to the boundaries of the Davidic–Solomonic kingdom, 'from Dan to Beersheba', as a definition of the geographical extent of Eretz Israel, a claim that will need to be examined in later chapters, betrays that it is the biblical perception of the past which is dominant. Rainey's claim, made in such a reasonable and matter-of-fact manner, that the term Eretz Israel is not just non-political but is the *only* non-political term for the region, is astounding in the context. The terms 'Palestine' and 'Eretz Israel' are not interchangeable but are in competition given the contemporary struggle for Palestine. The political nature of the term 'Eretz Israel', *contra* Rainey, is evident from the fact that it opens and is used throughout the Proclamation of Independence of the State of Israel issued in May 1948 (Laqueur and Rubin 1984: 125–8). The implications of the choice of terminology to define space become more obvious when it is learned that Aharoni's monograph was designed to replace W.F. Albright's classic treatment of thirty years earlier, *The Archaeology of Palestine* (1949). Just as the prehistoric and Canaanite periods have been superseded by the Israelite era, so Palestine has been supplanted and replaced by Israel.

Rainey acknowledges that the phrase Eretz Israel is anachronistic when applied to what he terms the 'prehistoric' and 'Canaanite' periods since it is the 'biblical period' and the 'Israelite period' which are the focus of attention.[8] This is revealing in light of the title of the work, *The Archaeology of the Land of Israel*, compared with the scope of the work which covers the Chalcolithic to the Persian periods. Thus a vast expanse of time before the appearance of any entity called Israel or the formation of an Israelite state is subsumed under the term 'the Land of Israel'. Aharoni (1982: 90) describes the Middle and Late Bronze Ages, his Middle Canaanite II and Late Canaanite (c. 2000–1200 BCE), as the first historical period for which there are documents preserved. However, he goes on to add that 'this is also the period in which the Hebrew tribes penetrated into various districts of the country and finally crystallized into the people of Israel, *the first and only people to make the country its natural homeland*' (Aharoni 1982: 90; emphasis added). While his view of the origins or emergence of Israel in the Late Bronze Age is now outdated in comparison with much recent research, as will be shown below, the significant fact is that he gives no justification for his view that it is 'the people of Israel' who are 'the first and only people to make the country its natural homeland'. The reader is given no explanation as to why it is Israel alone that can claim the territory as its 'natural' homeland. It is significant that the language Rainey chooses closely mirrors the Balfour Declaration of 2 November 1917 which committed the British government to viewing 'with favour the establishment in Palestine of a natural home for the Jewish people'. However much the discourse of biblical studies might profess its objectivity, it is easy to see that it is implicated in contemporary political struggles.[9] The claims of the modern state to the region as its 'natural homeland' are mirrored in a projection of the past in which Israel replaces Palestine and Israelite history supersedes prehistory and Canaanite history. Once again there are no ancient Palestinians, only prehistoric inhabitants or Canaanites, therefore there can be no such thing as Palestinian history.

The essence to the claim on the land and therefore the right to name it, which is to possess it, is made on the basis of nationhood and statehood. It is at this point that the modern struggle for Palestine coincides with the representation of the past in biblical studies. The choice of language, the naming of the land, is part of the manipulation of power in which relationship to the land is affirmed or denied. The political ramifications and problematic nature of the naming of space emerges in the discussion of nomenclature which took place at the Congress of Archaeology in Jerusalem in 1984. Moshe Dothan (1985: 136), responsible with his wife Trude Dothan for so much of the discovery and clarification of Philistine culture, rejected the term 'Holy Land' as too narrow in its application to biblical aspects of the past and a study of holy places. He rejected the use of the term 'Palestine' on the grounds that it was the official name for the country 'for only a mere thirty years under the British Mandate' (1985: 137), arguing that its origins in the fifth century BCE were restricted to a designation for the southern coast: he refers to it as a Greek simplification and generalization found in Herodotus. It was replaced by Yehud and Yehudah but reinstated in the Roman period and used after the Arab conquest. After the eleventh century CE, the term, according to Dothan, was almost forgotten, allowing him to conclude that:

Thus for nearly 700 years, the name *Palaestina* was hardly used. Only in the nineteenth century, with the awakening of European religious, historical and political interests, did the Latin name *Palaestina* reappear. We may conclude that the chronologically late and inconsistently used term 'Palestine' was apparently never accepted by any local national entity. It therefore can hardly serve as a meaningful term for the archaeology of this country.

(Dothan 1985: 137)

This denial of continuity between the use of the term Palestine and any past reality thereby denies any claims to a Palestinian history. Yet this is a denial of a use of a term which appears in Assyrian and Hellenistic sources, becomes the designation for the region in the Roman period, and was then used extensively in Arabic sources from the tenth century onward (Davies 1992: 23; Said 1992: 10). Once again the controlling factor is the nation state since it is the 'local national entity' which defines the space. Since the modern state of Israel is such a 'local national entity' it follows that 'Israel' is the appropriate label for the area. Dothan went on to argue that:

> The Israelites were the only ethnic group which, as a nation, succeeded in creating a state in this land, one that was neither dependant on some great empire nor belonged to a loose conglomeration of city-states like those of the Canaanite period.
> (Dothan 1985: 139)

Nation and land become synonymous in this analysis since the territory belongs to and is identified with the nation. Here it should be noted that once again it is the nation state, Israel, which has replaced Canaanite culture characterized as merely a loose conglomeration of city-states. Israel represents the ultimate in political evolution, the European nation state, and the pinnacle of civilization which surpasses and replaces that which is primitive and incapable of transformation. Thus Israel has replaced Palestine, and Israelite history thereby silences any Palestinian past. Dothan goes on to claim that the only terms that can be 'correctly applied' are 'the archaeology of Israel' or 'the archaeology of the Land of Israel'. He rejects the former on the grounds that it excludes areas outside the borders of the modern state of Israel, thereby concluding that 'the archaeology of the Land of Israel' is the most appropriate term. The existence of the modern state and its claims to continuity with some earlier state of the Iron Age is the determining factor in the choice of terminology. The claim to continuity means that other claims to existence, other perceptions of the past, are effectively silenced. We are left with the history of Israel, past and present. There is no Palestine and therefore there cannot be a history of Palestine.[10]

The term 'Palestine' has been divested of any inherent meaning of its own in biblical scholarship: it can only be understood when it is redefined by some other theological or political term such as 'Holy Land' or 'Eretz Israel'. But what is even more striking is that while the use of the term 'Palestine' might be widespread, albeit divested of any meaning of its own, the term 'Palestinians' as inhabitants of the land very rarely occurs in biblical scholarship. If we have a land called Palestine, why are its inhabitants not called Palestinians?[11] For the so-called prehistoric periods, the inhabitants are nameless except for designation by archaeological period: Neolithic, Chalcolithic, or possibly Ghassulian culture. There are no written sources by which to identify the inhabitants. But they are not 'Palestinians' or even 'Neolithic Palestinians', 'Chalcolithic Palestinians', or 'Palestinians of the Neolithic or Chalcolithic periods'. In the Bronze Age, it is the 'Canaanites' who become the inhabitants of the land. Archaeologists recognize the achievements of their culture, particularly for the Middle Bronze and Late Bronze Ages. Yet they are never said to have a national consciousness and their religion is presented, of course, as a degenerate fertility cult, lacking in the overarching ethical impulse of Yahwism, and therefore immoral. Such a presentation also draws a sharp contrast with the national consciousness and moral mono-theism of Western civilization. They are replaced by the Israelites who are a 'nation' or incipient nation who, according to Aharoni, are only claiming their 'natural homeland'. We have the paradox that 'Canaanite' culture was more advanced, as many archaeologists acknowledge, but their religion is portrayed as far inferior to the supreme religion which is the foundation of Judaeo–Christian tradition and thereby Western civilization. In the same way, Israel as a nation state is at the pinnacle of political evolution in contrast to a conglomeration of city-states in the region.

Palestine may exist, in name only, but it has no reality in terms of its history or inhabitants being Palestinian. Those inhabitants who are acknowledged before the beginning of the Iron Age are only temporary, mostly anonymous, awaiting Israel's arrival to claim its national heritage. Since it is difficult to deny the existence of inhabitants prior to the 'emergence' of Israel, the standard approach has been to denigrate their achievements or their right to exist. So the Bishop of Salisbury could address members of the Palestine Exploration Fund in 1903 with the following words:

> Nothing, I think, that has been discovered makes us feel any regret at the suppression of Canaanite civilization by Israelite civilization ... the Bible has not misrepresented at all the abomination of Canaanite culture which was superseded by the Israelite culture.

(cited by Said 1992: 79)[12]

The situation in antiquity as presented by biblical scholarship is remarkably similar to the modern period leading up to the foundation of the modern state of Israel. Scholarship seems to mirror the late nineteenth-century Zionist slogan for Palestine: 'a land without people, for a people without land.' What we have in biblical scholarship from its inception to the present day is the presentation of a land, 'Palestine', without inhabitants, or at the most simply temporary, ephemeral inhabitants, awaiting a people without a land. This has been reinforced by a reading of the biblical traditions and archaeological findings, interpreted on the basis of a prior understanding of a reading of the Bible, which helps to confirm this understanding. The foundation of the modern state has dominated scholarship to such an extent that the retrojection of the nation state into antiquity has provided the vital continuity which helps to justify and legitimize both. The effect has been to deny any continuity or legitimacy to Palestinian history. If there were no Palestinians in antiquity then there could not be a Palestinian history. The notion of continuity is reinforced by the assumption that European civilization, the pinnacle of human achievement, has its roots in this Judaeo–Christian tradition. Europe has retrojected the nation state into antiquity in order to discover its own roots while at the same time giving birth to the Zionist movement which has established a 'civilized' state in the alien Orient thereby helping to confirm this continuity in culture and civilization. The irony of this situation is that for the past there is a Palestine but no Palestinians, yet for the present there are Palestinians but no Palestine.[13] The politics of scholarship is brought home by the remark of Menachem Begin in 1969: 'If this is Palestine and not the land of Israel, then you are conquerors and not tillers of the land. You are invaders. If this is Palestine, then it belongs to a people who lived here before you came' (cited by Said 1988: 241). In the scholarship of the past and in the reality of the present, Palestine has become 'the land of Israel' and the history of Israel is the only legitimate subject of study. All else is subsumed in providing background and understanding for the history of ancient Israel which has continuity with the present state and provides the roots and impulse of European civilization.

DENYING TIME TO PALESTINIAN HISTORY

Time, like space, is a political concept, an 'ideologically constructed instrument of power' (Fabian 1983: 144), which has been manipulated in biblical studies to deny any temporal reality to Palestinian history. Fabian points to the common acknowledgement of the imperial construction of space, often as an 'empty land' to be occupied for the good of humanity. However, as he notes, this concentration on the imperialistic and political constructions of space has led to a failure to concede that time is every bit as much controlled, measured, and allotted by dominant powers. The discovery of 'deep time' has been at the heart of Western historiographical perceptions of the evolutionary development of culture and history. This emphasis on the inexorable progress of time's arrow has resulted in a perception of Israelite history, as the taproot of Western civilization, replacing all other aspects of historical reality in Palestine as part of the inevitable evolutionary process. The way in which this has been done is a further illustration of Césaire's dictum that Europe is the subject of all history.

Garbini (1988) has produced one of the most radical critiques of the historiographic perceptions of biblical studies in recent years. Nevertheless, he betrays the Eurocentrism of his own conceptions in the opening to his essay on the failings of standard biblical histories:

> The ancient Near East, with its civilization and its history, has been rescued from the oblivion of time by just over a century of European science. With it have appeared the remotest roots of Western civilization: before Paris, Rome, Athens and Jerusalem there were Babylon and Uruk.
>
> (Garbini 1988: 1)

According to such a view, there is no history without Europe and the significance of the history that has been rescued from the oblivion of time is that it provides the roots of Western civilization. Garbini is able to go on to talk about 'this now long past of ours' or claim 'the creative force of this civilization as now passing from Asia to Europe'. Ancient Israel then becomes the fulcrum for this transfer of civilization as 'the link between Asia and Europe'. The significance of Israel is ascribed to its mediation of Egyptian and Babylonian culture so that 'Israel returned to Jerusalem enormously enriched and transformed. When Greek culture arrived there, Hebrew thought was in a stage of further revision, the final result of which was transmitted to Europe by some brilliant men. This was the historical function of Israel' (1988: 1). The evolutionary scheme which links Babylon, Egypt, and Greece through Israel culminating in the triumph of Western civilization is so deeply ingrained that it pervades such a radical critique of recent histories of ancient Israel in biblical studies. Garbini's assertions are a perfect illustration of Asad's point (1993: 18) that the West's past becomes an organic continuity from the ancient Near East through Greece and Rome to the Renaissance and Reformation culminating in the universal civilization of modern Europe. From this perspective, there is no recognition that the history of the region, whether Israelite or Palestinian, might have a significance or value of its own. Europe is the subject of this history and it is Europe's conception of time which determines its course.

The entanglement of the disciplines of history and anthropology in the colonial enterprise has been instrumental in representing the triumph of the West and thereby silencing alternative claims to the past by indigenous cultures. Fabian's perceptive study of the way in which anthropology has defined time as part of the European representation of the Other exposes the role of the discipline in providing the intellectual justification for colonialism:

> It gave to politics and economics – both concerned with human Time – a firm belief in 'natural', i.e. evolutionary Time. It promoted a silence in terms of which not only past cultures, but all living societies were irrevocably placed on a temporal slope, a stream of Time – some upstream, others downstream. Civilization, evolution, development, acculturation, modernization (and their cousins, industrialization, urbanization) are all terms whose conceptual content derives, in ways that can be specified, for evolutionary Time. They all have an epistemological dimension apart from whatever ethical, or unethical, intentions they may express. A discourse employing terms such as primitive, savage (but also tribal, traditional, Third World, or whatever euphemism is current) does not think, or observe, or critically study, the 'primitive'; it thinks, observes, studies *in terms* of the primitive. *Primitive* being essentially a temporal concept, is a category, not an object, of Western thought.
>
> (Fabian 1983: 17)

The history of ancient Palestine has effectively been denied time of its own. Instead it is subject to the tyranny of biblical time through the periodization of the Hebrew Bible which has been an essential element of the discourse of biblical studies. The history of the region has long been seen as neatly compartmentalized into Patriarchal,

Exodus, Conquest, or Settlement periods followed by the United Monarchy of David and Solomon, the Divided Kingdoms of Israel and Judah, Exile, and then Restoration.[14] The history of the region is, then, the history of the principal characters and events of the biblical traditions: it is the classic pursuit of the history of great men and unique events. Palestinian history is effectively silenced by this tyranny of biblical time which has been perpetuated by Western scholarship.

This situation has not been changed by the agonized debate in recent years over the starting point of Israelite history which has seen the loss of the Patriarchal, Exodus, and Conquest periods in the wake of the conjunction of literary studies and archaeological data. Rather than reclaiming Palestinian time from the nineteenth through the thirteenth centuries BCE, it has only served to highlight the fact that Palestinian history is denied time. Soggin (1977: 332) may find his datum point with the rise of the monarchy, or Miller and Hayes (1986) provide their 'best guess' with the treatment of David, but the time which precedes this beginning for their accounts of Israel does not become Palestinian time. Rather it remains the domain of Israelite history and thus Western civilization as the prehistory or protohistory of ancient Israel (Malamat 1983; Soggin 1984). Noth's starting point for his history of Israel arrives with the occupation of Palestine by the 'fully united' tribes of Israel: it is only at this point that 'the real "History of Israel" can take its departure' (1960: 5). He claims that there is no information on the historical evolution (note the term) of Israel or 'primeval Israel' but 'only traditions about events in pre-historical times' (1960: 5). Ancient Israel, which only becomes a reality according to Noth with the twelve-tribe structure in Palestine, is able to reach back over centuries to lay claim to time thereby denying this temporal span to Palestinian history. Noth's attitude to the documentary and archaeological evidence from the region is representative of the discourse of biblical studies: he is able to state that the Amarna letters 'reveal clearly the historical background of the beginnings of Israel in Palestine and are thus one of the direct sources for the history of Israel' (1960: 19) or that the Ras Shamra finds 'help to illuminate the situation which the Israelite tribes found on their arrival in Palestine' (1960: 20). Palestinian history only has significance and meaning as the locus of, or background for, the development of Israelite history.

The debate over the problems of constructing the early periods of Israelite history has resulted in a switch of scholarly attention to the second Temple period. Yet once again it is the biblical conception of time which dominates and silences any other claims to the past. It has been common to refer to this period as the 'Intertestamental period', thus betraying the tyranny of biblical time in the understanding and presentation of the history of the region. Biblical scholarship for much of the century has presupposed an evolutionary scheme moving from the 'Old Testament' through the 'Intertestamental' period and culminating in the 'New Testament' era: a periodization which owes nothing to historical reality and all to theological presuppositions about the progressive nature of revelation. The theological conception of the 'Intertestamental' period is revealed in the striking judgement that it was all too often deemed to be 'a mere empty chasm over which one springs from the Old Testament to the New' (Wellhausen 1885: 1). The welcome re-evaluation of the seventh century BCE to the first century CE, the second Temple period from a biblical perspective, has shown this to be a crucial period in the formation and crystallization of the traditions which make up the Hebrew Bible. Yet the perspective has remained parochial and introspective. In the same way that the Amarna or Ras Shamra material has found its primary significance for biblical historians as background to understanding the emergence of Israel in Palestine, so the Dead Sea Scrolls and other extrabiblical materials have found their significance as the backdrop to the history of Israel. Biblical scholars have accepted the claims to monopoly advanced by the tiny province of Yehud, as Davies (1992: 58) has recently pointed out. The periodization of the history of the region has been dominated, then, by Judaeo–Christian theological concerns since the study of Israelite history has remained, and remains, the preserve of faculties of Theology, seminaries, and departments of Religion. The definition of time and the notion of historical progress, fundamental to European Christian teleology, is embodied in the belief that ancient Israel represents the origin of 'historical consciousness' and the agent of divine action within history. The progression of history is then traced to the development of European and Western societies which come to represent the pinnacle of civilization. The indigenous cultures of Palestine and the ancient Near East remain static and stagnate; they represent a failure in the divine scheme of historical evolution.[15] There is no history of Palestine because it is Israel and not Palestine which is the focus of theological attention. The progressive scheme of revelation coupled with the search for ancient Israel has combined to deny any temporal reality to Palestinian history.

An alternative to the tyranny of biblical time ordained by biblical scholars has been the archaeological periodization which has been developed throughout the century. This is a further expression of the evolutionary scheme of 'natural' time which moves in its inexorable fashion from the Stone Age through the Bronze and Iron to the present. It might seem at first sight that this schema is more neutral than the biblical periodization, thereby allowing time to Palestinian history. However, biblical historians, particularly in the wake of Albright, have tried to equate the periodization derived from the Hebrew Bible with the schema developed by archaeological research. Thus the Bronze Age becomes the time of the Patriarchs, while the Late Bronze Age is the era of the Exodus and Conquest or Settlement, and the Iron Age sees the emergence and development of the monarchy; the Exile or second Temple period is covered, of course, by the Persian, Hellenistic, and Roman periods. The denial of time to Palestinian history is confirmed by this attempt to claim the past for ancient Israel. This becomes more explicit in the alternative nomenclature for archaeological periods which has been developed by Israeli scholarship.

The classic treatment of Israelite archaeology by Aharoni (1982) is representative of the way in which time has been used in biblical scholarship. Aharoni begins his vast temporal sweep with the Stone Age (Paleolithic, Epipaleolithic, Neolithic) and Chalcolithic period. The Early Bronze Age is designated as the Early Canaanite I–IV, with the Middle Bronze as the Middle Canaanite, and the Late Bronze Age as the Late Canaanite I–II. Aharoni then follows the normal convention of Israeli scholarship by designating the Iron Age as the Israelite period. This is a strongly evolutionary scheme with a clear movement in which the 'prehistoric' and Canaanite periods are replaced by the Israelite. Aharoni describes the Early Canaanite period as significant in the 'history of Eretz-Israel' since it laid the foundations for Canaanite culture (1982: 49), although it is still a 'mute period' which is 'suitably called protohistoric'. Although this might be termed the Canaanite period, it is still claimed by the 'history of Eretz-Israel', confirming the interrelationship of time and space. His evolutionary scheme is made explicit with the designations prehistoric and protohistoric. The fully historic, he claims, is found in neighbouring lands which have a rich deposit of written documents: 'Eretz-Israel, located between them, remains in the shadow while the search lights of history are illuminating its neighbours' (1982: 49). The way in which the period is divested of any inherent significance of its own is revealed in his discussion of terminology (1982: 50): 'Therefore, it would seem to us that the name "Canaanite" is more suitable. This is the general name for the population of the country during the Israelite conquest, when more extensive historical illumination begins!' We only reach history with the appearance of Israel and the biblical traditions. His Middle Canaanite I (EBIV–MBI) 'concludes the protohistoric era in the history of Eretz-Israel' (1982: 80). When we turn to the Middle Canaanite II and Late Canaanite periods (2000–1200 BCE) we find that:

> From the standpoint of culture and history, they represent a continuity worthy of the name 'the Canaanite period', in the fullest sense of the term. This is Canaan in its rise, its flourishing, and its decline as reflected in ancient Israelite tradition. It is the first really historical period in Eretz-Israel for which written documents have been preserved – historical, administrative, and literary – that give flesh and blood to the sinews of the bare archaeological finds.
>
> (Aharoni 1982: 90)

He follows this immediately with his claim that this is also the period when the Hebrew tribes entered, being 'the first and only people to make the country its natural homeland'. The evolutionary presuppositions are now made explicit with the rise and eventual decline of Canaanite culture to be replaced by Israelites who claim the country as their natural homeland. It is not explained why the Canaanites, who according to Aharoni's periodization have been *in situ* for roughly a millennium, failed to make this their natural homeland. By comparison, the Israelite period lasts for six hundred years. The evolutionary process means that these 'temporary' inhabitants, no matter how long their length of residency, are replaced in the natural scheme of things by a higher culture and civilization. The effect of this is to deny time and therefore reality to Palestinian history: the past is either the domain of Israel or is claimed by Israel as its own prehistory or protohistory.

The debate over the starting point of Israelite history has meant that major blocks of tradition within the Pentateuch and Deuteronomistic History have been relegated to the prehistory of Israel. As we have seen, this has not meant that these periods are returned to Palestinian history. Israel's claim to the past has remained as strong as ever. Yet the concentration upon prehistory and protohistory also has profound implications for the conception of history, which in turn helps to silence and deny Palestinian history. The widely held distinction between history and prehistory embodies the common assumption, prevalent within biblical studies, that the writing of history is dependent upon the existence or, more accurately, the *accidental* preservation of written materials. Yet the ebb and flow of the historical process is not dependent on written materials. They are clearly a major source for the historian but their absence does not mean that the past must be abandoned. Clarke highlights the complex and misleading relationship between history and prehistory:

> The term prehistoric, while it serves a useful purpose in designating a period for which written records are available only for the concluding phase, is in some respects unfortunate. The roll of history is nothing if not continuous. It is only that different parts of it have to be read by different means. Prehistory is not merely an antecedent of history. In a broader sense it forms a part, indeed much the larger part of the story of man's past. From a temporal point, though not from an existential point of view, almost the whole of human history is prehistoric in the technical sense that it has to be reconstructed without the aid of written records. Only some five thousand out of the two million years are documented in this way and then only for a minute area. Conversely vast territories remained 'prehistoric' until 'discovered' by western man in recent centuries. Indeed the remoter parts of territories like Australia, New Guinea or Brazil remained outside the range of recorded history until our own generation.
>
> (Clarke 1973: xvii–xviii)

This insistence on the importance of written sources for the reconstruction of the past betrays the Eurocentric nature of the historical enterprise, as Clarke makes clear. It is an assumption which has informed biblical studies, dependent upon the canons of European historiography, leading to the insistence that Israel and its written traditions are the arbiter of history.

The removal of traditions from the grasp of the biblical historian by literary critics may have led to a crisis of confidence in the scholarly enterprise of writing a history of Israel but it has not resulted in a voice for Palestinian history. Palestine has, we are told, few written materials that have been preserved or unearthed by archaeologists. Thus it cannot have a history. Those which are well known, such as the Amarna or Ugaritic materials, are claimed as background to Israel's prehistory. Malamat (1983: 303) is typical in trying to come to terms with the problem of the Patriarchal and Conquest traditions. He draws a distinction between Israelite 'prehistory' and 'protohistory': 'prehistory' implies a time prior to Israel's existence, whereas 'protohistory' is restricted to the period when embryonic Israel took shape and eventually emerged as an ethnic and territorial unit in Canaan. He would include the so-called Patriarchal, Exodus, Settlement, and Conquest periods in this latter term. Thus for Malamat, as for Aharoni and many biblical specialists, vast spans of time do not belong to Palestine or Palestinian history but remain the preserve of Israel and its (proto-)history.

Palestinian history, if it is to emerge as a subject in its own right, has to be freed from both the tyranny of biblical time and the tyranny of prehistoric time which denies it substance and voice. Lucien Febvre exposed the fallacy of 'prehistory' in strikingly eloquent terms:

> Nevertheless the concept of pre-history is one of the most ridiculous that can be imagined. A man who studies the period in which a certain type of neolithic pottery was widespread is doing history in exactly the same way as a man who draws a map of the distribution of telephones in the Far East in 1948. Both, in the same spirit, for the same ends, are devoting themselves to a study of the manifestations of the inventive genius of mankind, which differ in age and in yield, if you like, but certainly not in ingenuity.
>
> (Febvre 1973: 35)

Or as Braudel (1989: 19–20) would have it: 'As if history did not reach back into the mists of time! As if prehistory and history were not one and the same process.' The history of Palestine will need to be written from the conjunction of written and material remains, and will need to be pursued for those periods where written materials do not exist (cf. Febvre 1973: 34).[16]

The pursuit of Palestinian history is dependent upon freeing it from the temporal constraints imposed upon it by the discourse of biblical studies. Braudel's concept of *la longue durée* offers a perspective which overcomes the neat periodization of biblical histories. It is a temporal perspective which helps to illustrate that Israel is but an entity in the sweep of Palestinian time. Concentration on the short term, the Iron Age to Roman period or the present, obscures the fact that Israel is but one thread in the rich tapestry of Palestinian history. It is the perspective of *la longue durée* which allows the historian to decide whether the settlement patterns of, say, the Early Iron Age in Palestine are unique or conform to similar patterns at other times. Only then is it possible to ask if there might be similar factors at work affecting the shift in settlement or whether it has to be explained in terms completely different from any other period in the history of ancient Palestine. From this perspective, Palestinian history becomes the pursuit of the whole gamut of social, economic, political, and religious developments within Palestine, rather than a primary or exclusive concern with how such developments relate to and explain the emergence and evolution of Israel.

The appeal to the Braudelian conception of time (1972; 1980), with its different levels of geographical, social, and individual time, however, again raises the problem of Eurocentrism. Braudel (1984: 18) places great emphasis on what he terms *world time* which is uneven in the ways in which it affects different areas: 'This exceptional time-scale governs certain areas of the world and certain realities depending on period and place. Other areas and other realities will always escape and lie outside it.'[17] He goes on to add that: '*World time* then might be said to concentrate above all on a kind of superstructure of world history: it represents a crowning achievement, created and supported by forces at work underneath it, although in turn its weight has an effect on the base.' Said (1985: 22–3) has criticized this conception of world time as growing out of the European colonial enterprise: 'What was neither observed by Europe nor documented by it was therefore "lost" until, at some later date, it too could be incorporated by the new sciences of anthropology, political economics, and linguistics.' It is important therefore to recognize and allow Palestinian history its own time. Said (1985: 22) argues that although 'the methodological assumptions and practice of world history' are 'ideologically anti-imperialist', 'little or no attention is given to those cultural practices like Orientalism or ethnography affiliated with imperialism, which in genealogical fact fathered world history itself'. The danger remains that in trying to free the history of Palestine from the tyranny of biblical time it will become replaced by a notion of world time which continues to deny Palestine its own inherent importance and coherence.[18] The reality of this danger can best be illustrated by Baly's remark that because of Palestine's position at the crossroads of three continents surrounded by barriers to settlement and movement it can 'be said to have had, properly speaking, no internal history' (1984: 1) during the Persian period.[19] Here is the problem of world time writ large so that it divests Palestinian history of internal worth and value.

Thus the history of Palestine should not be subsumed under 'world history' or 'world time' any more than it should be subsumed under Israelite history or biblical time. It has its own rhythms and patterns which are an essential part of its own history and which form part of any world history. Attention needs to be paid to the micro-environments of Palestine, the diversity which goes to make up the singularity we call Palestine. All too often in the past, discussions of the region have focused upon the nature and identity of 'Israel' to the virtual exclusion of other important historical entities except where they are thought to impinge upon Israelite history. Our standard 'biblical histories' have presented a conception of history almost exclusively in ethnic and religious terms, even though our understanding of ethnicity in antiquity is extremely problematical. Such classifications presuppose that the rightful concern of history is a series of unique events and individuals narrated as part of a linear, progressive history. The conception of Palestinian history advanced here would concentrate upon wide-ranging issues such as settlement, politics, economy, trade, ideology, and religion which need to be discussed in the broadest possible terms. By concentrating upon such broad themes the focus then is shifted away from the standard historical concern with great personalities and unique events to a concern with overarching factors that have shaped and been shaped by the history of the region.[20] Such a history would draw upon all forms of evidence, particularly archaeology and anthropology, including the Hebrew Bible, while being aware of the elaborate connections of such disciplines with the colonial enterprise that has shaped and distorted the history of the region. Written sources must take their place in the hierarchy of forms of evidence as they relate to particular issues under discussion. Such a history is not predicated on a notion of ecological determinism, as some claim, simply because it moves the focus away from the 'specific people and events' of the Hebrew Bible.

One of the major issues raised by such an approach is the relationship between the study of the history of the region and biblical studies in general. Clearly the term 'biblical history' is no longer appropriate for the kind of exercise being advocated here. The biblical text no longer forms the basis of or sets the agenda for the research in the same way that it has dominated past approaches to the problem. Syro-Palestinian archaeology broke away from the constraints of 'biblical' archaeology in the pioneering work of W.G. Dever. It is now time for Palestinian history to come of age and formally reject the agenda and constraints of 'biblical history'. Those scholars concerned with understanding the social and political milieu from which the Hebrew Bible arose must pursue research into the communities which gave rise to these traditions and their regional and interregional environments. But we must also recognize that the region possesses a legitimate history which is much wider than these communities or the texts to which they gave rise. Thompson (1987: 36) agrees that 'Israel's history (understood as distinct from biblical historiography), and the history of Israel's origin, fall unquestionably and inescapably into the context of regional, historical geographical changes in the history of Palestine'. Palestinian history must come of age through the pursuit of *all aspects* of the region's history regardless of whether or not it sheds light on the development and understanding of the text of the Hebrew Bible. It demands its own time and space denied to it for more than a century by the discourse of biblical studies.

It is the historian who must set the agenda and not the theologian. In the past the theologian has dictated the concerns and methods to be employed in the study of the history of Israel on the grounds that the Hebrew Bible is the only source of evidence and is their domain. Now the historian must claim the right to set the agenda and research strategies. Attempts by theologians or exegetes to try to understand and appropriate the results of such a history as they relate, if at all, to the interpretation of the text is a separate issue which remains the domain of biblical studies.[21] Palestinian history must be granted its own temporal and geographical domain outside the discourse of biblical studies. The discourse on the Palestinian past is, to adapt Said (1992: 8), a contest between affirmation and denial in which ancient Israel has taken control of Palestinian time and space. Furthermore, in reclaiming the temporal and spatial elements for such a regional history as part of world time, it has to be recognized for its own intrinsic value and not solely as the locus for the origins of European civilization. The invention and construction of America provides an analogy with the way in which Palestine has been appropriated, divested of meaning, and its history effectively silenced. O'Gorman (1961: 137) makes a similar point to those advanced above about the domination of all history by Europe in reference to the discovery and invention of America: 'Europe became history's paradigm, and the European way of life came to be regarded as the supreme criterion by which to judge the value and meaning of all other forms of civilization.' The invention of America by Europe is paralleled by the invention of ancient Israel by biblical specialists. What O'Gorman has to say about the invention of America could just as easily be applied to the discourse of biblical studies and its invention of ancient Israel:

> America was no more than a potentiality, which could be realized only by receiving and fulfilling the values and ideals of European culture. America, in fact, could acquire historical significance only by becoming another Europe. Such was the spiritual or historical being that was identified for America.
>
> (O'Gorman 1961: 139)

Just as America was 'invented in the image of its inventor' (O'Gorman 1961: 140), so ancient Israel was invented in terms of the European nation state; or, as Chakrabarty (1992: 2) put it, 'Europe is the silent referent in historical knowledge'. The dominant discourse of biblical studies has masked the means by which the term Palestine has been divested of spatial and temporal significance. Palestinian history has become one of the many excluded histories, divested of significance in terms of world history and relegated to prehistory. Europe, and later Zionism, has rescued the historical significance of the region in its search for ancient Israel: a search for its own cultural roots which has silenced Palestinian history. It is this invention to which we must now turn in order to illustrate the ways in which the dominant discourse of biblical studies has achieved this in the name of objective scholarship.

3

INVENTING ANCIENT ISRAEL

THE SEARCH FOR ANCIENT ISRAEL

Biblical scholarship has invested considerable intellectual and financial resources in its search for ancient Israel. The essential Israel of biblical scholarship has emerged not in the so-called Patriarchal or Exodus periods, though these have been important in the discourse of biblical studies, but in the Late Bronze–Iron Age transition. This is the period which is usually referred to as the 'emergence' or 'origins' of Israel, the period when Israel is considered to have taken possession of Palestine. The dispossession of Palestinian history has been completed in the representation of the reigns of David and Solomon in the Iron Age where a fledgling state is presented as becoming the major military power in the region in a very short period of time. These two periods, the 'emergence' of Israel in Palestine and the development of the Davidic–Solomonic state are of such importance within the discourse of biblical studies that they could be described as representing the defining moments in the history of Israel and thereby in the history of Palestine as a whole. The search for ancient Israel has been of such primary concern within the discipline because the historical critical assumption has been that it is these periods which provide the loci for understanding and defining much of the biblical material. The irony is, however, that current reassessments by Ahlström, Lemche, Coote, Whitelam, and Thompson are likely to lead to the view that it is the period of the Late Bronze–Iron Age transition which will come to be seen as the defining moment in the emergence of Palestinian history as a subject in its own right. Palestinian history became one of the 'excluded histories' with the invention of ancient Israel and its location in the Late Bronze–Iron Age transition: it is likely to regain its voice, its

71

right to representation, with the reassessment of this period brought about, ironically, by the volume and quality of archaeological data for the period which has been produced by Israeli scholars.

Debates have become increasingly acrimonious because the aura of objectivity which has been projected to cover the collusion of biblical studies in the dispossession of Palestine has gradually been exposed. The history of the debate on the emergence of Israel in Palestine illustrates quite clearly that the discourse of biblical studies has been shaped by contemporary political struggles over the question and future of Palestine. The debate on the origins or emergence of ancient Israel is typically presented as an argument over three major models or hypotheses; a debate which refuses to acknowledge its involvement in contemporary politics. Various surveys (Miller 1977; Ramsey 1982; Chaney 1983) provide an overview and critique of the major models in terms of their methodological assumptions, use of data, and general conclusions. However, such reviews and critiques have, by and large, failed to recognize just how closely these seemingly competing constructions of ancient Israel have mirrored the events of Palestine at the time at which they were formulated. The discourse of biblical studies, while ostensibly arguing over the origins or emergence of Israel, has mirrored and often adopted the language of contemporary struggles over Palestine.

The sustained critique of these dominant positions, which has taken place over the last decade or so, has led to increasingly acrimonious exchanges. As we have noted, the increasing acrimony has occasionally fractured the surface of objective, academic debate to expose underlying religious and political beliefs which have shaped the various constructions of the past. The struggle for the past is invariably a struggle for power and control in the present, as we have seen in the ideological construction of time and space in the previous chapter. While biblical studies could maintain the illusion that the debates over the three models associated with Alt and Noth, Albright and Bright, Mendenhall and Gottwald were essentially about the assessment and relative weight of various forms of data which led to the formulation, negation, or reformulation of hypotheses, then the exchanges between the main protagonists might be heated or forceful but retained the essential civility, except in odd cases, of academic discourse. Post-modernist discourses, however, have led to the realization of the essential subjectivity of the academic enterprise exposing the role of various academic disciplines in the colonial enterprise. This has led to the growing, but slow, awareness that the search for ancient Israel is not about some disinterested construction of the past but an important question of contemporary identity and power. The hypotheses formulated by German and American biblical specialists are presented as debates ostensibly over the nature of the emergence or origins of Israel. This is not a debate, so much, between competing claims to the past, as it is usually understood, but rather a debate over the identity of *which* Israel is to lay claim to that past. The different inventions of Israel proposed by these three hypotheses all lay claim to Palestinian time and space: it is always Israel's past, however one might conceive of Israel. There is no real competition within the discourse of biblical studies because Palestine and the Palestinians are denied any right to this past.

The critiques of the mid-1980s onwards, which have undermined the major models of Israel's past in the Late Bronze–Iron Age transition, focused upon the failure to account for the growing body of archaeological data in the region. They all, in varying degrees, tried to articulate alternative constructions of the Palestinian past. Their disavowal of a reliance upon the biblical traditions for understanding the archaeological and other data in their constructions of the 'emergence' of Israel has exposed, unwittingly, just how far the previous models were implicated in contemporary struggles for Palestine. The political nature of these constructions of the past is only now emerging as attempts to articulate a history of ancient Palestine placing Israelite and Palestinian pasts in direct competition. The contested past of the Late Bronze–Iron Age transition can no longer be divorced easily from competing claims by Israelis and Palestinians to the same land. It is no longer a debate, a purely academic debate, on the different understandings of the nature of ancient Israel. The continuum between past and present is broken, a fracturing which undermines contemporary claims to both knowledge and power. The consensus that had surrounded the periods of 'emergence' and the Davidic monarchy for so long has collapsed at such a startling rate in the last few years that there is a pressing need for a complete reappraisal of the end of the Late Bronze and the early Iron Age. It is the beginning of this reappraisal, above all, which has led to the growing realization of the need to reclaim time and space for Palestinian history in its own right. However, before considering the implications of this dramatic shift, it is important to consider the ways in which the search for 'ancient Israel' in the Late Bronze and early Iron Ages has dominated the history of the region and effectively silenced the search for a history of ancient Palestine. This is not a standard review of the relative strengths and weaknesses of German and American scholarship from the 1920s onwards, a function already provided by the many convenient reviews. It is an attempt to illustrate the theological and political assumptions which have contributed to the dominant definitions of Israel's past. It is designed as a commentary, using their own words, to illustrate just how far their constructions of the past have mirrored and are implicated in contemporary struggles for Palestine. What it reveals is a series of imaginative pasts which have been responsible for the silencing of Palestinian history in the name of objective scholarship.

CLAIMING PALESTINE 1:
IMMIGRATION INTO PALESTINE

Albrecht Alt's seminal essay 'Die Landnahme der Israeliten in Palästina', published in 1925 (1966: 133–69), led to the development of what has come to be called the Infiltration or Immigration model of Israelite origins, frequently characterized as the peaceful infiltration/immigration of Israelites into Palestine. This hypothesis, associated with German scholarship, notably Alt, Noth, and M. Weippert, has been very influential in the discourse of biblical studies, nearly three-quarters of a century after its classic formulation by Alt, not only in current reformulations of the hypothesis, but through a series of ideas which have been taken for granted in the discourse of biblical studies and therefore rarely articulated. It still retains considerable support, most notably in the recent important work of the Israeli archaeologist Israel Finkelstein (1988). However, it is a construction of the past, an invention of Israel, which mirrors perceptions of contemporary Palestine of the 1920s at a time of increasing Zionist immigration.

Alt's innovative insight was to recognize that in order to overcome the deficiencies of the Hebrew Bible for understanding the process of Israelite origins, it was necessary to investigate 'the history of [the] country's territorial divisions in complete independence of other aspects of the problem' (1966: 136). By this means, he intended to understand the settlement of the Israelites in Palestine at the end of the Late Bronze Age (thirteenth century BCE), the conditions which preceded it, and its effects upon the settlement history of Palestine. Alt, in effect, proposed to address the problem from the perspective of *la longue durée* by using Egyptian and cuneiform materials to construct 'the political geography of Palestine' (1966: 137). His findings stressed the important role played by small city-states with their 'petty' princes in defining this political geography: the Pharaoh exercised power through them and only dealt directly with them. The full development of this political system resulted in the extreme fragmentation of Palestine into a number of small city-states consisting of little more than the land surrounding the city and a few neighbouring villages. He drew an important regional distinction between the political geography of the coastal lowlands, where the majority of these city-states were located, and the highlands of Palestine where the lack of good arable land resulted in the fact that 'the settlement of the mountains, and the development of an advanced culture there, had not at this stage reached the same level' (1966: 149). He drew upon the Amarna archives concerning Labaya at Shechem to conclude that 'the existence of a political unity in the mountains north of Jerusalem is unmistakable' (1966: 153). This contrast between the plains and the highlands, which has been very influential in perceptions of the region, for him, 'clearly go back to a different political structure: in the first, groups of city-states close together, in the second, an extensive territory under a single ruler' (1966: 154). Jerusalem is characterized as an important exception in the hill country of a city-state that failed to extend its territorial control over a wide area.

He contends that with the collapse of Egyptian power at the end of the Late Bronze Age the 'political map of Palestine is completely changed' (1966: 157) leaving approximately only half a dozen states in the area. This can only be explained, according to Alt, by a complete shift of political power in the region. The dramatic decline of imperial Egypt is an insufficient explanation for the new forms of political life and territorial units which emerged at this time. Nor can it be explained by indigenous developments in response to the decline in imperial Egyptian control: 'When native politics were left to develop in their own way, their obvious course was to preserve the state of affairs that had grown up in the country over many centuries' (1966: 157). Alt's assumption is that the change can only be brought about by external influence, thereby denying inherent value to the internal history of the region. It is an assumption, as we have seen, that pervades the discourse of biblical studies: an assumption that coincides with common presentations of the events taking place in Palestine contemporary with Alt's research. Palestine for Alt, as for contemporary Western politicians, notably the British, was incapable of developing 'new forms of political life': 'The impetus towards the general re-ordering of the political organization of Palestine cannot therefore have come from there' (1966: 158). Notice how categorical Alt can be in his statement of the failure, the inability of the indigenous population of Palestine to cultivate innovative forms of political organization. Such forms *had* to come from outside. Similarly, Swendenburg (1989: 208) points out that Israeli historians tend to view Palestinian society of the 1930s as an internally fragmented tribal society incapable of national organization.[1]

What, then, are these innovative forms of political life which require external stimulation and which he attributes to the Israelites, Philistines, Judaeans, Edomites, Moabites, Ammonites, and Arameans? None other than the nation state. Here Alt sees for the first time the development of a national consciousness, something that the indigenous population are incapable of experiencing: 'the naming of states after their people also betrays a national consciousness which the earlier political formations, and the city-states in particular, never had and because of their political structure could not have' (1966: 18). There is no clear justification for his assumption that the growth of national consciousness could not have been indigenous but must be explained as an external import: his analysis of the city-state system does not justify such a categorical statement. However, Alt's work is set in one of the most crucial periods of modern Palestinian history: a period of increasing Zionist immigration into the area in the early decades of the century, along with aspirations of a national homeland, which completely changed the social, political, and demographic characteristics of the region (see Abu-Lughob 1987; Khalidi 1984). The central feature of Alt's construction, significant immigration of groups in search of a national homeland, needs to be considered in the context of these dramatic developments in Palestine at the time he was conducting his research – developments of which he could hardly have been ignorant.

The nation state might be the apex of political development but it was only certain peoples who were capable of evolving to this final stage. This is evident in his explanation of how certain groups failed ultimately to achieve this goal, unlike the Israelites. The Philistines, whom Alt (1966: 158) describes as acting as a unit, failed in their attempts to found a national state precisely because it was located in the coastal plain where the city-state system had its stronghold. Even though they may have extended its limits further than before, they were forced to retain the city-state system. In effect, this indigenous form of political organization 'imposed itself upon the new inhabitants' (1966: 159). The Philistines failed because they had been contaminated by such close contact with the indigenous population. It was left to the kingdoms of Israel and Judah to impose a new form of political organization on the region, thereby sweeping away the indigenous city-state system. This is the defining moment in the history of the region for Alt since he claims that 'the importance of this occurrence for the history of Palestine in general has not yet been fully estimated' (1966: 160). Alt then offers a striking description of the foundation of the Israelite state in which the indigenous population do not expect equal rights:

> The kingdom of Saul is simply the union of the Israelite tribes and their districts into one state, while the non-Israelite city-states remained outside or at least did not expect equal rights as part of the newly-founded kingdom. A glance at the map will show that although the nature of the Israelite state provided a basis for national unity, it had not succeeded in rounding off the borders of its territory, and the strategical situation before Saul's last battle is a clear example of this.
>
> (Alt 1966: 161)

It was the entry of the Israelites into Palestine which had altered the situation, preparing the way for the ultimate achievement of the foundation of a nation state under David and Solomon – an achievement beyond the capabilities of the indigenous Palestinians who, we are told, did not expect equal rights! No evidence is offered for such an assertion, which only serves to emphasize the superiority of Israel over an inferior indigenous Palestinian population. His famous account of the Israelite occupation of Palestine describes how they settled in those areas in the hill country where larger political units were already established and which were protected from contamination by the lowland city-state system. It was these thinly populated areas, described by Alt as politically ill organized, that were least capable of resisting the Israelite intruders. Only after the 'semi-nomadic' groups had settled to an agricultural way of life did their expansion lead eventually to the destruction of the city-state system.

In effect, the other main proponents of this model, Noth and M. Weippert, have modified Alt's views only slightly and have adopted and propagated the domain assumptions. Noth also assumes that 'naturally, the Old Testament tradition is unquestionably right in regarding the tribes not as indigenous to Palestine but as having entered and gained a footing there from the wilderness and steppe at a definite point in time' (1960: 53). Israel only became 'a final and enduring reality in Palestine' (1960: 53). He believes that these tribes brought with them important traditions from outside Palestine which contributed to the self-consciousness and faith of Israel as it developed in Palestine. His own description of Israelite settlement (1960: 55–6; 68) in the sparsely populated areas of the highlands is little more than a reiteration of Alt. His assumption, following Alt, is that these tribes were semi-nomadic in a protracted process of sedentarization 'the whole process being carried through, to begin with, by peaceful means and without the use of force' (1960: 69). The stress is constantly on the 'peaceful' means by which the land is appropriated. The implicit claim of this model is that Israel's infiltration into Palestine was not an act of dispossession but the possession of an empty, uninhabited land, or at least those areas which were uninhabited. It is only with the second phase of Israelite 'territorial expansion' that conflict with the Canaanite city-states takes place (M. Weippert 1971: 6).

The continued critique of Alt's hypothesis of Israelite origins and its various reformulations has illustrated the extent to which it is an imagined and invented past (see Ramsey 1982: 77–90; Miller 1977: 268–70; Mendenhall 1962; Gottwald 1979: 204–9). Literary approaches to the Hebrew Bible have seriously undermined the source-critical assumptions which Alt employed in his analysis of the biblical texts. The domain assumption that it is possible to identify particular strata in the texts, to date these, and then to use them for historical reconstruction has been put under sustained critique. Furthermore, it has become accepted that the fundamental assumption by Alt, along with most other biblical specialists of the time, that social change in the ancient past was necessarily the result of external invasion/migration by different ethnic groups who replaced the indigenous culture can no longer be sustained. In particular, the assumption that Israel was composed of nomads or semi-nomads in the process of sedentarization has been abandoned in light of the growing anthropological evidence showing that pastoralism is a specialized offshoot of agriculture in the ancient Near East. The growing body of archaeological evidence from the region, since Alt's initial research, has also illustrated quite clearly that the growth in settlements in the highlands of Palestine during the Late Bronze–

Iron Age transition can no longer be associated unequivocally with Israelite immigration.[2]

We might compare Alt's construction of Israelite settlement in Palestine with the political events of his own day within the region. His view of the imagined past is that the process of 'peaceful immigration' eventually resulted in the foundation of a nation state that swept away the inefficient, indigenous city-state system. He asserts, without any supporting evidence, that the indigenous population were incapable of any sense of national consciousness. Similarly, in the 1920s when Zionism with its strong sense of national consciousness was seeking a 'national homeland' in Palestine through immigration, it was common to deny any sense of national consciousness to Palestinian Arabs (Laqueur 1972: 248–50). Such an assertion has long been commonplace despite the denials of Antonius (1969) or even Elon (1983: 151–3). They show that a nascent nationalism was current among the Arab population in the region as early as the 1880s paralleling developments in Jewish nationalism. The widespread misrepresentation of the introduction of national consciousness and unity into the region as a result of immigration and the devaluing of indigenous political organization has permeated biblical studies since the time of Alt. Furthermore, it is important to bear in mind that Alt's own search for ancient Israel was informed by German nationalism and the search for the nation state (Sasson 1981). It is an imagined past that bears a strong resemblance to perceptions of the events in Palestine of the 1920s which saw increasing Zionist immigration into the area, the establishment of increasing numbers of settlements (*kibbutzim*), and a contrast between a growing Zionist 'national consciousness' and the inefficient, disunited groups of indigenous Palestinians/Arabs who were thought to be incapable of any such unified national organization. This imagined past, a mirror of Alt's own present, has had a profound and subtle influence on the discourse of biblical studies ever since. Biblical studies, in reiterating the unsubstantiated claims of Alt's construction, has participated in the struggle for Palestine by silencing any claim to the Palestinian past other than that of Israel.

CLAIMING PALESTINE 2:
THE CONQUEST OF PALESTINE

American scholarship, led by William Foxwell Albright, produced an alternative construction of Israel's emergence in Palestine which has been projected, within the discourse of biblical studies, as the diametric opposite of Alt's 'peaceful' immigration hypothesis. Albright was concerned to show that there was 'objective' evidence for accepting the picture presented in part of the biblical traditions of a external invasion and conquest. Alt and Noth had appealed to alternative traditions in Judges and parts of Joshua to support their construction of a protracted and largely peaceful immigration. Albright placed much greater emphasis on the increasing archaeological data to support the biblical tradition in Joshua of a short military campaign which devastated a number of the Palestinian urban centres. Albright's invention of ancient Israel has been of immense importance in twentieth-century biblical studies, propagated by a group of influential graduate students who rose to prominent academic positions throughout the USA. Yet, once again, it is remarkable how far his construction of Israel's past mirrors important perceptions of developments in the Palestine of his own day. Many of his ideas were forged during the very same critical period in the development of the region in the early decades of this century which is the temporal location for Alt's scholarship (see also Silberman 1993: 8).

Albright's philosophy of history, which is critical for understanding his perception of ancient Israel, was produced in 1940 and revised and reprinted three times. The 1957 revision includes the interesting statement that the book was published 'by agreement between Anchor Books and the Biblical Colloquium. The Biblical Colloquium is a scholarly society devoted to the analysis and discussion of biblical matters, and the preparation, publication, and distribution of informative literature about the Bible for the general reader as well as students.' Thus it is suggested to the reader that s/he can have complete trust in this excercise designed to provide the public with the fruits of objective scholarship. At the time, the Biblical Colloquium, the inflential gathering of Albright's graduate students, was actively involved in the propagation of his ideas with the express intention of seeing that they triumphed in American academic life.[3] In the 1957 introduction to the Anchor edition, he states explicitly that despite many discoveries since 1940, he has had no need to revise any of his conclusions with regard to the history of Israel: on the contrary, he has only been confirmed in these. This introduction also alerts the reader to Albright's evolutionary schema which informs his whole philosophy of history, divided into protological empirico-logical, and logical stages of development, thereby influencing his presentation of the Israelite past and leading to the silencing of Palestinian history (see also 1957: 84). This is confirmed in his attempts to articulate 'an organismic philosophy of history' concluding that:

> From the standpoint of the present study, this table reflects the writer's conviction that the Graeco–Roman civilization of the time of Christ represented the closest approach to a rational unified culture that the world has yet seen and may justly be taken as the culmination of a long period of relatively steady evolution. . . . It was, moreover, about the same time that the religion of Israel reached its climactic expression in Deutero-Isaiah and Job, who represented a height beyond which pure ethical monotheism has never risen. The history of the Israelite and Jewish religion from Moses to Jesus thus appears to stand on the pinnacle of biological evolution as represented in Homo Sapiens, and recent progress in discovery and invention really reflects a cultural lag of over two millennia, a lag which is to be sure, very small when compared to the hundreds of thousands of years during which man has been toiling up the steep slopes of evolution.
>
> (Albright 1957: 121–2)

He goes on to elaborate a broad classification of human history based upon human mental activity, 'as representing the highest religious and literary accomplishments of the historic past, seen in the perspective of the modern contrast between primitive tribes and civilized nations' (1957: 122). Notice that the high point of human development, the achievements of 'civilized nations', was a pinnacle that had already been reached by the Israelite and Jewish religions. Western civilization of his own day was returning to the crucible of its origins. Ultimately, he concludes that this evolutionary progression is not the product of random chance since history is the realm of divine revelation: 'The sympathetic student of man's *entire* history can have but one reply: there *is* an Intelligence and a Will, expressed in both History and Nature – for History and Nature are one' (1957: 126). The rhetorical use of 'sympathetic' is designed to undermine the views of anyone who does not profess to his theological schema. In the same way, recent revisionist histories can be deemed as beyond the bounds of acceptable, objective scholarship by being labelled 'unreasonable'. In Albright's synthesis it is not just that Israelite history belongs to the realm of theology, but that all history is theology.

Albright based his construction of Israelite origins on his unparalleled knowledge of archaeological results from Palestine and his reading of the biblical traditions. He saw a direct correlation between evidence for the destruction of numerous Palestinian urban sites at the end of the Late Bronze Age, their replacement by poorer settlements often marked by a change in material culture such as different pottery or architectural types, and the tradition in the book of Joshua of an Israelite invasion and conquest of Palestine (for convenient reviews and details, see Miller 1977: 212–79; Gottwald 1979: 192–203; Ramsey 1982: 65–98; Chaney 1983). Like Alt, he identified the growth of highland villages in the Late Bronze–Iron Age transition with Israel. This was not, however, a peaceful immigration but a sudden and violent eruption from outside which destroyed the urban culture of Palestine.

Albright's espousal of an Israelite conquest of Palestine combining biblical traditions and archaeological data led him to conclude that:

> The population of early Israelite Palestine was mainly composed of three groups: pre-Israelite Hebrews, Israelites proper, and Canaanites of miscellaneous origin. The Hebrews coalesced so rapidly with their Israelite kindred that hardly any references to this distinction have survived in biblical literature and the few apparent allusions are doubtful. The Canaanites were brought into the Israelite fold by treaty, conquest, or gradual absorption.
>
> (Albright 1957: 279)

Albright's description is remarkably reminiscent of the demographic distinction following the Zionist influx into Palestine with the indigenous Jewish population being assimilated ('coalesced') while the indigenous Palestine population were absorbed 'by treaty, conquest, or gradual absorption'.[4] There is no question raised here as to the legitimacy of Israel's right to the land or the rights of the dispossessed indigenous population. But what is most striking, and frightening, is that Albright not only does not raise the question of the rights of the indigenous population to the land but follows on with a remarkable attempt at justification for the extinction of this indigenous population. His discussion has such far-reaching consequences for the assessment of this act of dispossession that it needs to be quoted in full:

Strictly speaking this Semitic custom was no worse, from the humanitarian point of view, than the reciprocal massacres of Protestants and Catholics in the seventeenth century (e.g. Magdeburg, Drogheda), or than the massacre of Armenians by Turks and of Kirghiz by Russians during the First World War, or than the recent slaughter of non-combatants in Spain by both sides. It is questionable whether a strictly detached observer would consider it as bad as the starvation of helpless Germany after the armistice in 1918 or the bombing of Rotterdam in 1940. In those days warfare was total, just as it is again becoming after the lapse of three millennia. And we Americans have perhaps less right than most modern nations, in spite of our genuine humanitarianism, to sit in judgement on the Israelites of the thirteenth century B.C., since we have, intentionally or otherwise, exterminated scores of thousands of Indians in every corner of our great nation and have crowded the rest into great concentration camps. The fact that this was probably inevitable does not make it more edifying to the Americans of today. It is significant that after the first phase of the Israelite Conquest we hear no more about 'devoting' the population of Canaanite towns, but only of driving them out or putting them to tribute (Judges 1: *passim*). From the impartial standpoint of a philosopher of history, it often seems necessary that a people of markedly inferior type should vanish before a people of superior potentialities, since there is a point beyond which racial mixture cannot go without disaster. When such a process takes place – as at present in Australia – there is generally little that can be done by the humanitarian – though every deed of brutality and injustice is infallibly visited upon the aggressor.

It was fortunate for the future of monotheism that the Israelites of the Conquest were a wild folk, endowed with primitive energy and ruthless will to exist, since the resulting decimation of the Canaanites prevented the complete fusion of the two kindred folk which would almost inevitably have depressed Yahwistic standards to a point where recovery was impossible. Thus the Canaanites, with their orgiastic nature worship, their cult of fertility in the form of serpent symbols and sensuous nudity, and their gross mythology, were replaced by Israel, with its pastoral simplicity and purity of life, its lofty monotheism, and its severe code of ethics. In a not altogether dissimilar way, a millennium later, the African Canaanites, as they still called themselves, or the Carthaginians, as we call them, with the gross Phoenician mythology which we know from Ugarit and Philo Byblius, with human sacrifices and the cult of sex, were crushed by the immensely superior Romans, whose stern code of morals and singularly elevated paganism remind us in many ways of early Israel.

(Albright 1957: 280–1)

This justification, by one of the great icons of twentieth-century biblical scholarship, of the slaughter of the indigenous Palestinian population is remarkable for two reasons: it is an outpouring of undisguised racism which is staggering, but equally startling is the fact that this statement is never referred to or commented on, as far as I know, by biblical scholars in their assessments of the work of Albright.[5] Albright's characterization of the sensuous, immoral Canaanite stands in a long line of Orientalist representations of the Other as the opposite of the Western, rational intellectual. It is a characterization which dehumanizes, allowing the extermination of native populations, as in the case of Native Americans where it was regrettable but 'probably inevitable'; the claim is couched in terms of the progress that colonial or imperial rule will bring. This passage occurs in a chapter entitled 'Charisma and catharsis': remarkably, the foreword to the 1957 edition only mentions that in the original volume (1940) he failed to stress the predictive element of Israelite prophecy sufficiently in this chapter. Even after sixteen years, well after the full horrors of the Holocaust had been exposed, Albright felt no need to revise his opinion that 'superior' peoples had the right to exterminate 'inferior'. Nor did he acknowledge the startling paradox of his theology which fails to recognize the offensiveness of the idea that Israelite monotheism was saved in its 'lofty ethical monotheism' by the extermination of the indigenous population.

His interpretation of the archaeological data reinforces his claim to such a sharp distinction between Israelite and Canaanite culture:

Since Israelite culture was in many respects a *tabula rasa* when the Israelites invaded Palestine, we might expect them to have been influenced strongly by the culture of their Canaanite predecessors. Yet excavations show a most abrupt break between the culture of the Canaanite Late Bronze Age and that of the Israelite early Iron Age in the hill-country of Palestine.

(Albright 1957: 284–5)

Albright's identification of collared-rim ware and the four-room house type as markers of Israelite material culture has, of course, been fundamental to subsequent readings of the archaeological data or constructions of this period until very recently. Thus Palestinian time and space are replaced by Israelite time and space as part of the inevitable evolutionary development and replacement of cultures. This inevitable progress was to result in the foundation of an Israelite national state: 'Meanwhile the constant struggle between the Israelites and the surrounding peoples was slowly but surely hammering them into national unity' (1957: 286). Yet, it seems, the surrounding or indigenous populations were not similarly metamorphized by this conflict into a national unity. He concludes this discussion of Israel's conquest of Palestine with the remarkable assertion, remarkable in following so closely on his justification of the genocide of the indigenous population:

> When the Israelites address foreigners they use language suitable to their horizon and capable of producing a friendly reaction. There is nothing 'modern' about this principle, which must have been commonplace in the ancient Orient – though no other known people of antiquity can approach the objectivity of the Israelites in such matters, to judge from their literature.
>
> (Albright 1957: 288–9)

Israel, as the taproot of Western civilization, represents the rational while 'Canaan', the indigenous Palestinian population, represents the irrational Other which must be replaced in the inexorable progress of divinely guided evolution. Further justification for this is hidden away in a footnote in the epilogue:

> It is far more 'reasonable' to recognize that, just as man is being evolved by the eternal spirit of the Universe, so his religious life is the result of stimuli coming from the same source and progressing toward a definite goal. In other words, the evolution of man's religious life is guided by divine revelation.
>
> (Albright 1957: 401 n. 1)

Reasonableness is again the mark and the test of acceptance of his theological beliefs.

The evolutionary and theological assumptions which underlie his work, and which have been so influential in the discourse of biblical studies, are made explicit in the epilogue:[6]

A double strand runs through our treatment: first, the ascend-
ing curve of human evolution, a curve which now rises, now
falls, now moves in cycles, and now oscillates, but which has
always *hitherto* recovered itself and continued to ascend;
second, the development of individual historical patterns or
configurations, each with its own organismic life, which rises,
reaches a climax, and declines. The picture as a whole warrants
the most sanguine faith in God and in His purpose for man.

(Albright 1957: 401)

Albright's whole philosophy of history is underpinned by the notion
of the evolutionary development of organisms so that it is natural for
Israel to 'replace' the inferior indigenous population of Palestine, just
as it was natural for Christianity to replace 'inferior' religions. The
justification of genocide, the justification for the silencing of Palestinian history, is contained in his final assertion that:

Real spiritual progress can only be achieved through cata-
strophe and suffering, reaching new levels after the profound
catharsis which accompanies major upheavals. Every such
period of mental and physical agony, while the old is being
swept away and the new is still unborn, yields different social
patterns and deeper spiritual insights.

(Albright 1957: 402)

The intellectual and spiritual advancement which had been reached
by Greek and Jewish thinkers by the fifth century BCE was impeded
for a millennium and a half. Significantly, then, for Albright, 'Jesus
Christ appeared on the scene just when Occidental civilization had
reached a fatal impasse' (1957: 403). The intellectual and spiritual line
stretches, for Albright, from ancient Israel to modern Western
civilization, or that civilization as Albright conceives of it:

We need reawakening of faith in the God of the majestic
theophany on Mount Sinai, in the God of Elijah's vision at
Horeb, in the God of the Jewish exiles in Babylonia, in the God
of the Agony of Gethsemane.

(Albright 1957: 403)

His assertions and the theological beliefs which inform and dictate
his construction of Israelite history are presented in the name of
objective scholarship:

Throughout we have resisted the temptation to modify our statement of historical fact in order to produce a simpler – but less objective – picture. We have endeavoured to make the facts speak for themselves, though our care to state them fairly and to provide evidence to support them, where necessary, may sometimes have made it difficult for the reader to follow the unfolding scroll of history.

(Albright 1957: 400)

Albright, as the objective academic, the representative of Western rationality, assures the reader that what is being presented is a trustworthy construction of Israel's past. We might compare this with Freedman's remark that:

While, for those of us who came to the Hopkins fresh from Christian theological seminaries, the presentation and articulation of the data were quite congenial and the Oriental Seminary . . . seemed like a continuation of what he had already experienced, namely a strong Christian cultural bias, and an essentially apologetic approach to the subject of religion, especially biblical religion in (or against) its environment, nevertheless, the basis and the method were different.

(Freedman 1989: 35)

In stressing his orthodox and pietistic Methodist upbringing, his conservative stance towards biblical religion, and his sympathetic treatment of evangelicals and fundamentalists, Freedman insists that Albright was careful to present his work in terms of the history of ideas rather than the defence of a particular faith or branch of it. He did not make any effort to conceal his faith but, Freedman claims, it was not obstructive or intrusive. 'He never appeared to be personally involved, since the debate and defence were conducted on purely intellectual grounds' (1989: 35).

The theological underpinning of Albright's invention of ancient Israel as the cultural, intellectual, and spiritual root of Western society are evident throughout his writings. The failure of biblical discourse to discuss this in the reassessment of Albright's work is staggering given the justification he offers for the obvious superiority of some peoples over others. The paradox of all this is that he was recognized by the state of Israel for his scholarly achievements and for his involvement in helping many Jewish refugees escape from the horrors of Nazi persecution (Running and Freedman 1975). Yet he, and subsequent generations of biblical scholars, have failed to reflect upon the implications of his justification for the Israelite slaughter of the Palestinian population in the conquest of the land. In the collection of essays produced from the symposium 'Homage to William Foxwell Albright', sponsored by the American Friends of the Israel Exploration Society, van Beek states that 'for Albright, homage without honest appraisal would have been little more than flattery, and therefore without merit' (1989: 3). What might we conclude from the overwhelming reluctance within the discourse of biblical studies to acknowledge Albright's racist philosophy? Either it has been an issue too delicate to raise or the discipline has colluded in the enterprise: the failure to point out the objectionable nature of his views, of course, is part of that collusion. The views of Albright, quoted at length above, bear comparison with anything found in Said's critique of Orientalism. They cannot be dismissed simply as the views of someone of his time, as though it is unreasonable from our current perspective to expect anything more. Nor can they be divorced from the rest of his scholarship since this overriding philosophy of history is fundamental to his interpretation and presentation of the archaeological and historical data. What has to be remembered is that his conclusions, his construction of the past, shaped and continue to shape the perceptions of generations of biblical scholars, particularly American and British.[7]

Even in the late 1980s, Albright was presented as the icon of objective scholarship, a presentation which has been essential to the discourse of biblical studies and which has hidden its involvement in the colonial enterprise. As with Alt's invention of an imagined past, so Albright's construction has come under sustained critique which has shattered any illusion as to its cogency. Albright's hypothesis suffers from the very same weaknesses as Alt's in terms of attempts to isolate literary strata and then read off a simple correlation with the historical reality. Ironically, however, it is the new archaeological data itself, from excavations and regional surveys, which have completely undermined his invention of the past. The problems posed by the excavations of Ai and Jericho for his correlation of archaeological data and the biblical traditions are well known. Furthermore, the discovery of collared-rim ware and the four-room house type in different areas and earlier periods further undermined his identification of Israelite material culture or any notion of a sharp break with indigenous culture. In retrospect it is easier to see that his construction was just as much an imagined past tied to his own present as that of Alt. Yet the political implications of his work have remained largely unexamined, masked by the concentration on his achievements in archaeological fieldwork and biblical studies in general. Silberman, in his reassessment of Albright, is one of the few scholars to raise the question of the political implications of his scholarship:

> It is strange that today's Biblical archaeologists – or Syro–Palestinian archaeologists – who likewise take pride in wearing the public badge of scholarly impartiality, don't often acknowledge that there is something more to Albright's legacy than historical ideas. Can a scholar, who is also a product of a modern society, with a particular national, religious, and economic position, really enter a strife torn society (like Palestine was in the 1920s) without participating willingly or unknowingly in the political struggle that is going on? Can he or she obtain rights to an archaeological site (which is also part of the modern landscape), negotiate for goods, services, and government sanction, employ local workers, and most of all present a version of the past that is susceptible to modern political interpolation, without contributing – again, knowingly or unconsciously – to the modern political debate?
>
> (Silberman 1993: 15)

Biblical scholarship has attempted to remain immune from the intellectual currents which have shaken other disciplines, choosing to ignore or deny its intricate involvement in the political realm. The particular questions raised by Silberman have not formed part of the scholarly agenda.

Biblical studies has been and continues to be, despite the many protestations of innocence, involved in the contemporary struggle for Palestine. This is revealed in Albright's 1942 article in *New Palestine* entitled 'Why the Near East needs the Jews' in which he describes his changing attitudes to Jewish immigration at the time of his first visits to Palestine in 1919 and 1920. He professes himself to be a 'friend of the Arabs as well as the Jews'. He is clearly aware of the context of his work set within the contemporary struggle for Palestine. His oscillation between 'the causes of the two peoples' was eventually resolved as he became an increasingly warm supporter of 'cultural Zionism', claiming to remain neutral on the question of 'political Zionism'. He had by 1940 abandoned his neutrality in light of 'the monstrous reality of Hitlerism' – an interesting confession given his statement on the right of superior peoples to replace inferior. Albright had come to recognize political Zionism as the only alternative, invoking the 'historical right' of the Jewish people and its 'internationally recognized legal right' to Palestine. He then states that 'more important than the clear historical right is the tremendous emotional force of the movement to revive Zion. Palestine is the home of the patriarchs, poets, and prophets of Israel; Palestine is the workshop in which Jews forged three right instruments of Western culture; the Hebrew Bible, the New Testament, and the Second Law' (1942: 12). Israel is presented as the taproot of Western civilization while at the same time the direct continuum between past and present is stressed as justification of Israel's right to the land. In order to show his balance and objectivity, his sympathy for the Arab cause, he tries to argue that 'a Jewish Palestine' would not be an 'irritating alien body in the otherwise homogenous Moslem Arab world'. The Near East needs the Jews because of the rapid modernization brought about by American and European involvement and investment. What is being constructed is 'a center of European civilization – an immensely energetic and progressive focus of influence – in the heart of the Near East'. The region would then benefit from the technological, medical, and cultural benefits introduced into the region through Jewish immigration. Albright's Israel of the Iron Age was a mirror image of the Israel of his present: Israel is presented as the carrier of (European) civilization which can only benefit the impoverished region. No mention is made of the right of the indigenous population to the land, either in the past or the present. Albright is concerned only with the historic right of Israel. His construction of an imagined past has been one of the most influential in the history of the discipline, and still retains wide popular support and considerable influence particularly among Israeli scholars. As such, it is an influential construction of the past which has laid claim to Palestine for Israel, thereby denying any such claim by the indigenous population whether ancient or modern.[8]

George Ernest Wright, a senior figure in the Biblical Colloquium, attests to the importance of Albright's ideas in shaping the discourse of biblical studies in the twentieth century. His influential *The Old Testament against its Environment* opens with a foreword, written in 1949, describing the purpose of his Haskell Lectures as 'to examine and lay emphasis upon those central elements of Biblical faith which are so unique and *sui generis* that they cannot have developed by any natural evolutionary process from the pagan world in which they appeared. They cannot be explained, therefore, by environmental or geographical conditioning' (1950: 7). He takes issue with 'the extreme positions' of those who try to explain the faith of Israel in developmental terms. Here is a unique entity, for Wright, which is radically demarcated from its 'pagan' environment to such an extent that it cannot be explained 'fully by evolutionary or environmental categories' (1950: 7). Encapsulated in these opening sentences is the overriding theological and ideological assumptions of Western biblical scholarship which have silenced Palestinian history. Interestingly, he takes issue with the evolutionary assumption that it is possible to trace the developmental path of the biblical traditions since this leads to the misunderstanding that 'the idea of development lays emphasis inevitably upon the process of human discovery rather than on revelation, on gradual evolution rather than mutation' (1950: 11). Once again, we find the language of the growth of organisms. Israel, however, cannot be understood in terms of development because its roots cannot be traced to the indigenous population or culture. It is of such a unique status that it can only be described as a mutation brought about by divine intervention rather than random accident.[9] The key to understanding Wright's arguments is his belief that 'the living God, says the Bible, breaks into a people's life and by mighty acts performs his wonders in their behalf' (1950: 11).

He draws a sharp distinction between Israel and its environment, contrasting the mythic world view of indigenous culture with the logical deductions of faith in a deity revealed in history. Thus he is able to conclude that:

> These, then, are some of the distinctions which must be drawn between the God of Israel and the gods of the nations. Together they constitute the basis of the Israelite mutation which cannot be comprehended through the metaphor of growth. It is impossible to see how this God of Israel could have evolved slowly from polytheism. The two faiths rest on entirely different foundations. The religion of Israel suddenly appears in history, breaking radically with the mythopoeic approach to reality. How are we to explain it, except that it is a new creation?
>
> (Wright 1950: 28–9)

It is interesting to note that these words were being delivered at the time of the creation of the state of Israel. Wright's understanding of ancient Israel and its faith as a new creation completely different from its environment is parallel to frequent presentations of the state of Israel as something different, a civilizing influence, set off from its environment. He appeals to Alt and Noth to confirm the view that 'without question ... the early, pre-monarchical organization of Israel was utterly different from that of other contemporary people' (1950: 61). What underlies all of this is the fundamental assumption of the direct connection between the uniqueness of Israel and its faith and Christianity. Thus Wright (1950: 68) is able to state: 'The doctrine of election and covenant gave Israel an interpretation of life and a view of human history which are absolutely fundamental to Christian theology, especially when they are seen with Christ as their fulfilment.' He then acknowledges that history is progressive but that the goals have been set by God (1950: 72). Israel might have borrowed some aspects from its environment but these are not allowed to stain its uniqueness:

> What Israel borrowed was the least significant; it was fitted into an entirely new context of faith. What was once pagan now became thoroughly Israelite, or else became the source of dissension in the community. Consequently, the Christian and the Jew as well, look upon this distinctiveness of the Old Testament as proof of its claim for special revelation.
>
> (Wright 1950: 74)

Israel's conception of history, and, crucially, its own historical experience, was unique:

> Biblical man, unlike other men in the world, had learned to confess his faith by telling the story of what had happened to his people and by seeing within it the hand of God. Faith was communicated, in other words, through the forms of history, and unless history is taken seriously one cannot comprehend biblical faith which triumphantly affirms the meaning of history.
>
> (Wright 1962: 17)

Such an assumption about the uniqueness of Israel and its experience means that the experience or claims of other peoples become of secondary concern.[10] The dispossession of the indigenous Palestinian population is not a matter of concern when the meaning of history is viewed solely from the perspective of the authors of the biblical traditions. It is little wonder, then, that Wright could represent the origins of Israel in Palestine in terms of a dramatic, divinely inspired, irruption which presented a radical break with indigenous culture. In the prologue to *The Book of the Acts of God*, he states unashamedly that:

> The conquest of Canaan whereby Israel secured a land for itself, was interpreted as God's gift of an inheritance. The land was not interpreted as belonging to various individuals and families of Israel as a natural right, but was thought of as a gift of God. Thus there came about a special understanding of the meaning of property and of obligation in relation to God, the land, which was God's gift, would be taken away at a future time.
>
> (Wright 1960: 8–9)

No mention is made of the right of the indigenous Palestinian population's right to the land. Their rights, their voice, and their history are excluded in the relentless search for ancient Israel. Here it is not a conquest but a gift, it is not dispossession but possession ceded by God. Similarly one of the major sections of the book is entitled 'God's Gift of a Land (Joshua–Judges)'. Wright gives no thought to the dispossessed. He does not justify explicitly the conquest in terms of Albright's belief in the inevitability of evolutionary development; rather, he tries, in a remarkable passage, to justify the act of genocide in which the indigenous population are wiped out according to the Joshua narrative:

> Now we know not only from the Bible but from many outside sources as well that the Canaanite civilization and religion was one of the weakest, most decadent, and most immoral cultures of the civilized world at that time. It is claimed, then, that Israel is God's agent of destruction against a sinful civilization, for in the moral order of God civilizations of such flagrant wickedness must be destroyed. On the other hand, God has a purpose in the choosing of Israel and in giving her a land, a purpose stated in the promises to the fathers of Israel in Genesis.
>
> (Wright 1960: 109)

He takes it as read that there can be no argument about the immorality and decadence of the indigenous population or that Israel has the right to take the land and kill the occupants. Wright then tries to resolve the theological problem for the Christian that God 'fights for Israel' and so is responsible for the slaughter:

In other words, God has a purpose of universal redemption in the midst of and for a sinful world. He makes even the wars and fightings of men serve his end. In the case of Israel, his purpose as expressed in the patriarchal promises coincided at the moment of conquest with the terrible iniquity of Canaan. It was a great thing for Israel that she got her land; it was also a sobering thing because with it went the great responsibility and the danger of judgement. It was likewise a great thing for the Canaanites in the long run. Between 1300 and 1100 B.C. Israel took away from them the hill country of Palestine, while the incoming Arameans took away the whole of eastern Syria. The remnant of the people was confined to the Syrian coast around Tyre and Sidon and further north. After 1100 B.C., they began to develop one of the most remarkable trading empires in the world (the Greeks called them Phoenicians). Their colonies were spread all over the Mediterranean world, much to the benefit of that world; and this was done, not by conquest, but solely by the peaceful means of trading.

(Wright 1960: 110)

It is astounding that he should believe that it was to the benefit of the indigenous people that they were wiped out and their land appropriated by Israelites or Arameans. This is an even more extreme variant of Lord Balfour's speech to Parliament in June 1910, critiqued by Said (1985: 31–6), in which he argues that the British government of Egypt was exercised for the good of Egyptians and the whole of the civilized West. It forms part of the standard justification of imperialism and colonization in that the imperial power acts on behalf of the indigenous population. Equally astounding is Wright's view that this appropriation of land was in the long-term good of Palestine since the survivors were forced to remain on a thin strip of the coast where they became a great trading force. As Elon (1983: 150) points out, many early Zionists were of the unthinking belief that Zionism represented progress with the implied or expressed assumption that Jewish settlement would ultimately benefit the Arabs. In fact, the Arab population were considered to be potential Zionists and were expected to welcome the Jews as a matter of course. Elon concludes that this was so self-evident for most Zionists that they never considered any alternative perception of what was happening. Similarly, the facts of the past are so self-evident for Wright that he does not consider any alternative construction. The assumption that the event, the conquest of Palestine by the Israelites, is part of revelation and that it represents a divine gift of land to Israel, 'one of the great acts of God's goodness' (1960: 103–4) only reinforces the exclusion of Palestinian history and the taking of Palestinian space. It rapidly becomes, in the discourse of biblical studies, 'their homeland' (1960: 105). But equally revealing is his view that even after the Conquest Israel was vulnerable to invasion by surrounding peoples and lacked real security apart from divine intervention: 'The Book of Judges, then, presents the real problem of Israel: the problem of living within a covenant apart from which there is no security. It is also preparatory for the next event: the establishment of a king as an attempted answer to this problem' (Wright 1960: 112). The solution to the problem of insecurity was the establishment of a sovereign national state. The invention of ancient Israel in the discourse of biblical studies mirrors the contemporary situation where Jewish immigration into Palestine eventually resulted in the founding of the modern state of Israel in 1948 as the realization of Jewish national consciousness and a means of providing security against the threats of the indigenous Palestinian population and surrounding Arab nations.

The invention of Israel's past is confirmed in Wright's classic treatment, *Biblical Archaeology*, in which he points out that, with the meticulous development of archaeology in the twentieth century, it has become possible to differentiate 'between early Israelite towns and those of the Canaanites whom the Hebrews could not drive out, to trace the evidences of the Israelite Conquest of Canaan' (1962: 24–5). The key element here is the differentiation between Israel and the indigenous population. This is borne out by Albright's excavation of Bethel, in which Wright participated, and which revealed evidence of a massive destruction of the city. However, the conclusion he draws from this is revealing of his underlying assumption:

> The Canaanite city destroyed was a fine one with excellent houses, paved or plastered floors and drains. Compared with them the poor straggly houses of the next town were poverty itself. The break between the two is so complete that there can be no doubt but that this was the Israelite destruction.
>
> (Wright 1962: 81)

No evidence is offered for this dogmatic statement except the implicit assumption that the destruction layer and poor settlement which follow indicate that there must have been a dramatic break in culture which can only be explained in terms of external invasion. He confirms this with his explanation of the destruction of Tell Beit Mirsim: 'As was the case at Bethel, the new town founded in the ashes was so different from the preceding one that we must think of a new people having built it, a people who must have been Israelites, or closely related to them' (Wright 1962: 83). Once again, no evidence is offered for this conclusion and he goes even further with the assertion that the destruction 'must have been' the result of invading Israelites or some group closely related to them. The indigenous population is destroyed and its voice silenced in the relentless search for ancient Israel. He believes that he 'can safely conclude that during the 13th century a portion at least of the later nation of Israel gained entrance to Palestine by a carefully planned invasion' (1962: 84). The search for Israel determined the interpretation of the archaeological evidence so that material artifacts are given an ethnic label which allows them to be used to differentiate between Israel and the indigenous Palestinian population even though there is nothing in the archaeological record which would permit such a conclusion.

The corollary of this is the theological assumption that Israel, and thereby its spiritual heirs in Christianity, is a unique entity which can be confirmed by the archaeologist's spade:

> We can now see that though the Bible arose in that ancient world, it was not entirely of it; though its history and its people resemble those of the surrounding nations, yet it radiates an atmosphere, a spirit, a faith, far more profound and radically different than any other ancient literature.
>
> (Wright 1962: 27)

Israel of the ancient world is set apart from its environment just as modern Israel is often described as set apart from the rest of the Middle East. Its special status, then, means that the conquest of Palestine is not a problem: it is in fact part of the divine plan: 'The deliverance from slavery in Egypt and the gift of a good land in which to dwell were to Israel God's greatest acts on her behalf' (Wright 1962: 69). What it results in, following the ceremony at Shechem (Joshua 24), is 'a united Israel with a common national heritage' (1962: 78).

The culmination of the pervasive influence of an invention of an Israelite conquest of Palestine is to be found in John Bright's *A History of Israel*, first published in 1960, which has shaped the ideas and assumptions of generations of students and scholars.[11] Despite the fact that the Albright–Bright position has long been seen as in direct opposition to the Alt–Noth hypothesis, as we have noted, it is remarkable to note how many important assumptions they share. These are the very assumptions that emphasize the uniqueness and superiority of Israel and the inferiority of the indigenous Palestinian population: assumptions which underline Israel's right to the land and justify the dispossession of the Palestinians. In his opening remarks, when setting the scene, to his discussion of the Exodus and Conquest traditions, he refers to Israel as 'a peculiar people' (1960: 97). Strikingly, he then adds that by the end of the thirteenth century BCE 'we find the people Israel settled on the land that was to be theirs through the centuries to come' (1960: 97). Bright clearly assumes that the land, Palestine, belongs to Israel. No consideration is given to the claims to the land of the indigenous population. Although he argues that Israel comes from outside Palestine, there seems to be no question that the land naturally belongs to this 'peculiar people'. Underlying Bright's construction of this period, and all other periods, is the assumption, prevalent in the discourse of biblical studies, as we have seen, that Israel is unique and set aside from its environment. It informs every aspect of his work, as articulated in the preface:

> The history of Israel is the history of a people which came into being at a certain point in time as a league of tribes united in a covenant with Yahweh, which subsequently existed as a nation, then as two nations, and finally as a religious community, but which was at all times set off from its environment as a distinctive cultural entity. The distinguishing factor that made Israel the peculiar phenomenon that she was, which both created her society and was the controlling factor in her history, was of course her religion.
>
> (Bright 1960: 9)

The use of this volume as the standard textbook on Israelite history in British and American universities and seminaries has ensured that this classic statement on the concept of Israelite uniqueness, its separation from its environment, and by implication the contrast with indigenous culture, has been read and absorbed by countless numbers of students for two to three decades.

Bright acknowledges the material and cultural achievements of 'Canaan' with its impressive urban culture and the invention of writing (1960: 107–8). Yet its indigenous religion is immoral and corrupt: 'Canaanite religion, however, presents us with no pretty picture. It was, in fact, an extraordinarily debasing form of paganism, specifically of the fertility cult' (1960: 108). This is in contrast to Israelite religion which was 'quite without parallel in the ancient world'; it was this that 'set Israel off from her environment and made her the distinctive and creative phenomenon that she was' (1960: 128). Israel's moral purity is reinforced with his assertion that Palestine possessed 'the sort of religion which Israel, however much she might borrow of the culture of Canaan, could never with good conscience make peace' (1960: 109). The way in which Israel is set apart from its environment is reinforced by an assumption shared with Alt and Noth that the indigenous population was incapable of developing sophisticated political systems: 'Though a cultural unit, Canaan was politically without identity' (1960: 109). The evolutionary scheme, common to both hypotheses, and an integral part of the discourse of biblical studies, extends to political and religious institutions: Palestine represents a branch of the evolutionary tree which fails to reach the pinnacle of evolution, the nation state and monotheistic faith, the hallmarks of European and American civilization. It becomes inevitable, under such a scheme, that the degenerate and static native cultures were surpassed and replaced by Israelite and Western civilization.

Both models presumed a now outmoded evolutionary view of social and political development from nomads/semi-nomads to sedentary groups. The American hypothesis shared with its German counterpart the assumption that Israel settled at first in the scarcely populated hill country of Palestine. Bright sets the stage for his description of the Israelite conquest of Canaan by preparing the reader with the suggestion and assertion that Israel was about to introduce a moral and political order into the region in just the same way that the Israel of his own day was often presented as the bearer of (European/Western) civilization into a region that was politically divided and morally bankrupt. The cultural achievements of Palestine are only mentioned in passing to be overshadowed by the inabilities of a religiously corrupt population to form itself into a meaningful political organization, i.e. it was incapable of crossing the threshold to statehood. Palestine, before the intervention of Israel, was merely a patchwork of petty city-states under Egyptian control which was left 'disorganized and helpless' (1960: 109) with the collapse of Egyptian power. Furthermore, the real controlling assumption of Bright's conception of history, or at least Israelite history, is revealed in the following sentence: 'It was this, humanly speaking, that made the Israelite conquest possible' (1960: 109). Underlying this is the belief that it is the divine which controls the course of history.[12] Little wonder then that there is no need to question Israel's right to the land; it is, after all, the gift of God. Israel becomes both the progenitor and the carrier of European civilization which has to be introduced from outside the region if it is to develop along the evolutionary political and religious scale.

Bright (1960: 117) is in no doubt that the biblical tradition of a conquest is historical and 'ought no longer to be denied'; as it was, of course, by German scholarship following Alt and Noth. This is seen as the pivotal disagreement between the two major hypotheses which dominated the discourse of biblical studies for half a century from the early 1920s to the 1970s. Such a presentation has obscured the critical shared assumptions which have been instrumental in helping to silence Palestinian history. For Bright, as for his mentor Albright, the process is understood primarily in terms of the 'Israelite conquest' or 'Israelite occupation' of Palestine. Bright acknowledges the biblical traditions of a protracted and 'peaceful' process but argues that the archaeological evidence for the destruction of key urban centres in Palestine leads him to the conclusion that 'it may be regarded as certain that a violent irruption into the land took place in the thirteenth century!' (1960: 120). He follows the standard assumption that Israel first settled in the sparsely populated hill country and later defeated the urban centres of the lowlands. He provides a striking description of this process which could easily have been written about the consequences of the foundation of the modern state of Israel:

> The incompleteness of the conquest, however, is evident. Israel was unable to occupy either the coastal plain or the Plain of Esdraelon, while the Canaanite enclaves – such as Jerusalem (Judges 1: 21), which was not taken until the time of David (2 Samuel 5: 6–10) – remained in the mountains as well. Since most of these areas, however, were ultimately incorporated into Israel, this means that Israel was later to include people whose ancestors had not only not taken part in the conquest, but had actively resisted it!
>
> (Bright 1960: 122)

He does not go as far as Alt in claiming that these indigenous groups did not expect equality of treatment. None the less, Bright's model of ancient Israel is one which is remarkably similar to the modern state in which large numbers of Palestinians were incorporated into the new state boundaries, particularly in 1948 and then later after the conflicts in 1967 and 1974.

Israel's right to the land in Bright's construction is based largely upon the right of conquest, although he argues that there is evidence to support the view that Israelite elements were in Palestine prior to the main conquest (1960: 122). This view again is in remarkable accord with the modern situation where there was a significant Jewish presence in Palestine prior to the Zionist immigration of the late nineteenth and early twentieth century and the conflict which led to the founding of the state of Israel in 1948. His summary description of the process echoes Albright and Wright in ignoring the rights of the indigenous population:

> In the latter half of the thirteenth century there took place, as archaeological evidence abundantly attests, a great onslaught upon western Palestine, which, however incomplete it may have been, broke the back of organized resistance and enabled Israel to transfer her tribal center there. There is no reason to doubt that this conquest was, as The Book of Joshua depicts it, a bloody and brutal business. It was the Holy War of Yahweh, by which he would give his people the Land of Promise. At the same time, it must be remembered that the herem was applied only in certain cases; the Canaanite population was by no means exterminated. Much of the land occupied by Israel was thinly populated, and much inhabited by elements who made common cause with her. Israel's victories occasioned wholesale accessions to her numbers. Clans and cities came over en masse and were incorporated into her structure in solemn covenant (Joshua 24). Among those absorbed either at once or later were Khapiru elements and various towns of central Palestine, the Gibeonite confederacy (chapter 9), Galilean clans and towns, as well as groups (Kenizites, Kenites, etc.), many of them already Yahwist, who had infiltrated the land from the south and mingled with Judah. Though the process of absorption was to go on for some time, Israel's tribal structure speedily filled out and assumed its normative form. With this the history of the people of Israel may be said to have begun.
>
> (Bright 1960: 126–7)

Israel's history begins, while Palestinian history ends. The past belongs to Israel; the indigenous population, whether absorbed or slaughtered, has no claim on this past.

M. Weippert's survey (1971) and restatement of the Alt hypothesis stresses that the debate between the schools of Alt and Albright was not about historical details as much as the principles of historiography. This is true in the sense that it was a debate over the relative values of the biblical traditions and 'external evidence', particularly the growing body of archaeological data from the 1920s onwards. However, this obscures the fact that, in important aspects, both schools shared important assumptions about the nature of Israel and its occupation/conquest of Palestine. Neither questioned the right of Israel to the land or raised the issue of the rights of the dispossessed indigenous population. In both cases, they assumed a model of the past which was directly related to and shaped by their own time: in the case of the Baltimore school, this was particularly influenced by the evangelical Christian persuasion of its participants. The real methodological issues which influenced these constructions of ancient Israel were hidden from the reader and have remained hidden and unspoken throughout the whole discourse of biblical studies. The search for ancient Israel, by both German and American scholarship, had resulted in its invention at a critical point in the history of the region, the Late Bronze–Iron Age transition. These inventions served to silence and exclude the history of ancient Palestine. At this point, Israel was Palestine: Palestine and its history, Palestinian time and space, are completely subsumed by Israel and its claims to the past as presented by the major figures of Western biblical scholarship.

CLAIMING PALESTINE 3:
THE STRUGGLE WITHIN PALESTINE

George Mendenhall, a pupil of Albright's at Johns Hopkins, is credited with formulating an alternative explanation of Israelite origins which challenged, and eventually undermined, many of the underlying assumptions of Alt and Noth, Albright and Bright, who had invented ancient Israel in the image of an Israel of their own day. His original programmatic essay, 'The Hebrew conquest of Palestine' which appeared in the *Biblical Archaeologist* in 1962, was overlooked for some time before becoming the focus of a fierce debate in the 1970s and 1980s. It is widely perceived to have shaken the very foundations of the biblical discourse on the origins of Israel by helping to undermine the conquest and immigration hypotheses. This common perception, however, is misleading since the foundational assumptions of Mendenhall, linked as they were to many of Albright's fundamental ideas, were locked into the discourse of biblical studies concerned with the search for ancient Israel as the taproot of Western civilization, effectively inventing Israel in its own image and thereby silencing Palestinian history. The paradox of Mendenhall's work is that there are important aspects which appear to give legitimacy and a voice to Palestinian history, only for that voice to be withdrawn or excluded under the truth claims of Christianity.

Ironically, Mendenhall's starting point is in agreement with the central thrust of this volume: previous scholarship had constructed Israel in its own image by basing hypotheses upon outmoded 'models' or 'ideal models'. One of his professed aims, interestingly in the light of the post-modern debate, was 'to avoid the worst mistake of reading purely modern ideas into the ancient world. Nationalism, like racism, is for all practical purposes a nonexistent operational concept in ancient history' (1973: 184). The hypotheses of Alt and Albright were based upon the fundamentally mistaken assumption that ancient Israel was a nomadic society, analogous to bedouin society of the nineteenth and twentieth centuries, what he later terms 'the nomadic mirage' (1973: 150).[13] He argued also that there had been a failure to recognize the social and political 'prejudices' of scholars involved in the reconstruction of the Israelite past. Both previous models assumed that changes in the ancient past can only be explained in terms of ethnic migrations or conquests supplanting other ethnic or racial groups. He was concerned to expose these 'tacit or expressed assumptions' (1962: 67) of both the main models of Israelite origins by questioning, on the basis of biblical and extra-biblical evidence, the domain assumption that the early Israelites were nomadic. At first sight, he appeared to reject the strong evolutionary scheme which had informed the discourse of biblical studies by rejecting a pattern of development from nomad to village to city.[14] It led to a seemingly radical proposal which was to occupy biblical scholars for a considerable period of time:

> The fact is, and the present writer would regard it as a fact though not every detail can be 'proven', that both the Amarna

materials and the biblical events represent politically the same process: namely, the withdrawal, not physically and geographically, but politically and subjectively, of large population groups from any obligation to the existing political regimes, and therefore, the renunciation of any protection from those sources. In other words, there was no statistically important invasion of Palestine at the beginning of the twelve tribe system of Israel. There was no radical displacement of population, only of royal administrators (of necessity!). In summary, there was no real conquest of Palestine at all; what happened instead may be termed, from the point of view of the secular historian interested only in socio-political processes, a peasant's revolt against the network of interlocking Canaanite city states.

(Mendenhall 1962: 73)

This represented a radical departure from the previous two models which had assumed a major external conquest or immigration: Mendenhall assumed that the external element was a small group which acted as a catalyst for the dissatisfied and exploited Palestinian peasant population. For Mendenhall, the key feature of this 'biblical revolution', as he termed it, was not the indigenous peasant revolt, but the religious revolution. In fact, he later complained that the designation of his hypothesis of Israelite origins as 'the peasant revolt' model was unfortunate and misleading since this was 'but an incidental and possibly even accidental aspect of the "biblical revolution"' (1983: 31).

His views, however, embody an important paradox. His questioning of the domain assumption that the origins of Israel in Palestine were the result of a significant external influx of a new population appears to value the importance of indigenous culture and history in a way that had not previously been recognized. However, his emphasis upon the centrality of the new religion, brought from outside, immediately stifled any possibility of a new departure in the study of the history of the region. Furthermore, Mendenhall stressed the inherent corruption of the indigenous culture possibly even more strongly than Albright had done. He presented a stark contrast between the ethical and monotheistic faith brought from outside Palestine by Israel, however statistically insignificant, and the immoral and polytheistic beliefs of a corrupt city-state system indigenous to the region. His analysis of the political set-up presupposed the work of Alt:

The Hebrew conquest of Palestine took place because a religious movement and motivation created a solidarity among a large group of pre-existent social units, which was able to challenge and defeat the dysfunctional complex of cities which dominated the whole of Palestine and Syria at the end of the Bronze Age.

(Mendenhall 1962: 73)

Mendenhall's theological assumptions are the driving force behind his historical analysis:[15]

It was this religious affirmation of the value of historical events which is still felt to be the unique feature of Israelite faith, and quite correctly, but any cultic separation of religious values from the brute facts of historical reality must inevitably result in a radical transformation of the nature of religious obligation. It is for this reason that theology and history must be inseparable in the biblical faith; biblical theology divorced from historical reality ends in a kind of ritual docetism, and history apart from religious value is a valueless secularized hobby of antiquarians.

(Mendenhall 1962: 74)

This theological agenda, which draws a direct connection between the 'biblical revolution' and Mendenhall's own day, is set out clearly in the preface to his major study, *The Tenth Generation*:

What was important about this community was its radically new way of looking at God, nature, and humanity – and this was truly revolutionary. A revolution occurred that is just as relevant today as it was in the time of Moses, and one that is just as necessary.

(Mendenhall 1973: xi)

His stress upon the uniqueness of Israel on the basis of its faith, the faith which underlies Western civilization, allows him to maintain, and in effect sharpen, the common distinction between Israel and the indigenous culture of Palestine. Furthermore, it reflects the common presentation of the direct continuum between ancient Israel and the modern West as societies founded upon monotheism in contrast to the polytheistic Near East. Thus, far from Mendenhall's theory of internal revolt leading to an appreciation of the indigenous culture and so the history of Palestine, it results in an even more radical distinction between Israel and the 'Canaanite' population: a distinction which is equally effective in silencing Palestinian history. His radical distinction is expressed in the following terms:

> Early Israel thus cannot be understood within the framework of traditional academic ideas about a primitive society gradually becoming urbanized, and therefore civilized. Its very beginnings involved a radical rejection of Canaanite religious and political ideology, especially the divine authority underlying the political institutions, and the Canaanite concept of religion as essentially a phenological cultic celebration of the economic concerns of the group – the fertility cult. Only under the assumption that the groups involved had actually experienced at first hand over a period of time the malfunctioning of Canaanite kingship, can one understand the concept of God in early Israelite religion, for the usual functions, authority, and prestige of the king and his court are the exclusive prerogative of the deity. So, land tenure, military leadership, 'glory', the right to command, power, are all denied to human beings and attributed to God alone.
>
> (Mendenhall 1962: 76)

The land, it is stressed, is the property of the deity and therefore a matter of divine gift. The loss of Palestinian space to Israelite control is justified, therefore, in terms of the divine gift of the land to Israel. The immoral and corrupt indigenous culture simply had no claim to the land under this understanding. Israel's 'conquest of Palestine' is affirmation of that divine gift. Mendenhall then drew a further distinction between Israel and Canaan which has many echoes in contemporary justifications for the legitimization of the modern state of Israel in contrast to the failures of the indigenous Palestinian population: 'Another impressive concern of early Israelite religion which is a striking contrast to Late Bronze Age Canaan is the preservation of the peace over a large territory' (Mendenhall 1962: 77). Only Israel was capable of maintaining peace over a large territory because the indigenous system represented the corrupt exploitation of the peasantry by the urban elite. Canaanite, and thereby Palestinian, society was not capable of developing a civilized system of social organization: 'By making the struggle for power an illicit assumption of the prerogatives of God alone, the early Israelite religion laid the foundation for an internal peace which Canaanite society evidently could not do' (Mendenhall 1962: 78).

The emphasis upon the peasant revolt, for Mendenhall an accidental and unfortunate designation, has all too often obscured the radical distinction he drew between Israel and the indigenous culture. Mendenhall, as a pupil of Albright and a member of the influential Biblical Colloquium, makes explicit many of the underlying assumptions of biblical studies discourse which have contributed to the silencing of Palestinian history through the scholarly invention of ancient Israel. Mendenhall's radical distinction between the Israelite religious community and the corrupt socio-political regimes indigenous to Palestine continues to mirror the common representation of the modern state of Israel as a radically new development in the region, with its roots in European civilization and democracy, which has been able to transform the land so long neglected by a divided and indolent indigenous population.

One of the most striking features of Mendenhall's analysis is his questioning of the ethnic unity of Israel in relation to Canaan.[16] The vast majority of 'Israel' were for him indigenous groups and individuals who had rejected the exploitative socio-political regimes of Late Bronze Age Canaan. As noted above, it would appear, at first sight, that this ought to provide the basis for the articulation, at least, of the value of Palestinian history in its own right. However, although he rejected the strong evolutionary pattern of social and political development of Albrightian and Altian scholarship, he imposed an even stronger evolutionary pattern of religious development which silenced Palestinian history equally effectively:

> In the past, the discontinuity from the Late Bronze Age to the Iron Age has been explained on the basis of a hypothetical change or displacement of population: the Israelites displaced the Canaanites in part, the Phoenicians displaced the Canaanites elsewhere; the Arameans displaced still more, and so on down the line. All of these ideas are now untenable. If the Phoenicians are merely the continuation of Canaanite culture, with considerable changes of course, the Israelites also represent such a continuation with a change of a more radical sort (particularly in the religious and social system). As revealed by excavations, certainly it is true that there are only minimal differences between the two in material culture, and those differences are most readily explained as functions of the differences in the social, economic, and religious structure of the ancient Israelites.
>
> (Mendenhall 1973: 10)

Indigenous religion and culture were condemned in the strongest terms, being rejected as 'Late Bronze Age paganism'. The discourse of biblical studies has refused to recognize indigenous religious systems as having any kind of legitimacy.[17] The truth claims of Judaism and Christianity, the foundations of Western civilization, have been accepted unthinkingly to the extent that Palestinian religious systems have been continually presented as immoral and corrupt. Mendenhall prefers to talk in terms of the foundation of a religious community called Israel, a utopian society based upon ethical relationships. As such, his invention of ancient Israel is comparable with the Zionist pioneers' desire to found a 'new, just society' (Elon 1983: 143). The 'biblical revolution', the foundation stone of Western culture, is a radical replacement of a corrupt pagan system. Significantly, although the indigenous population is seen as being statistically significant in the destruction of the urban centres in Palestine at the end of the Late Bronze Age, the religious movement which makes this possible is external: it is brought by a small group of Israelites escaping from Egypt. The real civilizing influence which transforms Palestinian society is an external religious system:

Any history of the origins of ancient Israel must start with, or at least account for, the sudden appearance of a large community in Palestine and Transjordan only a generation after the small group escaped from Egypt under the leadership of Moses. At the same time, it must account for the fact that from the earliest period there is a radical contrast between the religious ideology of Israel and those of the preceding periods and neighboring groups. In spite of that contrast, virtually all specific *formal* elements in early Israelite culture and ideology have impressive analogues in pre-Israelite or other foreign sources.

(Mendenhall 1973: 25)

He stresses the 'mere formal continuities' with 'the old pre-Yahwistic "Canaanite" and Anatolian cultures which characterized the Palestinian scene' but this is prior to 'the socio-religious unification' (1973: 25, n. 93). The emphasis here is on the fact that it was only due to this external input that unification was achieved, something of which the indigenous population and systems were incapable without external direction. Thus Mendenhall, rather than shaking the very foundations of biblical discourse and providing a voice for Palestinian history, invents an ancient Israel which continues to deny value to Palestinian society and history.

What is potentially much more important for the development of Palestinian history in its own right is his questioning of the causal connection between the growth of highland settlements and the urban collapse:

> The destruction levels revealed by archaeology in Palestine would have been caused not by the Israelites, but rather are part of the common experience of the population that made vivid the desirability and need for a new community. This could bring about the peace and secure a new cooperation for rebuilding a shattered society and economy.
>
> (Mendenhall 1973: 23)

Thus the shift in settlement is understood as a result of the urban collapse rather than its cause (Mendenhall 1973: 63–4). Although his conclusions are tied to his theological scheme, his analysis of the archaeological data provides a very important starting point for the history of ancient Palestine as a study of the processes which brought about social change in the region. If we remove the distraction of the search for Israel and think more in terms of trying to explain the processes involved in the political and social upheavals of the Late Bronze–Iron Age transition and the accompanying settlement shift, then Mendenhall's analysis has much to commend it. The focus of attention is then switched to trying to investigate and understand the processes which contributed to this settlement shift and the accompanying economic decline throughout the region at the end of the Late Bronze Age. It is this type of approach which holds out the promise of the realization of the study of Palestinian history as a subject in its own right rather than as the backdrop for the theologically and politically motivated search for ancient Israel. The paradox embedded in Mendenhall's analysis offers an instructive analogy with a great deal of subsequent research, to be discussed in chapter 5, whereby the accumulating data from archaeological excavations and surveys which offer a voice to Palestinian history have been side-tracked by the discourse of biblical studies in its continued and forlorn search for ancient Israel.

Norman Gottwald developed many of Mendenhall's basic ideas in an expressly political formulation of early Israelite origins in his massive *The Tribes of Yahweh. A Sociology of the Religion of Liberated Israel, 1250–1050 B.C.E.* The title reveals the explicitly political nature of Gottwald's work, something which he has continued to develop in a series of studies. This is signalled by the dedication of his study 'to the memory and to the honor of the first Israelites' followed by an anonymous tribute to the people of Vietnam in which love and power are deemed necessary to destroy power without love. His preface opens with three quotations, including one from Marx and Engels and one from Mendenhall (1973: 12), which stress the importance of revolutionary movements for social change. He then explicitly states one of the major influences on his work:

> Two decades of involvement in civil rights struggles, in opposition to the war in Vietnam, in anti-imperialist efforts, in analysis of North American capitalism, and in the rough-and-tumble of ecclesial and educational politics have continued an ever-informative 'living laboratory' for discerning related social struggles in ancient Israel.
>
> (Gottwald 1979: xxv)

It is quite clear that Gottwald was well aware of the subjective influences of current politics in shaping a construction of the Israelite past.[18] The preface concludes with the oft-quoted line that 'only as the full *materiality* of ancient Israel is more securely grasped will we be able to make proper sense of its *spirituality*' (1979: xxv). His professed aim was to view Israelite religion as a part of a total social system by assembling 'the most reliable information about *the rise of Israel* as determined by the recognized methods of biblical science' (1979: xxii).

It is striking that given the expressly political nature of Gottwald's work, his Marxist-materialist analysis of history and explicit acknowledgement of his part in the anti-Vietnam movement, he never mentions the struggle of the Palestinian people for self-determination. In one of the most radical and controversial works of twentieth-century biblical studies, the question of Palestine remains unspoken. Similarly, Silberman can state, in his review of the hypotheses of Mendenhall and Gottwald, that: 'The "peasant revolt" theory of Israelite origins had obvious rhetorical power in the 1970s, a time of modern national liberation movements and Third World insurgency' (Silberman 1992: 29). Yet Silberman, attuned as he is to the political construction of the past, makes no attempt to connect this theory of Israelite origins with the most obvious of national liberation movements, the Palestinian struggle against Israeli occupation. The problem remains unspoken because the dominant discourse of biblical studies has silenced any notion of Palestinian history or expression of self-determination so thoroughly. Even though Gottwald in his radical critique, and Silberman in his acknowledgement of the wider political setting of such an hypothesis, see the connection with other struggles for national liberation, they are unable to draw out the implications of this construction of the past for understanding the contemporary struggle for Palestinian self-determination.

Gottwald's opening chapter, entitled 'Obstacles to a comprehensive understanding of early Israel', focuses upon Israel as 'a radical socio-religious mutation' (1979: 3). The obstacles, however, in achieving this comprehensive understanding are not due to any lack of industry or ingenuity in scholarly investigation but stem from the nature of the sources and a scholarly and religious aversion and hesitancy in conceiving ancient Israel as a social totality. In addressing this issue of the appeal to social scientific data and theories for understanding ancient Israel, he identifies a key problem:

> One root of this inhibition is the canonical sanctity that still surrounds ancient Israel as the forerunner of Judaism and Christianity. The very patterns of our thinking about Israel have been imbued with religiosity, or with its defensive counterpart, anti-religiosity. It is difficult not to think of Israel as a people wholly apart from the rest of humanity. While our scholarly or secular minds may know better, our psychosocial milieu impels us to look for abstract religious phenomena and for all-encompassing theological explanations as indices to the meaning of Israel. As a result, the radical historical mutation of Israel in human history is accounted for by the supernatural, or by retrojected theological meanings from later Israel, or simply not accounted for at all.
>
> (Gottwald 1979: 5)

The paradox of this is that while Gottwald eschews the key notion of the uniqueness of ancient Israel which has been central to the exclusion of Palestinian history from academic discourse, he refers to Israel as a 'radical historical mutation', picking up the key terminology used by George Ernest Wright which set Israel apart as unique from its environment. The overspecialization of biblical studies is condemned as contributing to the failure to conceive of Israel as a total social system which he traces back to intellectual, cultural, and sociological factors. His analysis represents a very strong attack upon the dead hand of theology in the study of Israelite history while decrying the failure of biblical studies to articulate and investigate the social, economic, and political factors which affect its scholarship. The key for Gottwald was 'the crucial factor of the social-class identity of the biblical scholar' (1979: 10): the location of biblical scholars within a capitalist middle class, espousing scholarly human-istic ideals, has produced a vision of society which has excluded many of its members (1979: 11). He acknowledges the subjectivity and limitations of the discourse of biblical studies, yet he does not go on to develop the way in which the domination of theology has constrained the study of the ancient Palestinian past; it is only perceived as an obstacle to a clear understanding of ancient Israel. His whole focus is upon Israelite society, particularly the role of religion in Israelite society, and remains firmly rooted to the dis-course which has silenced Palestinian history. The influence of Alt's analysis of the political situation in Palestine prior to the so-called emergence of Israel is evident throughout, particularly in his identi-fication of the settlement shift to the Palestinian highlands with Israel. He is reliant upon the analyses of Albright for the various material aspects of this 'Israelite culture', as identified in its ceramic and architectural traditions, unlike Mendenhall who had strongly denied the ethnic labelling of such material culture. Furthermore, Gottwald's analysis of the biblical traditions themselves is firmly rooted in the dominant discourse of biblical studies.[19]

He is able to refer to Israel as 'a recognizably novel and coherent system in Canaan' (1979: 34), stressing the relationship between 'Israel as a total social system and the prehistories of its component peoples' (1979: 34). The history of Palestine, either prior to or contemporary with the so-called emergence of Israel, is thereby reduced to the role of 'prehistory' for this later all-encompassing reality. Israel is allowed to dominate and exclude Palestinian history through his continual references to 'proto-Israelites' or 'Israelite prehistory' which claim Palestinian time for Israel. However, he offers a greater understanding of the value and worth of the history of the region with the recognition that 'Israel's origins are positioned in the midst of an ancient and highly developed arena of self-conscious civilization' (1979: 43). But the negative assessment of this internal history ultimately prevails since Israel is distinctive in its egalitarian social experiment and 'manages to do this in the face of the most serious threats from powerful surrounding systems of domination determined to prevent its liberation' (1979: 43). In essence, the reader is presented with a model of Israel as the carrier of traditions of liberation and democracy surrounded by powerful forces which seek to destroy it.

In his review and critique of the three standard models of Israelite origins, Gottwald (1979: 191–227) makes it clear that the identification of material culture is a key aspect of his understanding of the location of Israel in Palestine. He criticizes the Albrightian conclusion that the cumulative evidence of the destruction of many Late Bronze urban sites and the spread of poor, rural settlements

> points to a culturally less advanced population living in temporary encampments or in poorly constructed houses without fortifications. Assuming the new residents to have been the destroyers of the Late Bronze cities on whose ruins they settled, it is easy to see them as the technically impoverished, 'semi-nomadic' Israelites.
>
> (Gottwald 1979: 195)

However, although he recognizes that there are many possible explanations for the urban destructions, it is the identification of a distinct material culture associated with the increase in rural sites in the early Iron Age that remains important for his understanding of early Israel. He proposes an equally sharp distinction between Israel, as a socio-religious mutation, and the politically and economically oppressive Canaanite regimes. Indigenous Palestinian culture is denuded of any value and is seen as being transformed by Israel into something it was unable to become by itself.

The distinctive element of Gottwald's formulation of a revolt hypothesis is his stress upon the socio-political aspects of the model. As with Mendenhall's formulation, it would appear that this stress upon the socio-political conditions of Late Bronze Age Palestine offers a voice to Palestinian history. However, once again this voice is effectively excluded by the concentration upon Israel and the presentation of a corrupt indigenous socio-political system devoid of value:

> When the exodus Israelites entered Canaan they encountered this stress-torn Canaanite society, which was in still further decline a century after the Amarna Age. Population in the hill country seems to have tapered off in the Late Bronze period, and the city-state units seem to have been reduced in number and size from the preceding century. The advocates of the

revolt model for Israelite origins picture these Israelite tribes as immediate allies of the Canaanite lower classes. Both groups shared a lower-class identity. The former slaves from Egypt, now autonomous, presented an immediate appeal to the restive serfs and peasants of Canaan. The attraction of Israelite Yahwism for these oppressed Canaanites may be readily located in the central feature of the religion of the entering tribes: Yahwism celebrated the actuality of deliverance from socio-political bondage, and it promised continuing deliverance whenever Yahweh's autonomous people were threatened.

(Gottwald 1979: 214)[20]

Despite the common assumption that both Mendenhall and Gottwald stress an *internal* revolt, the domain assumption is that the indigenous system is corrupt or deficient in some significant way, that it can only be transformed by Israel and its religious and political ideology which comes from *outside*. While extending and altering Mendenhall's original formulation of what came to be known as the revolt hypothesis, he was greatly influenced by the assumption shared with Alt and Albright that the settlement growth and shift to small rural sites in the marginal areas of Palestine was to be identified with Israel. His explanation of the nature and origins of Israel as largely internal has tended to mask this fundamental shared assumption of the dominant discourse of biblical studies. It is this domain assumption which remains at the heart of the failure to give Palestinian history a voice during a time when the search for ancient Israel has been all-consuming.

Gottwald, like Mendenhall, does not view Israel as unified ethnically:

The coalescing Yahwists were astonishingly diverse ethnically and culturally, but they had common social and political experiences and were forging together a common life of mutual defense and self-development.

(Gottwald 1979: 215)

What is interesting about this view is that it sounds remarkably like a description of early Zionism where Jews from many different European countries, or more recently from the influx of American, Russian, and Ethiopian Jews, among others, 'diverse ethnically and culturally', have been welded together as a modern nation 'forging together a common life of mutual defense and self-development'. He adds later that 'the model may have to be adjusted to the possibility that some Canaanite settlements were not so much polarized by the entering exodus tribes as neutralized, thus adopting a kind of live-and-let-live policy which Israel was willing or obligated to accept' (1979: 219). This offers a striking analogy with the modern period where Zionist immigration produced a situation in which Palestinian and Zionist settlements were located in close proximity, along with periods of conflict in which many Palestinian settlements have been driven out and deprived of their land. This again is reflected in his understanding of the rise of an Israelite state which 'overthrew the entire balance of power between Israelites and non-Yahwistic Canaanites' (1979: 219).

The fact that this model, just as much as the immigration and conquest models, is about claiming the land is made abundantly clear by Gottwald's elaboration of key questions of social structure which he believes have been overlooked or ignored by biblical scholarship because of a reluctance to draw upon social scientific data or models. He talks in terms of 'Israel's occupation of the land' or 'how groups of Israelites came to hold the land' (1979: 220). He elaborates that 'the conflict over models of land-taking is in reality a much larger conflict over the proper understanding of Israel as a social system' (1979: 220).

> For the issue at stake is not simply the territorial–historical problem of how Israel took its land, e.g. the segments of Israel involved, the regions taken, the military or nonmilitary methods of occupation, etc., all the while being naively content with unexamined – or at best only partly examined – assumptions about the nature of Israelite society.
>
> (Gottwald 1979: 220)

The focus on Israel is so all-consuming that there is no question that this is Israel's land: the problem of the rights of the other indigenous groups to a land or history is not raised. This is surprising given Gottwald's sensitivity to contemporary struggles for liberation, especially given his own involvement in the anti-Vietnam protests and acknowledgement of the importance of this in shaping his views. Yet what it demonstrates above all is the overwhelming power of the search for ancient Israel within the discourse of biblical studies. It is so overwhelming, so powerful, so all-consuming, that even within a critique that is sensitive to all kinds of socio-political implications the problem of Palestine remains unspoken. Palestinian time is claimed as part of Israel's past with the insistence that those indigenous groups who rejected the oppressive socio-political regimes and joined Israel were in effect 'proto-Israelites' (1979: 30, 32–43, 77, etc.). The Israel of the past and present have combined within the discourse of biblical studies to silence Palestinian history by laying claim to its time and its land.

Gottwald, despite various provisos, perpetuates the domain assumption of the discourse of biblical studies that Israel is unique. He is well aware of the problem of theological explanations:

> How can we describe and account for the early Israelite mutation without falling into the miasma of *sui generis* religious "explanations" which in fact explain nothing, which are no more than tautologies, unassailable because untestable?
>
> (Gottwald 1979: 232)

Yet he continues to emphasize the radical distinction between social systems of Israel and Canaan which he sees, following Mendenhall, can only be explained on the basis of the novelty of Israel's 'religious movement and motivation': 'I find myself in almost total agreement with Mendenhall on this point. The cult and ideology of Yahweh, the god of Israel, are at the nub of Israel's uniqueness' (1979: 233). Although his distinctive emphasis is to stress the material aspect of Israelite culture in trying to make sense of the articulation and realization of this religious ideology, it is clear that he remains rooted to the dominant view which professes the uniqueness of Israel, implying a lack of value in indigenous culture or history. His disagreement with Mendenhall is that he had imagined a community which attributed power to its god but did not wield power itself: for Gottwald, Israel took power for itself while attributing the source of that power to Yahweh (1979: 233). Yet even though he characterizes religion as 'the unmoved mover of the Israelite mutation', he is essentially wedded to the central role of the uniqueness of Israelite religion in distinguishing it from its Palestinian context.

The paradox inherent in Mendenhall's work is equally apparent in Gottwald's alternative formulation of the revolt hypothesis. His insistence upon the central role of Canaanite peasants throwing off the control of the urban elite appears to offer a voice to Palestinian history. In fact, he goes so far as to say that 'it is only in the literature of early Israel that the revolutionary consciousness of the Canaanite underclasses finds an articulate voice' (1979: 409). These groups are only given voice by Israel. Thus, Israelite tribalism is described as the result of a conscious choice by individuals and groups to reject the Canaanite centralization of power. Although his insistence upon 'retribalization' (1979: 325) is a distinctive aspect of Gottwald's proposals, it is little more than a variant on the fundamental assumption that has informed the discourse of biblical studies since the time of Alt, that Israel's political system is different from and fundamentally superior to that of the indigenous culture. The indigenous forms of organization were disjointed and incapable of unified action: 'we know of no such sustained collective leadership among the older Canaanite city-states which, even when faced with extreme external threats, had been capable only of episodic alliances markedly unstable in their membership and longevity' (1979: 412).[21] While there is an important focus on the conflict between indigenous groups, it is never articulated in terms of Palestinian history. It is only given voice as part of the history of Israel:

> To the contrary, Israel, with a mutant sophisticated tribal mode of organization, made an "appearance" within the social system and territorial domain of Canaan. The people who came to be Israelites countered what they experienced as the systemic aggression of centralized society by a concrete, coordinated, symbolically unified, social-revolutionary action of aggressive self-defence.
>
> (Gottwald 1979: 326)

The choice of the phrase 'aggressive self-defence' is particularly noteworthy since it mirrors apologetic language often used to describe the modern state of Israel in its foreign adventures into Lebanon, or elsewhere, in striking back against what it perceives as terrorist actions. This is not to suggest that Gottwald supports such aggression but simply to point out the way in which influential contemporary language and ideas become part of the vocabulary used by historians to construct the past.

The past is seen to be every bit as much a struggle for self-determination and the control of land as the present:

> Appropriating the land and economic modes of production, this body of people organized its production, distribution, and consumption along essentially egalitarian lines. The specific historic rise of old Israel was thus a conscious improvisational reversion to egalitarian social organization that displaced hier-archic social organization over a large area previously either

directly or indirectly dominated by Canaanite centralization
and stratification for centuries.

(Gottwald 1979: 326)

Here is an invention of the Israelite past which mirrors the ideological projection of the present of the modern state of Israel which
contrasts its democratic (egalitarian) ideal with the undemocratic
(centralized and stratified) Arab states which surround it. His
understanding of Israelite origins in the Late Bronze–Iron Age
transition provides a striking parallel with conceptions of the Zionist
movement prior to the founding of the modern state. Gottwald, in
rejecting the validity of Noth's amphictyonic hypothesis, makes the
striking claim that *'the Israelite confederacy was a consciously
contrived surrogate state for its peoples'* (1979: 383; his emphasis). His
description of this imaginary Israelite past could quite easily function
as a description of early Zionism prior to 1948 in which Israel is
perceived as 'an egalitarian, extended family, segmentary tribal
society with an agricultural-pastoral economic base' (1979: 389). Ben-
Gurion wrote, before leaving Russia, that he wished to create 'a
model society based on social, economic, and political equality'
(cited by Elon 1983: 81). Similarly, Elon adds that 'the pioneers of
the second wave saw themselves less as nation builders than as
chalutzim of a new social order' (Elon 1983: 112). We might compare
this with Gottwald's emphatic statement of the nature of ancient
Israel:

> *Together, the societal segmentation and inter-group bonding of
> early Israel were adaptively related to the fundamental aims of
> these segmented but cooperating people to escape imperialism
> and feudalism imposed by outside powers and to prevent the
> rise of feudal domination within their own society.*

(Gottwald 1979: 389; his emphasis)

This could quite easily serve as a manifesto of early Zionist ideals in
the construction of a society by those fleeing the persecution and
racism of Europe, a broad collection of imperial powers ranging from
the modern nation states of Western Europe to the feudalisms of
Eastern Europe.[22] It is a view of an egalitarian society, however,
which fails to deal with the rights of the indigenous population.

In discussing the importance of Israelite religion he takes issue
with Bright's view that Israel was not unique in the way that it took
possession of the land and that its uniqueness stemmed from its

religion. Instead, Gottwald (1979: 593) argues that 'Israel's socio-political egalitarian mode of life, involving an entire populace of formerly oppressed peoples, was unique in its explicitness and in its spatio-temporal effectiveness' (Gottwald 1979: 593). His complaint against Bright is that he isolates Israelite religion from its social setting. Similarly, he rejects Mendenhall's view of Israelite religion as idealist in the way it places it in 'an asocial and ahistorical vacuum' (1979: 601). Nevertheless, Gottwald does agree 'with Bright that Israel's religion was innovative in the ancient world in significant ways' (1979: 594). He claims that it is misleading to speak of Israelite religion as 'unparalleled ' or 'unique' and prefers to use the phrase 'Israel's innovative distinctiveness' (1979: 595). It is innovative and distinctive, for Gottwald, precisely because it is the expression of an egalitarian social revolution. Despite Gottwald's dispute with Bright, he is open to the very same criticisms as Albright, Wright, Bright, and Mendenhall in undervaluing the indigenous value system which can only be transformed from outside since the religious ideology is carried by the small group of Exodus Israelites. He does not deny that there is some continuity or comparability but suggests that this has been transformed in a way that simply was not possible without outside intervention.

Gottwald's programme of 'cultural-material research into early Israel', which he proposes towards the end his massive volume (1979: 650–63), highlights the central paradox of the volume: these proposals are crucial to the realization of a Palestinian history in its own right. The pursuit of settlement history, demography, economy, etc., in broad detail over a long period of time must be at the heart of any reappraisal of the Palestinian past. The irony here is that it is again Gottwald's distraction with the search for early Israel which does not allow him to see the need for the wider application of such a programme and prevents him from giving voice to Palestinian history. As with the Conquest hypothesis of Albright, it is the ever-increasing range and quality of archaeological data from the region which has shown that Gottwald's proposal, including various reformulations, is an imagined and invented past. Although there are important features of Gottwald's work which are essential to the realization of a Palestinian history in its own right, it fails to achieve this because of the distraction with ancient Israel. Any Palestinian claim to the past is effectively silenced by the pursuit of ancient Israel: it is a past that has no self-definition apart from its definition in relation to Israel.

CONCLUSION

The changes in perspective on reading the Hebrew Bible which have raised serious questions about standard historical critical assumptions and use of the biblical traditions for historical reconstruction, along with the accumulating archaeological data from single site excavations and regional surveys in Palestine, have shown these various models or theories to be inventions of an imagined ancient past. The increasing inability of the three major constructions of Israelite origins to deal with this growing body of evidence, along with the undermining of its notion of a text, has highlighted the extent to which Israel has been invented. It is only in retrospect that it becomes possible to ask how this has come about. The driving force of biblical studies has been the need to search for ancient Israel as the taproot of Western civilization, a need that has been reinforced by the demands of Christian theology in search of the roots of its own uniqueness in the society which produced the Hebrew Bible. This has been reinforced with the foundation of the modern state of Israel, giving rise to a search by Israeli scholarship for its own national identity deep in the past.

Biblical scholarship, in its all-consuming search for ancient Israel, has reflected the myopia of the West, in general, and the early Zionists in particular, in ignoring the indigenous population and its claims to the land or the past. Elon's descriptions of the attitudes of early Zionist settlers could easily be applied to biblical scholarship:

> There are few instances in modern history where the image of things overshadows reality as thoroughly as it did in Palestine during the first half of the twentieth century. One can think of no other country where a utopian state of mind persevered for so long a time. If the Arabs shut their eyes to reality, many pioneers of the second wave shut their eyes to Arabs. They lived among themselves in workers' camps – closed communities that often resembled isolated religious orders. Contact with the Arab natives were few. It was as if the *chalutzim* deliberately banished the Arabs from their minds.
>
> (Elon 1983: 123)

Biblical scholarship has also remained blind to the indigenous population; very often when it is acknowledged, it is dismissed as unworthy, immoral, corrupt, or primitive, thereby lacking any rightful claim to serious consideration. Elon's continued description finds similar striking parallels with the discourse of biblical studies:

> The political imagination, like the imagination of the explorer, often invents its own geography. The settlers did not, of course, consider the country 'empty', as did some Zionists abroad. What they saw with their own eyes contradicted the ludicrous dictum attributed to Israel Zangwith, 'The land without people – for the people without land', which was current in Zionist circles abroad at least until as late as 1917. Yet even if there were people living in the country, the settlers saw that it was populated only sparsely. They believed they were operating in a political void; and not until the end of World War I were they fully cured of this naive illusion.

> (Elon 1983: 149)

It is now becoming clearer that biblical studies has invented its own geography in trying to construct various versions of the past, heavily influenced by a variety of social, political, and religious factors which shaped the scholars' vision of the past and present. Just like the early Zionist settlers, they have believed, or at least tried to convey the belief, that biblical scholarship was operating in a political void. The self-delusion of the pursuit of objectivity continues to operate. Attempts to raise the spectre of subjectivity or the political implications of biblical scholarship for the contemporary struggle for Palestine have met with a hostile reception. Just as the First World War was a watershed, in Elon's view, in exposing the naivety of Zionist myopia, so post-modernism has exposed the fallacy of biblical studies' self-delusion to be interested only in 'objective' scholarship or its denial of any responsibility for or connection with contemporary struggles for Palestine. 'The public badge of scholarly impartiality', in the words of Silberman (1993: 15), continues to be used to mask the political implications and responsibilities of biblical studies.

It is striking, yet understandable, that all the models have invented ancient Israel in terms of contemporary models. This is not to suggest that this has been self-conscious or deliberately misleading or that all the scholars mentioned explicitly support the dispossession of the Palestinians. It exposes, rather, the power of the discourse of biblical studies which has projected an aura of objective scholarship when it is quite clear that subjective and unconscious elements have played a key role in constructions of the imagined past of ancient Israel. It helps to demonstrate the tyranny of the present which has silenced Palestinian history. The discourse of biblical studies is implicated in this process. The acknowledgement of these implications is a necessary prelude to the freeing of the Palestinian past from Israelite control. The realization of this proposal continues to be hindered by the perpetuation of many of the domain assumptions which were the foundations for the invention of ancient Israel in the Late Bronze–Iron Age transition. The edifice of the models may have crumbled, but what is being built in their place often utilizes the very same foundations. However, before examining the new search for ancient Israel and the ways in which it has continued to exclude Palestinian history from scholarly discourse, it is important to consider how this has been achieved by the other defining moment in the history of the region, the creation of an Israelite state.

4

THE CREATION OF AN ISRAELITE STATE

CREATING A STATE: CLAIMING THE PAST

The protracted search for, and location of, ancient Israel in the Late Bronze–Iron Age transition provides only one of the defining moments in the history of Palestine. The creation of an Israelite state, which the biblical traditions associated first with Saul and then particularly David and Solomon, is for biblical scholarship *the* defining moment in the region's history. It takes on an importance which derives from but ultimately overshadows the period of so-called emergence during the Late Bronze–Iron Age transition. The creation of a state not only signals the realization of the ultimate in political development but also demarcates Israel as an *autonomous* and *sovereign* nation state independent of imperial control. The labours of biblical scholarship in pursuit of the Davidic monarchy are not merely of antiquarian interest given that the modern state of Israel traces its historic and natural claim to existence back to this Iron Age state. The Proclamation of Independence of the State of Israel issued by the Provisional State Council in Tel Aviv on 14 May 1948 refers to 'the re-establishment of the Jewish State' (Laqueur and Rubin 1984: 126). Any attempts by biblical scholars to divorce themselves from the implications of their research, to claim a disinterested objectivity in the past divorced from the realities and struggles of contemporary politics, are exposed in the opening sections of the Proclamation:

> The Land of Israel was the birthplace of the Jewish people. Here their spiritual, religious and national identity was formed. Here they achieved independence and created a culture of national and universal significance. Here they wrote and gave the Bible to the world.

Exiled from the Land of Israel the Jewish people remained faithful to it in all the countries of their dispersion, never ceasing to pray and hope for their return and the restoration of their national freedom.

Impelled by this historic association, Jews strove throughout the centuries to go back to the land of their fathers and regain their statehood. In recent decades they returned in their masses. They reclaimed the wilderness, revived their language, built cities and villages, and established a vigorous and ever-growing community, with its own economic and cultural life. They sought peace, yet they prepared to defend themselves. They brought the blessings of progress to all inhabitants of the country and looked forward to sovereign independence.

(Laqueur and Rubin 1984: 125)

The right to the land is advanced on the basis of historic precedent of the existence in the area of an ancient sovereign and independent Israelite state. It is this state, above all, which has the right to the land since this is the ultimate expression of political development and supersedes any other forms of political organization in the region – developments that are inevitably seen as inferior. Explicit in the claim is that in the modern period Jewish settlers had 'brought the blessings of progress to all the inhabitants' prior to the formation of a national state. These very same implicit and explicit assumptions underlie many of the constructions of the imagined past of Israelite emergence in Palestine, as we have seen. The explicit claim to the land, or reclaiming of the land, on the basis of this historic precedent is a widely held view that has long informed political and popular perceptions of modern Israel and its right to the land. A memorandum produced by Lord Balfour two years after his famous Declaration of 1917 which committed the British government to favouring a 'national home in Palestine for the Jewish people' contained the following statement:

The four Great Powers are committed to Zionism. And Zionism, be it right or wrong, good or bad, is rooted in age-long traditions, in present needs, in future hopes, of far profounder import than the desires and prejudices of the 700,000 Arabs who now inhabit that ancient land.

(Khalidi 1971: 208)

It is a claim, of course, that is embodied in the frequent modern-day references to 'historic Eretz Israel'. It finds expression in the 1948 Proclamation of Independence with the claim to 'the re-establishment of the Jewish State'. This is a significant rephrasing of Balfour's Declaration thirty-one years earlier which talked of 'the establishment of a national home in Palestine for the Jewish people'. Weizmann's concern to rephrase Balfour's terminology (Said 1992: 86) finds its fulfilment in the Proclamation which makes explicit the right to a Jewish State, no longer simply a national home, on the basis of historic precedent; it is the 're-establishment' of what was once there.

The context of claim and counter-claim over the possession or dispossession of land means that biblical scholarship, in its construction of an ancient Israelite state, is implicated in contemporary struggles for the land. The Zionist struggle for the realization of a sovereign and independent state has dominated the history of the region throughout this century. What has not been sufficiently appreciated is just how far this contemporary contest for Palestine has influenced the way in which the ancient past has been imagined. Even though the Zionist struggle was not realized until 1948 with the founding of the modern state of Israel, events earlier in the century have made an indelible mark upon the conscious and largely unconscious assumptions of biblical scholars as they have imagined the Davidic past as a golden age of Israelite history.[1] If nations are narrations, in the words of Homi Bhabha, then narrations of the past are intricately linked to the realities of the present excluding other possible representations or creations of the past. Biblical specialists and archaeologists have searched for and constructed a large, powerful, sovereign and autonomous Iron Age state attributed to its founder David. It is this 'fact' which has dominated the discourse of biblical studies throughout this century, providing a location for the development of many of the biblical traditions at the royal court – 'a fact', more than any other, which has silenced Palestinian history and obstructed alternative claims to the past.

It is, of course, not new to say that Palestine has been subject to outside control for the vast majority of its history; it is accepted as a given in most historical accounts. However, the Late Bronze–Iron Age transition is considered by most 'biblical historians' to be an exception to this rule. It is this period which sees the collapse of the Mycenaean, Egyptian, and Hittite empires and the so-called 'emergence of Israel'; 1200 BCE is viewed as a watershed in the history of the region, marking the dramatic decline and then conspicuous absence of imperial control.[2] More significantly, it is presented, as we have seen, as an important watershed, as the period in which the autonomous entity Israel emerges on the scene of Palestinian history, crossing the threshold to statehood in a remarkably short time. It is this entity, rather than the imperial powers of Egypt, Assyria, Babylonia, Persia, Greece, and Rome, which, in our standard 'biblical histories', comes to dominate the history of the region. The period of 'emergence', which, as we have seen, defines the essential nature of Israel, is followed by the rise of an Israelite state under David and Solomon which, it is argued, takes advantage of the international power vacuum to become the defining entity in terms of the geographical extent of Israel. Although the later Hasmonean period is seen as a brief interlude of autonomous control which manages to throw off the otherwise constant of imperial domination, it is the Davidic monarchy which becomes the dominant feature of the history of the region.

John Bright's (1972) classic treatment of the rise of the Israelite state, the 'united monarchy' of David and Solomon, provides a useful illustration of the way in which it comes to dominate and obliterate Palestinian history for the early Iron Age:

> The crisis that brought the Israelite tribal league to an end came in the latter part of the eleventh century. It set in motion a chain of events which within less than a century transformed Israel totally and made her one of the ranking powers of the contemporary world. This rather brief period must occupy our attention at some length, for it is one of the most significant in Israel's entire history.
>
> (Bright 1972: 179)

The claim as to the status of the Davidic and Solomonic state as 'one of the ranking powers of the contemporary world', a phrase that could just as easily be used of the modern state, shows just how remarkable this entity is thought to have been. It would appear from Bright's narration that the inhabitants of small, rural, materially poor villages in the highlands of Palestine had outstripped the great riverine civilizations of Egypt and Mesopotamia to claim a place as a world-class power. This is a claim which will need to be examined later in the chapter. For the moment, it is the claim that this period, one of an absence of imperial interest in the region, is 'one of the most significant in Israel's entire history' which, though related, is of primary concern. It is of such overwhelming concern that, once the

Philistine threat has been dealt with by David, the Davidic state *becomes* the history of Palestine for the period. The reason for this implicit assumption is not hard to find since Bright (1972: 197) presents the period as one of consolidation of the dynastic state and the building of an 'empire': 'But in the end David was the master of a considerable empire.' Here was an 'empire' that included Ammon and Syria in the north, Edom and Moab in the east, such that Bright (1972: 200) is able to conclude that 'with dramatic suddenness David's conquests had transformed Israel into the foremost power of Palestine and Syria. In fact, she was for the moment probably as strong as any power in the contemporary world.' Here was an 'empire' whose borders stretched from the Gulf of Aqabah to the Mediterranean, from the Wadi el-'Arish in the south to the Lebanon range and Kadesh on the Orontes in the north. In effect, according to Bright's account, David had managed to inherit the Asiatic empire of New Kingdom Egypt.[3] The borders of this 'Davidic empire', maintained more or less successfully by Solomon (Bright 1972: 207–10), meant that the history of the Israelite state *becomes* the history of Palestine.

What Bright has constructed is a biblically inspired view of 'Greater Israel' which coincides with and helps to enhance the vision and aspirations of many of Israel's modern leaders. Ben-Gurion expressed the view that the borders of Israel ought to include southern Lebanon, southern Syria, Jordan, all Cisjordan, and the Sinai. Chomsky notes Ben-Gurion's view that:

> The acceptance of partition does not commit us to renounce Transjordan; one does not demand from anybody to give up his vision. We shall accept a state in the boundaries fixed today, but the boundaries of Zionist aspirations are the concern of the Jewish people and no external factor will limit them.
>
> (cited by Chomsky 1983: 180)

Ben-Gurion even referred to the founding of 'the Third Kingdom of Israel' following the 1956 capture of the Sinai (cited by Chomsky 1983: 163 from Nar-Zohar 1978: 91–2; 166; 186–7; 249–50). Any scholarly construction of the Israelite past, particularly the construction of the Israelite monarchy and its boundaries, has to be read in this contemporary context since it is both informed by and informs contemporary claims and aspirations. The implications of biblical scholarship for the world of politics, whether the scholar acknowledges this or not, are brought out in Begin's statement following the establishment of the state in 1948:

The partition of the Homeland is illegal. It will never be recognized. The signature institutions and individuals of the partition agreement is invalid. It will not bind the Jewish people. Jerusalem was and will be forever our capital. Eretz Israel will be restored to the people of Israel. All of it. And forever.

(cited by Chomsky 1983: 161)

The biblically inspired political vision and claims of the modern world are confirmed, for the most part, by the construction of an imagined past of the ancient Israelite state within the discourse of biblical studies. Furthermore, here ironically is an imperial control, constructed by the Hebrew Bible and modern 'biblical historians', which mirrors the dominant theme of empire in the history of the region to such an extent that Palestinian history no longer exists: all we have is a history of an imagined imperial Israel.[4]

Confirmation of the importance which the discourse of biblical studies has always placed upon this period can be found in Soggin's assessment of the inauguration of an Israelite monarchy:

With the formation of a united kingdom under David, the history of Israel leaves the realm of pre-history, of cultic and popular tradition, and enters the arena of history proper. The kingdom under David and Solomon constitutes a datum point from which the investigation of Israel's history can be safely begun.

(Soggin 1977: 332)

Soggin's view is noteworthy for several reasons since he had argued against the possibility of using the biblical traditions to construct early pre-monarchic Israel, the essential Israel of biblical scholarship discussed in the previous chapter. His *History of Israel* was one of the first to take seriously the growing objections to standard assumptions about the historicity of the biblical traditions. For Soggin, the search for Israel in the Late Bronze Age had to be abandoned since the source material was not available. Instead the real starting point for a history of Israel was, for him, the foundation of a monarchy. However, it is clear that he is working with the common assumption in biblical studies that 'history proper' can only be written on the basis of written documents. Without such documents we are condemned to 'pre-history' which somehow does not carry the same weight, is not real somehow, and so these periods and their peoples are silenced. This is the principle of Western historiography of the nineteenth century as it developed in the context of the nation state. It is now reinforced in the construction of Israelite history by the fact that it is only with the Israelite state (nation state) that we enter the realm of 'history proper'. History, in effect Palestinian history, before this time cannot be 'proper'. For most other scholars, who have been content to date parts of the biblical tradition much earlier or argue that late traditions still accurately reflect a much earlier historical reality, the 'emergence' of Israel, as we have seen, is the other defining moment in the history of Palestine.

It is not simply the assumption that the rise of an Israelite state, and in particular the Davidic monarchy, brings us to history proper but that this is the defining moment of Israelite history and so of the region as a whole. The assertion of Bright (1972: 179) that Israel under the monarchy became 'one of the ranking powers of the contemporary world' and that this is 'one of the most significant in Israel's entire history' is representative of a common view in biblical studies. The emphasis on the crucial nature of this period is found throughout our standard histories and reference works. It is necessary to trace the discourse of biblical studies in relation to the invention of an Israelite state or 'empire' in the context of the Zionist agitation for and eventual realization of a modern state of Israel.[5] The two processes are intricately linked in that the scholarly discourse has been conducted in the context of the struggle for a state in the first part of this century and then dominated by the existence of that state ever since. If 'politics is everywhere', as Said (1994b: 16) claims, then the discourse of biblical studies has steadfastly refused to acknowledge that the construction of the past is a political act. Biblical scholars and archaeologists have sought to escape to the haven of objectivity effectively ignoring, or even denying, the context in which they work and the contexts in which their work is received and read. The cumulative effect of frequently circulated ideas and values both shapes and is shaped by their findings. This is particularly true of any history of ancient Israel and particularly one which deals with the creation of a state. The attachment to place, the claim of 'historic right' to the land, excludes any counter-claims. Biblical studies in imagining a past dominated by an Israelite state, elevated to the rank of a world power, simply adds to the legitimacy of the claim of 'historic right' by excluding any other possible construction of the past.

Furthermore, as we saw with the discussion of the so-called

emergence of Israel, there are a number of domain assumptions which have permeated considerations of the inauguration of an ancient Israelite state. The presentation, invariably, has been in terms of objective scholarship divorced from the sordid realities of the world of politics. It has not been seen as a matter worthy of comment that biblical scholarship's discussion of an Israelite state in the past has no bearing upon or implications for claims in the present for the land of Palestine. It is simply assumed that biblical studies has no part in contemporary struggles for identity and land, when in fact the very silence, the fact that the 'problem' of Palestine and the existence of a Palestinian past remains unspoken in the discourse of biblical studies, has only served to legitimate Israel's claims to the past and the exclusion of any alternative competing Palestinian claims. The discourse of biblical studies has imagined an ancient Israelite state that is remarkably similar in many aspects to the modern state. What is striking are the recurrent themes, images, and phrases which appear throughout this discourse from the 1920s onwards to the present day: the Davidic monarchy as the defining moment in the history of the region, the existence of a Davidic empire to rival other imperial powers in the ancient world, the defensive nature of David's state, the paradox of the alien nature of the monarchy to Israel, and Israel as a nation set apart from surrounding nations.

IMAGINING AN ANCIENT ISRAELITE STATE

Just as with the study of Israel's emergence, Alt's seminal work (1966) on the Israelite monarchy, originally published in 1930, represents the classic formulation of the formation of an Israelite state in Palestine which sets and continues to set the agenda for the study of the history of the period. The underlying presupposition that the history of the region must be understood in terms of national entities is set out in the opening sentences of his study. He states that the time during which the tribes of Israel were migrating from 'the southern wastelands in the mountain regions of Palestine' (1966: 173) coincided with the arrival in the lowlands of Aegean groups including the Philistines. He claims that it is not possible to 'understand the history of Palestine during the following centuries without first grasping the difference in the way of life and in the achievements of the two nations after they had settled in Palestine' (1966: 173). The claim that subsequent Palestinian history can only be understood from this vantage-point emphasizes that this is the defining moment in the history of the region. Furthermore, it is a struggle between the expression of Israelite national consciousness and the Philistines. Yet the Philistines are not responsible for this defining moment. This is a claim that must be reserved for Israel. The Philistines' failing is that they are identified with indigenous political structures. They more or less adopted the existent form of political organization: 'we are justified in seeing in the little states of the Philistines and the other Aegean peoples in the plains of Palestine the heirs and successors to the early Canaanite system of city-states' (1966: 174). Although he admits that they developed a distinctive form of political organization which could not be attributed to the Canaanites, ultimately they failed because they were contaminated by indigenous political structures. As we have been told repeatedly, indigenous political structures could not compare with external forms of organization. Indigenous 'states' were always small. The defining moment in the history of the region was dependent upon a political system of a completely different order, the formation of an Israelite state. His explanation of this development and the ultimate failure of the Philistines is very revealing:

> During their wars of migration, the collective nature of their every undertaking had been of vital importance, and even when they annexed Palestine they were to owe a great deal of their success to their strong cohesive unity. Naturally the other Aegean tribes had entered into the alliance during the nomadic period, or had individually founded similar organizations; after their occupation of Palestine, however, they seem to have rapidly fallen victim to the disunity effected by the system of tiny city-states which they adopted, so that in the Israelite tradition they are never again called by their tribal names and the only reference is to their cities. The Philistines, on the other hand, were able to preserve their combined organization for some time, and because of it were in a position to develop a political and military strength with a wide influence beyond the immediate area of their settlements. This would inevitably lead them to a position of political domination in Palestine, where the old Egyptian régime was now practically without influence. To this extent, they can actually be described as being the successors to the Pharaohs; even though their power was

always confined to a far smaller area than had been that of the Egyptians previously, it was as a result much more effective.

(Alt 1966: 174–5)[6]

Interestingly, the indigenous peoples cannot be considered to be a nation in contrast to Israel. He then goes so far as to say that the Philistines had the opportunity to create 'an empire of the first rank' (1966: 175).[7] This is to be contrasted with the slow, mostly peaceful, immigration of Israelite tribes into the hill country of Palestine in which they were separated by chains of non-Israelite tribes, as we have seen in chapter 3. He stresses their nomadic origin, lacking the military superiority of the Aegean groups. Yet it is Israel who is able to create an 'empire', not the Philistines. Israel of the imagined past, as of Alt's own present, claims to take possession of an empty and unpromising land:

> Already the difference between them and the Aegeans was as great as it could be; these, as we saw, moved immediately into the older civilized regions, and took possession of its riches; on the other hand, the Israelite settlement in Palestine was really in undeveloped territory which was at first necessarily isolated from civilization. Immediately after the occupation it held the Israelites apart from the native Canaanite system, giving them time to develop their own civilization more vigorously in its new homeland, whereas the Aegean culture very quickly degenerated into that of the occupied country.
>
> (Alt 1966: 176)

It is not just that they take possession of this empty land but because they remained isolated they do not suffer the same fate as the Philistines who are dragged down by the indigenous Canaanite system.

Alt was writing, of course, well before the realization of a modern state of Israel. But the context in which he worked is not an insignificant factor in determining his conception of the past, as we have seen (Sasson 1981). His guiding principle is that it is the nation state which defines history: thus the struggle for national self-determination and self-consciousness is the key element in Israel's imagined past. This articulates well with Alt's own training in German historiography, itself a product of the struggle for German unification, and is reinforced by the contemporary struggle in Palestine, at the time he was writing, of the Zionist struggle for a 'national homeland'. The themes of national awareness and self-determination inform his work throughout.

Alt (1966: 177) goes on to stress that Israel's nomadic past contained 'some rudimentary functions of a national nature' – we are not told what these are – but that their settlement in a 'civilized country' made the development of 'national functions' almost inevitable. This provides an interesting contrast with more recent studies of state formation which stress that crossing the threshold to statehood is by no means inevitable.[8] Yet we find that Israel's move to statehood is 'almost inevitable'. For Albright and much of subsequent American biblical scholarship, this inevitability is explained in terms of evolutionary development in the context of a divine providential plan. Alt offers no explanation for the inevitability of Israel's move to statehood beyond the assertion of its inevitability. However, he stresses the Philistine threat as the crucial factor which pushed Israel towards state formation but in so doing emphasizes just how far this is the defining moment in the region and in terms of world history:

> As regards the Israelites themselves, however, it involved them directly in a completely different manner and to a far greater degree in the course of the history of their country and the world than at the time of their emigration, imposing on them a new and unavoidable intercourse and participation in the life of the surrounding culture, from which they were unable to withdraw again by their own power.
>
> (Alt 1966: 182)

The language here suggests that this 'unavoidable intercourse' with surrounding cultures was distasteful, an unavoidable contact which threatened the very existence and distinctiveness of Israel just as it had corrupted the Philistines. The crucial difference here is that Israel, unlike the Philistines with their military superiority, was not dragged down by the indigenous circumstances but managed to transform the region and the world. Here is a triumph against all the odds. Israel was able to defeat the 'oppressive rule' (1966: 183) of the Philistines and establish a state despite the contaminating influence of the corrupt Palestinian setting.

The other striking feature of Alt's construction, which has continued in biblical scholarship, is his stress on the foundation of an Israelite 'national-state' (1966: 185). Notice he refers to it a few pages later as the 'first unified national state' (1966: 187) and a 'nation state'

(1966: 191). The claim of 'historic right' to the land is reinforced, of course, by the claim of priority and exclusivity to statehood in the region. An equally influential idea has been his view that the Israelite state was founded for defensive purposes only, an attempt to deal with the Philistine military threat: 'it was a kingship for the sole purpose of defence against the Philistines, and the idea of establishing a dominion over non-Israelite areas was far removed from it' (1966: 196). This notion of the defensive nature of Israel is a theme that runs throughout the discourse of biblical studies on the Israelite state and which articulates closely with Zionist claims and later apologetics following the foundation of the modern state of Israel. The modern state is frequently described as being defensive in nature: a view that is expressed in the Proclamation of Independence: 'They sought peace, but they prepared to defend themselves.'[9]

It is 'scarcely conceivable' (1966: 197) for Alt that Israel could have been influenced by Canaanite states. Instead it was influenced much more by what Alt describes as the 'national foundations' (1966: 200) of Edom, Moab, Ammon, and Aram:

> The kingdom of Israel came on the scene as one of the last of this series of closely similar political structures, and so played its own part in the sweeping change in the political map of Palestine which came to its conclusion in the tenth century B.C. From the purely chronological point of view, one might consider the much later development of the Israelite state as a mere imitation of the long-established nation-states east of the Jordan. But it is intrinsically improbable that the connection can be explained in such a mechanical way. In both cases we are dealing with related peoples, who were led from their common desert home by a similar route into the various parts of the civilized region of Palestine. If, as far as we can see, all these nations show in the formulation of the state traces of the same creative principles in operation, and if this is in fact a principle which was unknown to the previous inhabitants of the territory in which their new states were set up, then we should be able to recognize with greater confidence the consequences of a tendency which was common to all the new intruders, and which sooner or later, and according to individual circum-stance, brought into being the same type of national structure, without one nation first having to learn from the others.
>
> (1966: 200–1)

All of this is simply a working out of the major assumptions which inform Alt's understanding of the emergence of ancient Israel, the expression of the essential Israel. The real civilizing influence in the region was therefore external. The indigenous cultures were simply incapable of structuring themselves in such a way. The other striking feature of this construction is just how close it is to the modern period with the creation of nation states by the European imperial powers. The boundaries of the region were fixed, however artificially, by Europe: the indigenous peoples were unable to organize themselves in such a 'civilizing' manner. The indigenous peoples were devoid of this so-called 'creative' principle, a creative principle which amounts to little more than the ability to organize and co-operate. For Alt, the nation state is the pinnacle of civilization; it is unknown to the region until introduced by outsiders of which Europe is the heir.

Israel is seen as a special case because of its greater isolation in an area 'influenced by the ancient and completely dissimilar city-states of Palestine' (1966: 201). The form of the state might have been similar to its Jordanian neighbours at first but it developed independently. The critical stage is seen as the reigns of David and Solomon who are credited with extending their control 'further than any native power of earlier times known to us, even the Philistines' (1966: 225). The 'great men' view of history is encapsulated in Alt's influential conclusion that 'the whole of Palestine was incorporated into a very complicated system of dependencies, the only focal-point of which was the person of David and Solomon' (1966: 226). Alt's conclusion at the end of his article illustrates many important points about the assumptions of biblical scholarship. David and Solomon are seen as departing from the founding principle of Saul's kingdom based upon national organization to that of a supra-national power based upon personal allegiance. The recently formed 'national states' remained in existence but were incorporated into this wider structure. However, the national principle reasserted itself against the personal union:

> History here has something very significant to say; it shows the empire created by David and Solomon with such amazing speed to be a swing of the political pendulum, which went too far, beyond the prevailing inclinations and capabilities of the people of Palestine at the time, to make possible for it to stay longer, let alone permanently, in this position, and it makes it

apparent that actually only the principle of the nation-state, which was a very early, if not the earliest, type of political organization in the country, fulfilled the requirements of the peoples concerned and enabled some sort of balance to be set up between them.

(Alt 1966: 237)

The notion of the nation state dominates Alt's construction to such an extent that it is to be seen as the essential principle underlying the political organization of the region. But it is a principle which has had to be introduced from outside. Even more amazingly, he claims that this was an early, 'if not the earliest', type of political organization in the country. This suggests that the indigenous peoples of Palestine were incapable of *any form* of political organization until the introduction of the nation state by nomads infiltrating from outside!

These and other important trends in biblical scholarship were continued and perpetuated by Alt's most distinguished pupil Martin Noth. His construction of the period of the formation of an Israelite state followed closely the outlines of the biblical traditions. He articulated a problem which has exercised the minds of many biblical scholars relying for their constructions of the period on traditions contained within the Hebrew Bible: namely that the inauguration of the monarchy denies the essential theocratic nature of Israel. Furthermore, Israel's uniqueness, its claim to priority in the formation of a state in the region, is compromised by the acknowledgement that it had adopted this political structure from surrounding cultures:

> But the very fact that the monarchy in Israel was based on a model that had proved its worth in other peoples inevitably made it a problem for Israel. Was it right for Israel to try to be a nation like other nations and to install a king on the model of foreign monarchies and, in spite of its distress, to embark on the road to political power? Modest though the first steps which it took in this direction were, it was a fundamentally new departure for Israel.

(Noth 1960: 172)

Traditional constructions, based upon the biblical text, have failed to resolve this paradox: it is seen to be alien to Israel and a rejection of its essential theocratic nature while becoming the defining moment in Israelite history which determined its national boundaries and autonomy.[10]

Noth portrays Saul's reign in typically biblical terms as a failure, 'a mere episode': the Philistines established sovereignty in Palestine and the result of Saul's reign was 'as hopeless for Israel as it could be' (1960: 178). The nature of the defining moment is expressed by Noth as the reign of David in which 'Israel's progress to political power entered a completely new and decisive phase' (1960: 179). He also states that the newness of the situation is confirmed by the introduction of a 'new historical tradition' in the Old Testament, a 'historical record, a work of scholarship'. The connection between the rise of modern historiography and the nation state with an emphasis upon the uniqueness of great statesmen and the importance of state archives is confirmed in Noth's representation of this imagined past. The connection between past and present is also assured by the contemporary scholar's study of this ancient 'work of scholarship'. It is, of course, a guarantee of objectivity as well as a product of disinterested scholarship. He states that the development of political power and the active participation in historical events was the precondition for the beginning of historical writing. This is to assume, of course, that his proposed twelve-tribe amphictyonic structure or the reign of Saul were not 'political'! Interestingly, it seems, only states are political and only states provide the foundation for historical records. Yet at the same time biblical scholarship can deny or ignore the political context and implications of its research.

One of the major historical puzzles about the biblical accounts and constructions based upon them is that the Philistines who are presented as such a potent threat to the very existence of Israel under Saul are not just defeated by David but virtually disappear from the historical record.[11] Thus Noth is able to say that:

> The Philistines made no further attempt. They were forced to surrender their supremacy in the land. The period of their predominance had come to a rapid end. Henceforth they were limited to their old possessions in the southern part of the maritime plain and formed one of the small neighbouring states which gave trouble to Judah and Israel as occasion offered but were no longer able to make any decisive historical interventions. David's decisive victories over the Philistines were the fundamental and the most lasting successes of a life that was rich in success. They gave him freedom to develop and elaborate his political system along his own lines.
>
> (Noth 1960: 189)

The Philistines are, interestingly, confined to 'the southern part of the maritime plain', the modern Gaza strip. They are no longer able to participate in historical events whereas the region is defined in terms of the Davidic monarchy. Indeed, what we see here is the elevation of Israel to the point where it silences Palestinian (Philistine) history. The choice of Jerusalem as the capital of what Noth terms 'the greater kingdom Israel' (1960: 189), the combination of Israel and Judah, was crucial. The allusion to 'Greater Israel' is particularly significant, as we have seen, in considering the subtle influence of the present on the imagined past. The phrase has been of crucial significance in the period since 1948 (see Chomsky 1983). It is a phrase that we see used by Alt, now Noth, and which becomes common parlance in the discourse of biblical studies. The capture of Jerusalem also helps to define the crucial moment in the history of the region:

> It was near the main north to south road over the hills, which followed the watershed, but lacked good communications with the east and the west. It was in no sense the obvious centre of the land and the natural features of its position did not mark it out as the capital. What it became under David, and what it has meant in history right up to our own day, it owes not to nature but to the will and insight of a man who, disregarding the natural conditions, made a decision that was right in a particular historical situation.
>
> (Noth 1960: 190)

The guiding principle, once again, is that it is great men who write history. Yet the view expressed does not correspond to any known historical reality in terms of the size and importance of Jerusalem at the time of the supposed reign of David.[12] Yet its meaning is carried through to the present day. For Noth (1960: 7), as for most biblical scholars and certainly for the Zionist movement, there is a direct continuum between the Davidic and modern states. The claim of Israel's inviolable right to Jerusalem as its capital, espoused most vociferously by Menachem Begin and many other Likud leaders, has its roots in this imagined Davidic golden age. The opening sentence of Avigad's popular report (1980) on the archaeological excavations in Jerusalem from 1969 to 1981 shows the political context in which such work needs to be understood: 'The reunification of Jerusalem in 1967 was not only a great historical event ... but was as well an event that will long be remembered as a turning point in the archaeological exploration of the city' (1980: 13). The significance is then said to be the fact that this allowed Israeli archaeologists access to locations previously inaccessible. Yet the fact that he describes the result of the 1967 war as 'a great historical event' shows that the archaeological enterprise is not just an academic exercise. Jerusalem is described as 'a symbol of deep emotional significance for the Jewish people and for much of mankind' (1980: 13). Avigad completes his study with the observation that the excavators were able to witness a further historical process in accord with the patterns of the past: the restoration of the Jewish quarter. It is clear that Avigad sees a direct continuum between the past and present of Israel which centres on the political and religious significance of Jerusalem for the Jewish community.[13] The direct continuum between past and present which is invoked, or implicitly assumed, in biblical scholarship and in the realm of politics means that the two spheres are intricately related.

The mirage of the Israelite monarchy as some all-consuming entity, claiming the past and thereby legitimizing the present, which defined and dominated Palestinian history, is further emphasized by Noth's contention (1960: 193) that David 'created a great empire extending far beyond the confines of the Israelite tribes, and well rounded-off on all sides, including a greater part of Palestine and Syria'.[14] This recurrent theme of 'empire', the image of 'Greater Israel' shows a complete misunderstanding of the nature of empire or the potential of Palestine itself in relation to surrounding areas. Noth even refers to the Aramean territory of the northern land east of the Jordan as far as Damascus as a 'province of the empire of David'.

> The whole realm had become an extremely complicated political structure and had grown far beyond the confines of a purely Israelite state. It had become a Palestinian–Syrian empire united in the person of the king and embracing numerous different peoples. David's political organization was the first great independent power structure on Palestinian–Syrian soil of which we have knowledge, embracing directly or indirectly most of Palestine and Syria: a tremendous phenomenon from the point of view of world history and basically the achievement of one intelligent and uncommonly successful man. The general historical situation in the Orient had been in his favour. In Egypt and Mesopotamia there was at that time no greater

power which might have encroached on Palestine and Syria and enforced a claim to rule over it.

(Noth 1960: 195)

The imperial power vacuum in the area had allowed David's 'empire' to develop in Syria–Palestine just as the Zionists were able to exploit the power vacuum create by the British resignation of UN mandatory powers. This is the defining moment not *just* in Palestinian history but in world history. The 'historic' claim of Israel to the past and the present, advanced through the notion of priority, is confirmed in Noth's vision of a Davidic empire: 'the first great independent power structure on Palestinian–Syrian soil of which we have knowledge.'

The cult of personality, the reflex of German historiography that it is the great men who shape history, so evident in Alt's work, finds further expression in Noth's view that 'the existence of David's empire was so dependent on the strong personality of its founder that its survival beyond his death only seemed assured provided a successor of more or less equal stature could be found' (1960: 199). This is reinforced with his final statement on the reign of David that any successor was faced with an 'extraordinarily difficult' task in holding together this 'complicated empire' (1960: 199).

Noth's understanding of the Israelite state under David and Solomon is clearly a reflection of the ideals of the European nation state:

The historical events which took place in the reigns of David and Solomon occasioned extremely great changes in the Israelites' conditions of life. A strong monarchy had relieved them of concern for self-preservation in their particular historical setting and they enjoyed the advantages of living in a state that was not merely powerful but also well governed.

(Noth 1960: 216–17)

Noth is able to state that it is well governed even though he admits (1960: 217) that 'we are told almost nothing of the administrative measures of David's reign, and even for Solomon's we are merely told a few things connected with his buildings and the royal household'. No evidence is offered. The statement could easily have been made of the modern state as the haven for European Jews, represented as the ideal of democracy, strong and well governed. While the state is the defining factor of this imagined past, it is a particular form of state, not one like the monarchies round about. It is this notion of the ideal of democracy embodied within the Israelite state which provides a solution to the paradox of the monarchy as a denial of the essential theocratic nature of Israel. In terms of the region, Israel is to be distinguished from its neighbours:

> These great descriptions of episodes from the history of David have also a special significance in so far as they have established once and for all the fact that the monarchy represented an institution on the soil of Israel which had emerged in history long after the Israelite tribes had settled in Palestine and consolidated their position, and that, after the episode of Saul, David was the first to establish and bequeath to his son the monarchies over Judah and Israel which continued to exist in the history of the people. It was therefore difficult for the idea to emerge in Israel that the institution of the monarchy as such and the actual monarchies in Judah and Israel were elements of the unalterable and everlasting world order. If it is also borne in mind that the problematical nature of the monarchy in general was also felt among the Israelite tribes possibly from the very beginning and with ever-increasing force as time went on ... it will be realized that the monarchy was bound to appear in very different light than was the case in the rest of the ancient Orient and, above all, in the ancient oriental empires where monarchy was regarded as an essential element in an everlasting, divine order of things.
>
> (Noth 1960: 223)

Israel of the past as well as the present was a nation set apart, particularly set apart from its own social and political world. Thus Noth continues:

> In Israel the monarchy was bound always to be regarded as an institution that had evolved in the process of history and it was precisely under the influence of the historical emergence of the monarchy that the form of historical writing arose in Israel to which there is no counterpart in the world of the ancient Orient. It was the result of Israel's unique historical consciousness which was based on the special nature of its experience of God. It is therefore wrong to apply without question to the monarchy in Israel the ancient oriental ideas of a sacral divine monarchy, with the attendant religious observances.
>
> (Noth 1960: 223)

It is remarkable how closely this is echoed in the perceptions of the modern state of Israel as a nation set apart from its political and cultural context, a civilizing influence in the region. It is the result of 'Israel's unique historical consciousness' which is divinely inspired.[15]

The formulation of a 'Solomonic Enlightenment' by von Rad represents the culmination of the view of the Israelite monarchy as a golden age which defined all subsequent moments in the history of the region. This became the setting and stimulus for the development of Israelite historiography and other wisdom traditions which were to form a major part of the Hebrew Bible:

> Thus the golden age of the Hebrew monarchy produced genuine historical works. No other civilization of the ancient Near East was able to do so. Even the Greeks achieved it only at the height of their development in the fifth century, and then as quickly fell away again. Here, on the contrary, we are dealing with a nation which had only just become civilized. The factors which were conducive to this, including the easily learned script, came to them as to the Greeks from the former occupants of their land; but this only makes their achievement the more astonishing. Here, as in all historical situations, we have the insoluble problems of innate ability. By virtue of their achievement in historical writing, realized independently and fully grown from the start, the civilization of Israel must be ranged alongside that which was achieved on the soil of Greece to a richer and fuller degree some centuries later.
>
> (von Rad 1965: 285–6)

The reader is presented with the astounding claim that it is through 'innate ability' that Israel is able to produce historical works 'fully formed' even though it had only just become civilized or learned the alphabet. Noticeably, the mark of civilization is statehood. This is indeed a unique culture with which other ancient Near East civilizations do not bear comparison. These other civilizations, it should be remembered, include the great riverine civilizations of Egypt, Assyria, and Babylonia with their magnificent monuments, graphic art, and extensive literary remains.[16]

John Bright's *A History of Israel*, a paradigm of 'biblical history', takes the world context of the region possibly more seriously than any other work of this genre. The incursions of the ever-changing imperial powers are carefully catalogued and interwoven into the narrative of the history of Israel. It forms an important backdrop to understanding the discrete history of Israel. However, the inter-connections between the rise and fall of empires and Palestine's place in this dynamic of world power need to be explored further. Imperial control is a constant in the kaleidoscopic history of Palestine but it is usually treated in discrete terms, as part of the unique, unrepeatable events of traditional history, Braudel's *'l'histoire événementielle'*. Yet the concentration on the incursions and battles of various Pharaohs, Assyrian or Babylonian kings, or Persian and Roman generals reveals only a part of the story of this recurrent theme of the region's history. The history of Palestine reveals quite clearly that from the Late Bronze Age to the Roman period, one could say through to the present day, there has been a shifting dynamic of world power which has seen economic and military superiority fluctuate from region to region. The imperial episodes in Palestinian history need to be treated from a comparative perspective in order to reveal their similarities and dissimilarities. The apocalyptic liter-ature of the region often adopts a rigid schema of the succession of empires, a schema mirrored in the reconstructions of our modern 'biblical histories' which then posit a Davidic empire in the power vacuum of the early Iron Age. The failure to appreciate the dynamics of world power and its effect upon the history of the region lies behind the assertion of many biblical scholars and archaeologists of the existence of a Davidic empire. This failure will be explored briefly later in the chapter.

For the present, it is enough to acknowledge, as we have seen above, that Bright's (1972: 179) classic treatment of the rise of the Israelite state, the so-called 'united monarchy' of David and Solo-mon, which eradicates all other narrations of Palestinian history for the early Iron Age repeats the recurrent themes found in the works of Alt and Noth. Bright (1972: 224) presents the paradox of an Israelite monarchy in even starker terms than Noth. What is fascin-ating is that although Noth and Bright are represented as prot-agonists in the discourse of biblical studies in respect of their constructions of the emergence of Israel in Palestine, they share remarkably similar views when it comes to a consideration of the inauguration of an Israelite state. Their disagreements over the use of archaeology disappear since there is little archaeological evidence pertaining to the so-called periods of David and Solomon. Strikingly, they both accept that the biblical texts are basically historically trustworthy and use them as the major source for their constructions which amount to little more than the précis of the narratives of the books of Samuel and Kings. The model of the nation state, the locus of state archives which are the basis of history writing, becomes so dominant that their constructions of the imagined past of Israel coincide.

Herrmann's history (1975), which stands in the tradition of the scholarship of Alt and Noth, is interesting because he states explicitly that Israel in the pre-monarchic period did not 'as yet form a "state" in any way' (1975: 131). He detects the beginnings of the 'equally modern conception of a united "people"' but again states that the stimuli for the movement to statehood were external. We are not told how Herrmann is able to detect such things. Again we find the paradox of the essentially alien nature of monarchy to Israel but also the claim that this change in organization brought with it 'a new degree of mutual awareness' (1975: 132). Again no justification is offered for such a claim. He then follows the standard practice of paraphrasing and expanding the biblical text in his construction of the reign of Saul. The vexed question of the extent of Saul's kingdom is revealing of some underlying assumptions:

> When he became king, he did not take over a clearly defined territory; he was merely acclaimed by a group of tribes about whom unfortunately we know no further details. Saul's 'kingdom' was a national state in the original sense of the word, a hegemony over clans and tribes of the same origin; it was not at the same time a territorial state with fixed boundaries and an independent administration.
>
> (Herrmann 1975: 140)

Here is the conception of Israel as a nation seeking out a territory which has pervaded so much of biblical scholarship.[17] It becomes transformed and confirmed with David: 'He ruled over a "national" group which was in one sense limited, but whose territory and purpose was far more closely defined than Saul's complex "empire"' (1975: 152). David, on this account, is the founder of a nation state. Herrmann (1975: 156) cites Alt's view that with David's capture of Jerusalem 'almost overnight the stunted city-state becomes the centre of a kingdom which embraces the whole of Palestine'. He moves from this to argue that David is the creator of the nation state:

> We may conclude from this that David succeeded where Saul failed in taking the step from a national to a territorial state, to a 'kingdom' with more or less fixed boundaries, to a territory

and not just a tribal alliance, under the authority of the king.
(Herrmann 1975: 157)

Revealingly, we are told that this state had to incorporate other 'ethnic groups': 'The result was that the so-called "Canaanite problem" became not only an acute domestic political difficulty but also above all a religious danger' (1975: 157). This has been the critical problem for the modern state following the wars of 1967 and 1973, both of which preceded the publication of Herrmann's history. His choice of phraseology is intriguing: he refers to the 'Canaanite problem' faced by the Israelite state. It parallels the 'Palestinian problem' confronting the modern state of Israel which was apparent for all to see in the early 1970s, and earlier, but which remained unspoken in the discourse of biblical studies. Significantly, for Herrmann, the problem is not one of the rights of the 'Canaanites' but the danger which they pose from inside to the unity and security of the Israelite nation state.

For Herrmann, also, the period of the Davidic–Solomonic monarchy becomes the defining moment in the region's history. He refers to 'the ideal extension of the empire of Israel and Judah' (1975: 159) as represented in 1 Kings 5: 1, the text which informs Ben-Gurion's vision of 'Greater Israel', but argues that this never corresponded to the reality of David's power. Nevertheless, 'David's historical achievements certainly do not pale in the light of so ambitious an ideal' (1975: 159) since his control over a variety of territories meant that it is appropriate to refer to a Davidic 'empire'.[18] Herrmann stands firmly in the tradition of 'biblical histories' which imagine a Davidic 'empire' founded upon the cult of personality, the result of 'the personal achievement of the king'. He even goes so far as to talk in terms of an 'imperial ideology' (1975: 162). He sees it as highly probable that the conception of an 'all Israel' stems from the period of David. It is clearly the defining moment in the history of the region:

> But the ordering of the traditions and the formation of them into a consistent idea of a 'people' with ethnic and national contours, with its own national awareness, *could only* be developed to the full under the impact of the formation of the Davidic state.
>
> (Herrmann 1975: 163; emphasis added)

The indigenous culture, it seems, was incapable of such national awareness or the formation of written traditions. The paradox of trying to represent the Davidic monarchy as both unique and a part of mundane history is brought out clearly in his discussion: 'The Davidic empire was a unique creation, but a product of history, subjected to conflicting trends from within and threatened by dangers from without' (Herrmann 1975: 167). Israel was set apart. Its national state was unique but still a product of history. The only evidence for this uniqueness is derived from a paraphrase of the biblical traditions which are conceived to be the product of the Davidic court. Herrmann's evidence for his assertions of the existence of a Davidic empire and its territorial boundaries are procured, therefore, from a self-serving narrative of the Davidic bureaucracy. Herrmann, like other biblical historians, offers no corroborative evidence to support such a construction of the past.

Soggin (1984: 41) also refers to an 'empire' and follows Alt's thesis that it was held together by 'personal union'. He follows the standard pattern of presentation claiming that 'the region was unified for the first and last time in its history, though only for a short while, under a single sceptre, instead of being divided into dozens of autonomous entities' (1984: 42). The uniqueness of the Davidic monarchy is therefore that it unites the region for 'the first and last time in its history'. Again this confirms – unwittingly, it seems – the claim to the 'historic right' to the land on the principle of priority. He is more cautious about the extent of this entity than others, acknowledging that the existence of an empire is not confirmed by outside sources but that it is 'quite probable' given the decline of Egyptian power and the absence of Assyrian influence.[19] Why this imperial vacuum does not allow for the possibility of an Ammonite or Moabite empire but permits 'the possibility of an Israelite empire' is a question which is not addressed. He then concludes that the Davidic monarchy exploited the political vacuum to create an empire in Palestine and Syria for approximately seventy years at the beginning of the tenth century BCE before succumbing to the reappearance of the 'great empires' (1984: 44). What had been at first a possibility, with no external evidence to confirm it, has become a reality which survived for three-quarters of a century. It is an imagined past which corresponds to the biblically inspired modern concept of 'Greater Israel' in control of the West Bank, Gaza, and southern Lebanon. Biblical scholarship cannot divorce itself from the realities of the present which inform and are informed by such powerful imagined pasts.

Just how powerfully the present imposes itself upon the imagined past, whether consciously or unconsciously, is made apparent in Meyers's study (1987) of the Davidic–Solomonic periods. Meyers (1987: 181) follows in the long tradition stemming from Alt in presenting the Davidic–Solomonic periods as 'the Israelite empire', a brief period in the history of the region when Palestine had a unified government.[20] Here is the presentation of history as the result of the actions of 'great men' *par excellence*. The period is presented as being exceptional in 'the pre-modern Levant'. Notice how it is implied that the modern period, the creation of the modern state of Israel, is the only parallel to this exceptional unification of the region. She goes even further in arguing that the biblical sources in their concern for the emergence and dissolution of the 'United Kingdom' 'tends to obscure the fact that (sic) kingdom was not a simple self-contained national state but rather was the seat of an empire' (1987: 181). Although it might have been modest in comparison with Egypt or Mesopotamia, it was an empire nevertheless: 'Yet Israel during the time of David and Solomon, during the Golden Age of the United Monarchy, was nonetheless a minor imperial power' (1987: 181). Surprisingly, in light of the above, she claims that this has not been appreciated by biblical scholarship. She is concerned with reassessing the role of Solomon, who is usually portrayed as of secondary importance to David. In doing this, she describes David as 'the first Israelite "emperor", a brilliant initiator who unified the region' and Solomon as the second and last Israelite 'emperor' 'who held the disparate territorial components together for an unprecedented period of stability, who created a glorious cosmopolitan capital and built up a series of royal cities throughout the land' (1987: 182). This is described as a 'brief and uncharacteristic Levantine political configuration' (1987: 182). Clearly other indigenous powers were incapable of such an uncharacteristic achievement. She argues that social scientific studies of empires show that 'we must place the Davidic state within the category of a pre-modern empire, that is, a supranational state with a centralized bureaucracy ruled by a monarch with claims to traditional-sacred legitimacy' (1987: 184).

Meyers takes one of Alt's influential themes, the notion of the Israelite state as defensive, and develops it to an extreme not witnessed elsewhere, as far as I know, in the discourse of biblical studies. The novel aspect of her presentation is an attempt to deny that this 'Israelite empire' was aggressive or that it could be described as 'imperialistic'. She argues (1987: 184) that the most difficult problem in defining an empire is that of describing the motivation for its establishment. The key factor, it seems, is whether or not it was motivated by an ideology of superiority which results in pure aggression and which could then be designated as 'imperialistic'. But if the motivation was economic, self-interested but not superior, it would still surely be described as an empire. This she terms as 'accidental imperialism' and cites Rome, surprisingly, as a case in point:

> The Davidic expansion clearly can be classified among the empires arising from the defensive or accidental sort of empire-building. It should thus escape some of the opprobrium that attaches to imperialistic states.
>
> (1987: 184)

Her definition seems to confuse the definition of empire and the use of the term 'imperialistic' to describe aggression and exploitation. This parallels various descriptions of the modern state of Israel as involved only in defensive wars and not as an occupying power whether in the West Bank and Gaza or in southern Lebanon (see Chomsky 1983). Here we have a description of the Davidic monarchy which is a mirror image of the kind of apologetic offered to justify the modern state's occupation of the West Bank, Gaza, and the southern Lebanon.

Meyers presents the period of Solomon's succession and rule as that of a period of consolidation of David's territorial gains by diplomacy and ideology, the result of which was that:

> Jerusalem became, not simply the capital of a nation state, but rather the 'center' of an empire and the locus of activities and structures that impinged upon the 'periphery', upon territories removed from the Israelite state in which Jerusalem was located.
>
> (Meyers 1987: 189)

She then argues that the Solomonic temple was critical in providing the ideological justification for the right to dominate foreign territories. Even though, as she acknowledges, there is no archaeological evidence for this important symbol of power, the comparison of the biblical description (1 Kings 6–8) with sanctuaries from Syria and Palestine shows it to be 'the largest and grandest' of its kind. This leads her to the conclusion (1987: 190) that 'this striking fact is fully in accord with the Solomonic empire's unique position as the most extensive polity to have existed in ancient Syria–Palestine'. Her view of history, as presented in this article, as the result of the actions of great men is reinforced with her pronouncement on the achievements of David and Solomon (1987: 195): 'If it took the charisma and genius of a David to create an empire, against major economic, political, and historical odds, the maintenance of that empire for another regal span rested upon Solomon's unique gifts of wisdom and of successful diplomacy.'

What is remarkable about Meyers's imagined past, and those pasts of other major scholars reviewed above, is the way it accords with the realities of the present of a modern state of Israel which from its very existence has claimed to be involved only in defensive wars, a claim that has been maintained, officially at least, despite the invasion of Lebanon and eventually Beirut in 1982. The various works which have been cited above and commented upon are but an influential and representative sample of the discourse of biblical studies on the creation of an Israelite state in the Iron Age. They need to be read in the context of the contemporary struggle for land and identity which involves a struggle for the past. This representative sample of biblical scholarship shows that it has endorsed one particular creation of the past – what can only be described as an imagined past, in the light of available evidence – which has silenced or blocked any Palestinian claim to that past. The influences are subtle, not easy to substantiate, but the accumulation of recurrent themes and phrases which become assertions of fact, often on the flimsiest of evidence or in the absence of any evidence at all, helps to confirm common claims to the land advanced in the political realm. Biblical scholars and archaeologists are participants, however unwittingly, in the claims and counter-claims between Israel and the Palestinians: they are part, at the very least, of what Said (1994a: xxvi) terms a 'passive collaboration' which has silenced Palestinian history. The weight of biblical scholarship presents a past which conforms to and confirms the claims of the modern state. This silencing of Palestinian history arises out of the social and political context in which the work has been done, for it has arisen out of European historiography and imposed a model of the European nation state upon the ancient Middle East which has been confirmed by Europe and the West's sponsorship of the modern state. It forms an important part of that 'massed history' which has presented the public with a remarkably uniform view of the past. Palestinian history has no claim upon the past because it does not exist. It has been excluded by the discourse of biblical studies.

It might be argued that Ahlström's *The History of Ancient*

Palestine (1993) invalidates any such claim. Surely here we have a voice for Palestinian history in contrast to the domination of the Davidic empire? This is a work that explicitly questions the historicity of the biblical traditions proposing to present a history of the peoples of Palestine rather than of Israel and Judah alone. He questions the historicity of the texts which deal with the monarchy, arguing that they were edited from a Davidic perspective and are often late. Nevertheless, he stands broadly within the tradition of the historical critical movement in excavating the texts for historical information. His discussion of this period contains many elements found in standard 'biblical histories'. He discusses the period in terms of great men: Samuel, Saul, David, and Solomon. The only distinguishing feature of his presentation is a much more positive appraisal of Saul than standard histories of Israel which are more closely wedded to the presentation of the biblical narratives. He argues (1993: 434) that, although it had been difficult for chiefdoms in the hill country to develop into military powers that were able to oppose Philistine military power, 'one man succeeded, however, and freed for some time the hill population from Philistine rule: Saul'.[21] Although Ahlström provides this more positive appraisal of Saul, his interpretation of the period as providing a defining moment in the history of the region is broadly in line with more traditional treatments: 'Saul had created a territorial state that the greater Palestinian region had never seen before. Saul can therefore be regarded as the first state-builder in Palestine' (1993: 449).[22]

Ahlström goes so far as to say that Saul ruled over most of Palestine and Transjordan. In effect, he attributes (1993: 449) many of the achievements in bringing about this defining moment in the history of the region to Saul whereas, as we have seen, this is usually reserved for David. Similarly, Saul took advantage of the power vacuum created by the decline of the traditional powers in the region. Ahlström (1993: 454) recognizes that this is an unusual state of affairs which reverses the normal course of events in Palestine but, nevertheless, sees this as a period in which the history of the region was transformed by an indigenous power. In his view (1993: 454), three tried – Hadadezar of Aram-Zobah, Nahash of Aram, and Saul of Israel – but only Saul succeeded for a short time though ultimately he failed in the face of the Philistine threat. But he does not depart radically from standard treatments and eventually presents David as the key figure in this defining moment:

From the wing of the political stage a fourth man soon entered, one who managed to become the master of Palestine and parts of Syria: David. For a few generations the peoples of Syria–Palestine would be part of an artificial political unit.

(Ahlström 1993: 454)

The fact that he recognizes the artificiality of such an indigenous power points all the more to its uniqueness and the outstanding nature of its achievement. Although he refers to 'a great kingdom' (1993: 470) rather than an 'empire', his analysis is little different from that of the works he opposes.[23] His description of David's achievement is broadly similar to those of standard 'biblical histories':

As mentioned before, Palestine was not a country that encouraged the creation of larger political units. Historically, the political and cultural centers were in Anatolia–Mesopotamia in the north, and in Egypt in the south. Geographically Palestine was a connecting link and as such was always a point of contention among the great world powers. David's kingdom represents an exception, a parenthesis on the history of the ancient Near East. The achievements of David were possible because there was a power vacuum at this time.

(Ahlström 1993: 487)

He acknowledges that it was short-lived but unique as 'an exception' in the region. Its importance, however, stretches far beyond this:

But even if it was shortlived, it was never forgotten by the Jerusalemite writers and some Judahite prophets. David and his kingdom became for them the ideal that in some way distorted the historical reality, as well as creating wishful dreams about the future.

(Ahlström 1993: 488)

He might have added that it has also affected the ways in which the history of the region has been understood and presented: the kingdom or empire of David has become the dominant element in the history of the region, excluding any discussion of Palestinian history. For the Solomonic period, he argues (1993: 501) that because of the lack of extrabiblical materials it can 'only be presented by use of the subjective opinion of the biblical writers combined with archaeological remains. The latter are impressive compared with the preceding period.' Although there is some typical royal hyperbole, he believes (1993: 539) that a king would not have been built up to such an extent unless there was some basis for it, a remarkable statement given the history of hyperbole and propaganda in the ancient and modern worlds in service of 'great men'. He describes Solomon (1993: 538) as 'a king the likes of whom was produced neither before or after by that little country'. In short, it is difficult to distinguish Ahlström's narration from that of standard 'biblical histories' despite his claim to represent the history of ancient Palestine. As with our standard histories of Israel and Judah, the history of Palestine is little more than the history of Israel as presented in the biblical traditions.

QUESTIONING THE ISRAELITE STATE

Although the recent volume by Miller and Hayes (1986) represents the pinnacle of modern 'biblical histories', it is interesting to note that their construction of this period is much more guarded than the presentations considered above. They accept that their attempts to understand the reign of Saul are highly speculative. They provide a much more critical attitude to the biblical text, questioning the historicity of the David narratives (1986: 152) to a much greater extent than Soggin or any of the standard 'biblical histories' and particularly Meyers, for instance.[24] Thus they provide an interesting contrast with the broad scholarly tradition that sees this as a critical period in the history of the region:

> David founded a dynasty that was to rule from Jerusalem for over four centuries. Even after Jerusalem fell to the Babylonians in 586 B.C.E., which ended the long line of Davidic kings, many of the people of Jerusalem and Judah (including many scattered abroad at the time) continued to hope for a restoration of the days of old when the house of David was secure on the throne. Thus it is not surprising that David received so much attention in the biblical materials or that there was such an obvious effort on the part of the ancient Judaean compilers of these materials to present him in a favorable light.
> (Miller and Hayes 1986: 149)

They do, however, question the notion that the reign of Solomon was a 'golden age' (1986: 189). Although they note that archaeological evidence at Hazor, Megiddo, and Gezer indicates Solomon's building activity, they qualify this by describing these achievements as 'rather modest' when compared to Mesopotamia and Egypt but also when compared with the Omrides (1986: 189–90). They provide a much more sober assessment of the reign of Solomon:

> Solomon was probably an unusually wealthy and powerful ruler by the standards of Early Iron Age Palestine. Yet viewed in the broader context of the ancient Middle East, he is to be regarded more as a local ruler over an expanded city-state than as a world class emperor.
>
> (Miller and Hayes 1986: 199)[25]

They describe Solomon's kingdom as having consisted of the bulk of western Palestine and a large part of northern Transjordan but excluding the bulk of the Mediterranean coast which would have been in the hands of the Philistines and Phoenicians (1986: 214). Although they still place an important emphasis upon the reigns of David and Solomon, they are much more tempered than many of the extravagant claims which we have seen above. They do not articulate an alternative history of Palestine, it is not part of their aim, but they do at least recognize that the Israel of David was not the sole entity in the region. The recognition of the possibility of alternative claims to the past, the Philistine and Phoenician possession of the 'bulk of the Mediterranean coast', is at least implied. The fact that their work has been hailed as the pinnacle of 'biblical histories' and that they perceive it to stand in the tradition of Alt–Noth–Albright–Bright indicates the extent to which the changed perceptions of and approaches to the biblical texts have begun to erode the confidence of the dominant discourse of biblical studies.[26] The implications of this challenge will need to be considered later in the chapter. For the present, it is enough to concentrate upon a series of recent works which appear at first sight to offer a challenge to the dominant discourse but which in effect only serve to emphasize the silencing of Palestinian history.

One of the most distinctive treatments of the Israelite monarchy, as with the study of Israelite origins, has been supplied by Mendenhall. Once again in a seminal article (1975), he articulated a series of ideas which appear to challenge conventional understandings of the Israelite monarchy. He argues that the development of the Israelite monarchy followed the model of 'a typical Syro–Hittite state' introducing 'a paganization into the political and social history of Israel with fateful and lasting consequences' (Mendenhall 1975: 155). In effect, he pushes the notion of the paradox of the Israelite monarchy as both alien but peculiarly Israelite to its logical conclusion by drawing a sharp distinction between the essential Israel of the 'biblical revolution' and the reintroduction of Canaanite paganism through the monarchy of David and Solomon. Mendenhall suggests that the Davidic monarchy was a complex merging of 'Canaanite, North Syrian, Anatolian and East Syrian cultural traditions of the Bronze Age' with a few features derived from Egypt. This corrupt 'Canaanite paganism', it should be noticed, is internal and has to be contrasted with the purity of the biblical revolution of pre-monarchic Israel. He goes so far as to claim that 'this new insight is not only revolutionary so far as biblical studies and theology are concerned, it is potentially of crucial importance to the survival of modern civilization and its dense population' (Mendenhall 1975: 155). He argues that there is 'abundant evidence for a systematic reversion to Bronze Age paganism with the rapid evolution of the Jerusalem kingship, and that reversion took place in less than two generations' (Mendenhall 1975: 157). He sees this as a denial and reversal of the religious ethic of the Mosaic period to a system of the political monopoly of force which was subjected to critique by the prophets of the Hebrew Bible. The royal bureaucracy and its specialists, including religious specialists, were taken over from Canaanite states.

It is noticeable, however, that for Mendenhall such a bureaucracy was 'essential to a large political state and empire like that of David' (Mendenhall 1975: 160). Whatever its origins, it is still conceived of as an 'empire': it is the structure that dominates the history of Palestine, even though for Mendenhall it is judged negatively. In fact, he concludes that 'the biblical narratives tell us that most of the old Palestinian power-centres (or what was left of them) were incorporated by military power into the kingdom of David' (Mendenhall 1975: 160). Notice that the kingdom of David supersedes and incorporates Palestinian history. The bureaucracy that David inherited did not have its 'roots in the soil of ancient Israel, but rather in the impoverished regimes of Bronze Age Canaan' (Mendenhall 1975: 161). Yet it is important to make clear in what ways they could be considered to be impoverished. They provide the intellectual and literate elite to run David's kingdom, the Palestinian urban centres produced fine pottery and well-crafted artifacts, whereas the Israelites, according to most biblical specialists and archaeologists, lived in small rural sites with a poor, pragmatic material culture. The impoverishment can only be in terms of the religious system and values which for Mendenhall are paramount. Interestingly, for him, the Israelite monarchy is corrupted by the indigenous culture just as for Alt the Philistines had failed to dominate the history of the region but for different reasons. The contrast here, however, is between the essential Israel and a paganization of the Davidic monarchy which denies this essential nature.

Mendenhall's condemnation of the politicization of religion, and implicitly, I suspect, a work such as this which argues that the political aspects of scholarship have to be recognized clearly for their influence upon results, is stark:

> The Old Testament Constantine, King David, represents a thoroughgoing reassimilation to Late Bronze Age religious ideas and structures. These readapted the authentic traditions of Israel just as radically as the later Achemenids readapted New Testament Christianity. All three cases are entirely analogous, illustrating (to put it as provocatively as possible) the dissolution of religion into politics.
>
> (Mendenhall 1973: 16)

All except the truth claims of his own religious tradition are denounced as paganism. All indigenous religious developments are therefore inferior and to be replaced by this higher revelation which reaches its pinnacle in the Sermon on the Mount. Although Mendenhall provides a radically different appraisal of the reigns of David and Solomon from much of biblical scholarship, it is still the case that their reigns dominate the history of the region. They still remain the defining moment in the history of the region and of humankind, but for very different reasons from those traditionally advanced.

A series of works appeared in the 1980s which attempted to re-evaluate the inauguration of the Israelite state. Most of these works appealed to social scientific studies of state formation (Cohen and Service 1978; Claessen and Skalnik 1978; 1981; Haas 1982) attempting to apply these findings to the fragmentary data available for understanding the move to statehood in ancient Israel. In particular, they questioned the historical reliability of the biblical traditions, the view that the monarchy was alien to Israel or inevitable, and the view that the Philistine threat was a sufficient cause to explain this move to statehood. Hauer (1986), Coote and Whitelam (1987), and Whitelam (1986) all appealed to Carneiro's (1970) theory of environmental and social circumscription in order to understand the processes at work in the move to Israelite statehood. The Philistine threat is seen as no more than a catalyst to state formation (Coote and Whitelam 1987: 142; Frick 1985: 25–6). According to Coote and Whitelam (1987), Hauer (1986), and Frick (1985), it was the social and environmental factors of the hill-country settlements which led to a build-up of pressures which counteracted the natural tendencies of smaller polities to fission and led to increasing centralization and ultimately the development of an Israelite state. They argue for a complex feed-back process involving all forms of economic, social, political, and religious organization in contrast to standard interpretations which saw the Philistine threat as primary cause in the move to statehood (Frick 1985: 32; Coote and Whitelam 1987: 145). Whitelam (1986: 61) summarizes this as the social and geographical circumscription of the Palestinian highlands which places significant restraints upon the limits for expansion, increasing the competition for available land. The mechanisms which eventually led to the formation of the state were triggered once the dispersed rural settlements began to expand or multiply. In particular, the nature of farming strategies, devoted to terracing and commercial tree crops, required residential stability. This restriction on adaptability to increasing environmental and social pressures must have been an important factor in the move to centralization. They offered alternative explanations for the rise of the Israelite monarchy which challenged conventional understandings, stressing the combination of internal and external factors (Coote and Whitelam 1987: 142), questioning the oft-repeated notion that the monarchy is alien. Coote and Whitelam are able to conclude that:

> The standard interpretations of the rise of the monarchy, regardless of the position adopted on the origins of Israel, fail to pose or answer the major question of why it is this particular area which centralized and introduced an effective Israelite monarchy. Why is it the population of the highlands which succeeded in subduing and incorporating into its own political structure the surrounding, especially lowland, areas despite the seeming military and economic advantages of urban Canaan or the Philistine pentapolis? The monarchy, far from representing some alien cancer in the Israelite body politic, was fundamentally determined by the nature of the origins of Israel in the hill country and was the result of internal stimuli in response to social and environmental circumscription.
>
> (Coote and Whitelam 1987: 147–8)

Their conclusion reveals how far they were distracted by the search for ancient Israel. The processes of historical change for studying Palestinian history are appropriate but the concern is with the search for and location of ancient Israel. It is assumed, on the basis of the discourse of biblical studies, that Israel is to be identified with the highland settlements of the early Iron Age and that the development of an Israelite state can be traced from there. The power of the discourse of biblical studies is illustrated in Frick's conclusion that 'the emergent Israelite society in the highlands was ... a revolutionary development when viewed over against the Late Bronze Age Canaanite city-state system which had prevailed in the plains' (1985: 196). The appeal to social scientific data and theories has not freed these studies from Alt's domain assumption that Israel's political development represents a radical break with and replacement of (inferior) indigenous political structures. Furthermore, all these studies assume, however minimally, the broad outline of the biblical traditions for their constructions of the past.[27] Although they might be said to have contributed to the general climate which has led to a more radical questioning of this dominant discourse and its assumptions about Israel's claim to the past, they have failed to escape the stranglehold which that discourse has exerted over our understanding of this past. Coote and Whitelam (1987: 164) do provide a proviso in trying to see the creation of an Israelite state as part of the study of Palestinian history: 'The emergence of Israel and the inauguration of the monarchy must be seen as part of the long-term trends and processes if progress is to be made towards a more realistic appraisal of this phase of Palestinian history.' However, it is a Palestinian history dominated by Israel, it is a Palestinian history in name only: in reality it is no more that the study of Israelite history, admittedly seen at least as part of wider Palestinian history, but no nearer the realization or articulation of such a history.[28] Yet even these modest proposals which raised the possibility of a challenge to the dominant construction of the past and which questioned the dominant role of Israel could not be allowed to go unchallenged.

Finkelstein (1989: 43–74) offers a response to these reappraisals of the emergence of the monarchy in Israel in which the dominant discourse reasserts itself. The opening paragraph of the article indicates that, despite an appeal to new archaeological data, his understanding of the significance of the development of an Israelite state stands firmly within the discourse of biblical studies since the time of Alt:

> The emergence of the Israelite monarchy at the end of the eleventh century BCE was one of the most crucial events in the history of Palestine. The political unification of the hill country under Saul, followed by David's conquests and the creation of one powerful state throughout most of the country, virtually changed the historical development of the entire region. For the first time a local independent political entity was established in Palestine – a national ethnic state with a distinctive ideological and religious identity.
>
> (Finkelstein 1989: 43)

Here is a picture of the European nation state transposed to Palestine. We are told, without need for justification, that 'for the first time' the region reached the pinnacle of political evolution, the pinnacle of civilization, a national ethnic state with a '*distinctive* ideological and religious identity'. Presumably, all other political entities in the region prior to this event were not distinctive. The claim to the land on the basis of 'historic right' is reinforced with the notion that this is the first 'powerful state' and 'local independent entity' in the region. The underlying assumptions, drawn from the biblical traditions and the dominant discourse of biblical studies, have been reached before he begins his re-examination of biblical scholarship in light of 'the most important archaeological dimension for tracing processes of this kind – the study of settlement patterns' (1989: 43).

Again he is reliant upon 'the Land of Ephraim' survey to provide the archaeological data which had not been available to previous scholars. He contrasts the distribution of settlement at the beginning of Iron I (twelfth and eleventh centuries BCE) with that during the eleventh century BCE, and with the Iron II settlement pattern. The problems inherent in his attempt to define 'Israelite settlement' on the basis of archaeological evidence alone will be reserved for chapter 5. Clearly Finkelstein is heavily dependent upon his reading of the Hebrew Bible for this conclusion: a fact that places his work firmly within the mainstream of the discourse of biblical studies. He concludes that over 75 per cent of early Iron I sites were located in the eastern half of what he terms 'the Ephraim territory' (1989: 57). The settlement process in the western half intensified during Iron I with 62 per cent of the sites established in the latter phase of the period situated on the slopes and foothills; 76 per cent of the population lived in the eastern units (63 per cent of the population of all Iron I sites) at the beginning of Iron I with 46 per cent of the inhabitants of sites established in late Iron I living in western units. In comparison, 'for the first time in the demographic history of the land of Ephraim' (1989: 58), the western units (51 per cent) out-numbered eastern units. This shows an increase of 95–100 per cent in the number of western sites with 54 per cent of the large villages and 53 per cent of the population. He concludes that the western expansion 'meant a struggle with the harsh topography' (1989: 58) of the western part of the area. He notes that Zertal detected a similar process in his survey of 'Manasseh' and Kochavi's survey of 'Judah and Benjamin'; again the terminology is important. Thus it appears from his data, assuming that his chronological conclusions are correct, that 'Israelite settlement' initially took place in the desert fringes and in the central range between Jerusalem and the Jezreel Valley. Settlement increased in the western areas only in the latter stages of the eleventh century with the intensification reaching its height in Iron II: 'However, the ultimate "conquest", that of the ecological frontier of the central hill country – the western slopes of Samaria and the Judaean hills – took place only in Iron II' (1989: 59). As with his study of the 'emergence of Israel', he is reliant upon his reading of the biblical traditions in order to determine that this settlement shift represents 'Israelite settlement'. Noticeably, the area of demographic expansion which he is interested in is located on the 'western slopes of Samaria and the Judaean hills', the West Bank. He is then able to conclude that the 'Israelite population' in the early Iron I sites west of the Jordan was in the region of 20,000, excluding non-sedentary groups, 'while the settled Israelite population at the end of the eleventh century BCE is estimated at c. 55,000' (1989: 59). His appeal to his earlier study (1988: 27–33) for an understanding of the term 'Israelite' means that his work suffers from the same weaknesses. He has assumed that this settlement shift is Israelite and related to the internal and external conditions which contributed to the emergence of an Israelite monarchy. This is Israel's past alone.

The catalogue of statistical information he puts forward is very impressive. Yet the crucial point is that his assumption that these data relate to Israelite settlement immediately asserts a claim to the land and to the past – an impressive claim at that given the nature of the statistics. But what if this settlement shift is referred to as 'Palestinian' and not 'Israelite', what if we see it as a continuation of the transformation and realignment of Late Bronze Age Palestinian society? Immediately, the change of terminology and the change of perspective offer an alternative construction and claim on the past. The data he puts forward are essential to the examination of crucial processes in the continuing transformation and realignment of Palestinian society in the early Iron Age. He notes, for example, that the switch to a more specialized agriculture in the horticultural regions encouraged the villages of the desert fringe, eastern central range and parts of the foothills to specialize in grain growing and animal husbandry, and to intensify efforts to produce greater surpluses (1989: 60). Such an economic system, he reasons, 'necessitated a certain level of organization, which served as the springboard for public administration' (1989: 60). The production of surpluses led to stratification and the emergence of central sites resulting in a 'crucial shift of the Israelite population from a rural society of small isolated groups to the beginning of organization into larger socio-political systems' (1989: 60). It may be possible to infer from the archaeological evidence that such sociopolitical developments took place at this time but it moves way beyond the evidence to conclude that this is 'Israelite settlement' or the emergence of an Israelite state in the terms it is described in the Samuel traditions in the Hebrew Bible. His focus is solely upon an imagined Israelite past which helps to underpin claims to the land, 'historic Samaria and Judaea', the modern West Bank, which is crucial to modern conceptions of identity and a claim to the land on the basis of 'historic right'. Finkelstein's construction of the period, following his presentation of the data, is a reassertion of the domain assumptions of the discourse throughout this century: he is able to conclude that 'at this point, part of the "classic" reconstruction of the monarchy's incipience should be accepted' (1989: 62–3).

His construction of the imagined past stands firmly in the mainstream of the discourse of biblical studies. This is confirmed with his assertion that:

> In this context one can claim that the actions of one strong personality were responsible for the emergence of the monarchy (Samuel or Saul) – what is known as the theory of the 'Great Man' in human evolution.
>
> (Finkelstein 1989: 63)

He tries to temper this with the qualification that such a 'Great Man' can only arise under suitable socio-historical circumstances. Yet there is nothing in his presentation of the archaeological data for settlement shift and development in the Palestinian hill country and desert fringes which allows for an identification with Saul or Samuel. This is assumed, at no point argued, on the basis of his correlation of the biblical traditions and the archaeological data. He is able, then, to go on to confirm that it was only with David that 'the national state of Saul became a strong and large territorial state' (1989: 63). All this is predicated on the inference that the expanding villages need to produce larger surpluses, thereby increasing stratification and eventually moving towards centralization. Yet we suddenly move from this inference to find that what is really being discussed is a 'national state' which is carved out by Saul and completed by David. Then we find that 'the expansion of the monarchy into the coastal plain, the fertile northern valleys and Galilee united most of the country *for the first time in its history* under one local rule' (1989: 63; emphasis added). Finkelstein's presentation of new archaeological data is little more than a reiteration of the series of domain assumptions from the time of Alt which has invented an imagined Israelite past, the defining moment in the history of the region. The processes discussed in the settlement shift are crucial to any pursuit of Palestinian history for this period. However, such a history has been silenced by the continuing search for ancient Israel in the Iron Age. This is true of all the apparent re-evaluations of the emergence of an Israelite state which have appeared in recent years. Although they have challenged particular aspects of the dominant construction, they remain located firmly within a discourse which has effectively excluded Palestinian history from the academic sphere.

CHALLENGING THE DAVIDIC EMPIRE

The consensus presentation of the Davidic monarchy, although still dominant within the discourse of biblical studies, has gradually begun to fracture in recent years. Some of the reassessments of the formation of the monarchy, referred to above, have helped to contribute to a critical climate, but have fallen short of a sustained critique of the dominant discourse. The dominant construction of the past has begun to fracture as a result of the same convergence of factors which led to the reassessment of the 'emergence' of Israel; the implications of these earlier studies on the 'emergence' of Israel have been applied only slowly to the study of an Israelite monarchy in the early Iron Age. The guarded discussion of Miller and Hayes indicates that by the mid-1980s the convergence of factors which had challenged the dominant constructions of the origins of Israel had begun to produce cracks in the projection of an Israelite empire that dominated Palestine in the Iron Age. The overwhelming factor has been the sea-change in literary approaches to the Hebrew Bible which at first undermined standard historical-critical assumptions pertaining to the period of Israel's emergence and to a lesser extent the re-evaluation of archaeological data. The shift in approaches to the emergence of Israel was brought about by the convergence of these newer literary approaches and new archaeological data which raised serious questions about previous constructions of the Late Bronze–Iron Age transition. What is interesting about the creation of an Israelite state in the Iron Age is that there is very little unambiguous archaeological evidence which pertains to the so-called period of the Israelite monarchy. Thus the discourse of biblical studies has created this entity solely on the basis of a reading of the biblical traditions, supplemented by extra-biblical documentary evidence.

One of the most sceptical assessments of the biblical traditions along with the notion of some glorious age of Israelite empire is Garbini's (1988: 1–20) sharp critique of modern 'biblical histories' as little more than paraphrases of the biblical text stemming from theological motivations. His critical perspective is taken from a philological stance within Assyriology, attacking what he sees as a remarkably uncritical attitude of modern biblical historians to the text of the Hebrew Bible. He also provides a sharp critique of the standard presentations of the reigns of David and Solomon as that of an empire and golden age (1988: 21–32). He finds it remarkable that biblical scholarship has failed to recognize that 'the historical framework gives the impression of being nearer to the mythical vision of an original golden age than to a convincing reconstruction of human actions' (1988: 21). Although he raises important questions about the nature of the text which throw doubt on its historical veracity and usefulness for construction, sounding a suitably sceptical and critical note, he is not always well informed as to the debates within biblical scholarship on these issues.

It is the work of Gunn (1978; 1980), Alter (1982), Fokkelmann (1981; 1986), Eslinger (1985; 1989), and Polzin (1980; 1989), among others, which has opened new vistas on appreciating the literary qualities of the Hebrew Bible in general and the text of Samuel in particular, which has helped to fracture the dominant discourse. Most of these studies are not explicitly concerned with questions of historical reconstruction: some are unashamedly ahistorical, while others are interested solely in the artful construction of narrative. Whether implicitly or explicitly, they have served to undermine the confidence in standard reconstructions of the history of Israel and the early monarchic period, in particular by questioning domain assumptions which have underpinned the historiographic enterprise throughout this century. The circularity of source-critical approaches from the time of Wellhausen which identified pro- and anti-monarchic sources within Samuel have been exposed to questions of different voices in the text and reader-response criticism which have helped to undermine notions of text and the relationship between the text and history.

Leach has produced an equally trenchant criticism of the historical use of these narratives from a structural anthropological perspective. A dominant theme in his work is that the Hebrew Bible as a sacred text does not provide a historical source nor does it necessarily reflect past reality. For Leach, it represents a justification of the past which reveals more of the world of the story-tellers than of any past reality. He asks very important questions which raise misgivings about standard presentations of the reigns of David and Solomon questioning the historicity of this crucial period as presented in the biblical traditions:

> Personally I find this most implausible. There is no archaeological evidence for the existence of these heroes or for the occurrence of any of the events with which they were associated. If it were not for the sacredness of these stories their historicity would certainly be rejected.

> (Leach 1983: 10)

Underlying his approach is the belief that the traditional historical-critical approach has misunderstood the nature and purpose of the Hebrew Bible (Leach 1983: 10). He is more interested in the social setting of texts, particularly in contrast with many recent ahistorical approaches to the Hebrew Bible, concluding that the concerns of later communities responsible for the production of the Hebrew Bible are enshrined in the traditions rather than the product of some monarchic bureaucracy in the early Iron Age. This increasing interest in the social production of the biblical traditions in the second Temple community and the way in which conflicting traditions might reflect competing factions and their concerns rather than being reflections of some historical reality of the early Iron Age has helped to fracture the history of the period as it has been presented traditionally. Garbini and Leach have remained marginal voices within the discourse of biblical studies precisely because they have challenged the construction of an imagined ancient Israel which has been invented in terms of a model of the present, the European nation state, and tied to the struggle for the realization of a modern state of Israel. The discourse has been powerful and persuasive precisely because it is tied so closely to the question of social and political identity. The implications of these shifts towards the text of the Hebrew Bible and the questioning of the dominant construction of the past have not, however, led to a recognition of the shaping of this past in terms of the present of the modern state of Israel. It is instructive to consider the 'evidence' which has sustained the construction of the past in terms of the creation of an Israelite state which dominated and defined Palestinian history.

The most striking feature of the discourse is the overwhelming silence of the archaeological record concerning this defining moment in the history of the region. It is a silence which has contributed in the main to the strong consensus in the projection of this imagined past precisely because it has confirmed the prejudice of biblical historians that the writing of history is dependent upon written sources. But once again, as Garbini, Leach, and Flanagan have intimated, it is this silence of the archaeological record which raises the most serious questions about the presentation of an Israelite empire as an expression of a glorious renaissance culture and which suggests that we are dealing with an invented past. Any meaningful notion of a Davidic empire, the realization of 'Greater Israel', continually presented as an exception in the history of the Levant which is said to change the course of history, could reasonably be expected to have found corroboration in the bureaucratic output of surrounding cultures or ought to have left a significant impact on the material remains of the region.[29] It is often pointed out that although Solomon is reported in the biblical text as having married the daughter of the Pharaoh, a remarkable achievement given that this was denied to Hittite kings, there is no mention of this noteworthy event in any extant Egyptian records. Ahlström (1993: 488) attributes the lack of references to David's and Solomon's kingdoms in other ancient Near East texts to the political weakness of Egypt and Assyria which meant that they did not come into contact with the indigenous power in Palestine. However, even if this was the case, it is more difficult to explain the overwhelming silence of the archaeological record since such a large state, let alone an empire, would require significant changes in social and political organization which ought to have left some trace in the archaeological record. Yet Ahlström (1993: 541) believes that despite the lack of corroborative evidence, and even allowing for the exaggeration by the biblical writers, 'the historicity of the Davidic–Solomonic kingdom should not be doubted'. His final assessment does not differ from the standard presentations: 'Nevertheless, the period of the united monarchy was something exceptional within the history of Canaan, something that never happened before nor happened since' (1993: 541).[30] Here is an 'exception' in the history of the region for which, despite the investment of vast resources in the archaeological invest-igation of the Iron Age, little material evidence has been discovered to corroborate confident pronouncements such as Ahlström's, which are typical of biblical studies, as we have seen.

The power of the discourse to shape the interpretation of the past is shown by the history of the search for the location of Saul's capital at Gibeah. Albright was able to declare triumphantly after his excavations at Tell el-Ful in 1922–3 that he had located the 'Citadel of Saul': his excavations had revealed what he took to be an Iron I tower in the south-west corner of a fortress which he dated to the time of Saul. This conclusion was undermined by Lapp's later exploration of the site (1965) after which he concluded that the fortress was little more than conjecture. Nevertheless, he went on to conclude that Tell el-Ful was to be identified with the fortress of Saul. The rush to interpret supposedly objective, extrabiblical data on the basis of assumptions drawn from the biblical text is typical of the history of the search for ancient Israel. A much more sober assess-ment of the evidence has been provided by Arnold (1990: 52) who concludes on the basis of the archaeological reports that Iron I Tell el-Ful 'possessed a typical Palestinian watchtower with a few outlying buildings'.[31] This is remarkably different from the claims of most of our 'biblical histories' and the confident pronouncements as to the existence of an early state ruled by Saul.[32] Similarly, the so-called 'empire' of David, as Noth and others have presented it, has left little or no archaeological trace that has been unearthed and identified by professional archaeologists. Even one of the recent conservative handbooks has noted that despite the biblical description of a forty-year reign for David 'ironically enough, we have very few archae-ological remains from the Davidic period. There are no monuments that can positively be identified as Davidic' (Mazar 1984: 43). Mazar assumes that most of the Hebrew Bible was written during the period of the monarchy and asks the question whether or not Israel was as creative in the material realm as the spiritual.[33] He acknowledges that in comparison with surrounding cultures – the Aramean and Neo-Hittite kingdoms of Syria, the Phoenicians in Cyprus and in their various colonies overseas, and especially Assyria and Babylonia – the extant material remains 'in the Land of Israel are very poor'. He notes the lack of monumental reliefs and statues in the monarchic period along with magnificent palaces, delicately carved ivories, jewellery, crafted metal objects, or vessels of local manufacture. He points out that the vast majority of art objects were imported. Similarly Kenyon is able to state that:

> The united kingdom of Israel has a life span of only three-quarters of a century. It was the only time in which the Jews were an important political power in western Asia. Its glories are triumphantly recorded in the Bible, and the recollection of this profoundly affected Jewish thought and aspirations. Yet the archaeological evidence for the period is meagre in the extreme.
>
> (Kenyon 1979: 233)

This is typical of the discourse of biblical studies which has chosen to ignore the lack of archaeological evidence in making extravagant claims about this imagined past. Wightman (1990) provides an interesting critique of attempts to identify 'Solomonic archaeology' on the basis of the biblical traditions. He argues that this notion developed from an idea which was predicated on a reading of the archaeological data under the influence of assumptions drawn from the biblical traditions about Solomon. This notion rapidly became represented as fact in dating and identifying 'Solomonic' structures such as the gate-complexes at Megiddo, Hazor, and Gezer. Wightman exposes the circular reasoning often used in discussing this period and archaeological data, a circular reasoning which has become part of the general discourse and protected from further critical evaluation. The need for a critical evaluation of the whole period has been added to by the recent work of Jamieson-Drake (1991) which helps to expose the mirage of the Davidic–Solomonic 'empire'. Although his work is ostensibly a study of scribal schools in Judah, his investigation of the archaeological remains of the period has demonstrated quite forcibly that there was very little evidence of even basic state structures in the tenth or ninth centuries. He finds little evidence that Judah functioned as a state prior to the eighth century BCE increase in population, building, production, centralization, and specialization (1991: 138–9).[34] Even then, the archaeological evidence only points to a remarkably small state structure. Thompson, following Jamieson-Drake, believes that the evidence, or lack of evidence, now suggests that Jerusalem did not become a regional state capital until the seventh century BCE (1992a: 410) and was expanded to the capital of the nation state only in the Persian period. He questions the existence of the biblical 'united monarchy' on the grounds that Judah did not have a sedentary population, 'but also because there was no transregional political or economic base of power in Palestine prior to the expansion of Assyrian imperial influence into the southern Levant' (Thompson 1992a: 412). The discourse of biblical studies has ignored the silence of the archaeological record in constructing an Israelite empire which has defined and dominated the history of the region.

The recent discovery of part of a stele in Aramaic on Tel Dan has been greeted by many as confirmation and justification of the standard construction of this glorious past.[35] It has been proclaimed, by some, as a final rebuttal to the revisionist histories which have questioned the historicity of the biblical traditions (Rainey 1994; Lemaire 1994). The mention of the 'house of David' in line 9 of the inscription is seen as not only proving the existence of the historical David but of vindicating the biblical accounts of King David. This is in contrast to the more measured approach of the excavators in their original publication of the fragment:

> The nature of the biblical sources on the one hand and the fragmentary state of the Dan inscription on the other, do not allow us to draw a definite conclusion. There may be other possible scenarios, and only the recovery of additional pieces of the stele may provide an answer to the problems raised by the discovery of our fragment.
>
> (Biran and Naveh 1993: 98)

Subsequent claims have been much more exaggerated and concerned less with the interpretation of the inscription than the politics of scholarship. It has been heralded as dispelling the cynicisms of the 'Biblical minimizers' (Shanks 1994). Even if it is accepted that this is a reference to the Davidic dynasty and not a place name, as some argue, it is similar to the Merneptah stele in revealing very little in terms of usable historical information which we did not already possess. It is a further instance of the way in which the political and religious assumptions which have shaped and dominated the discourse of biblical studies can be brought to the surface. An isolated reference in such a stele may confirm the existence of a dynasty which is traced back to a founder named David but it cannot confirm the biblical traditions in Samuel about this founder. Attempts to disparage alternative constructions of the past by the use of pejorative labels or by questioning the integrity of scholars reveal that what is at stake are perceptions of the past which are closely tied to social and political identity in the present. It is part of the long-standing discourse of biblical studies to claim the past for Israel. The existence of a Davidic state as portrayed in the biblical traditions is vital to this enterprise, hence the virulence with which any questioning of this master narrative is attacked. The 'objectivity of scholarship', in defence of empire, is represented by Rainey's attack upon Davies:

> Davies represents what he and a circle of colleagues call the 'deconstructionist' approach to Biblical traditions. The present instance can serve as a useful example of why Davies and his 'deconstructionists' can safely be ignored by everyone seriously interested in Biblical and ancient Near Eastern studies.
>
> (Rainey 1994: 47)

Rainey's ostensible disagreement is with Davies' objections to the reading of the phrase 'house of David' as a reference to the Davidic dynasty and his claim that the lack of a word divider suggests that this might be a place name. It is used instead as an attack upon the shifts in historical studies which threaten Israel's control of the past. The rhetorical use of a phrase such as 'everyone seriously interested' is designed to signal that Davies or anyone linked with him cannot be 'serious' and can 'safely be ignored'. It is the emphasis on 'safely' which signals to the reader that it would be dangerous even to contemplate questioning the representation of the past presented in the biblical traditions and championed by Rainey. The reader is then given further severe warnings of the dangers of this route:

> Davies's objections are those of an amateur standing on the sidelines of epigraphic scholarship. Naveh and Biran cannot be blamed for assuming a modicum of basic knowledge on the part of their readers. They are not used to dealing with the dilettantism of the 'deconstructionist' school. Competent scholars

will doubtless take issue with some of Naveh and Biran's interpretations, but Davies can safely be ignored.

(Rainey 1994: 47)

Here the full weight of the discourse of biblical studies is brought to bear in an effort to silence alternative claims to the past. It is now a question of competence and integrity, not of Davies's reading of the inscription, but of any questioning of the biblically inspired construction of the past. The final vitriolic attack confirms that it is these wider issues which are at stake. The reader is informed that lay persons and teachers of the Bible want to know what the inscription 'really signifies': its real significance can only be determined by an 'authority' such as Rainey:

> On the other hand, as someone who studies ancient inscriptions in the original, I have a responsibility to warn the lay audience that the new fad, the 'deconstructionist school', represented by Philip R. Davies and his ilk, is merely a circle of dilettantes. Their view that nothing in Biblical tradition is earlier than the Persian period, especially their denial of a United Monarchy, is a figment of their imagination. The name 'House of David' in the Tel Dan and Mesha inscriptions sounds the death knoll to their specious conceit. Biblical scholarship and instruction should completely ignore the 'deconstructionist school'. They have nothing to teach us.
>
> (Rainey 1994: 47)

The reader is never informed as to the identity of these dilettantes apart from a reference to Thompson. This personal and vitriolic attack upon Davies is used as an opportunity to disparage the shifts in historical studies which have been taking place in the discipline. This movement, however, can be 'safely ignored' because not to ignore it would undermine the construction of the past promoted in the discourse of biblical studies which has sustained Israel's claim to the past and its success in excluding Palestinian history. The stele might confirm the existence of a Judaean kingdom in the ninth or eighth centuries but what it does not do is confirm the construction of the extent of that kingdom or the belief that the monarchy under David represented a first-rank 'empire'. The kingdoms of Judah and Israel still need to be understood as part of Palestinian history rather than the only elements in that broader regional history.

It is clear that biblical scholars and archaeologists have been aware of the lack of archaeological evidence for a long time but have persisted in constructing the massive edifice of a Davidic empire as one of the major powers in the ancient world.[36] Thompson's (1992a: 412) point about the lack of a transregional political or economic power base in Palestine has been blithely ignored by the discourse of biblical studies in its blind pursuit of the Israelite state in the early Iron Age. A study of the wider aspects of imperialism ought to have led to a more cautious approach which should have tempered the extravagant claims that the Davidic state was one of the foremost powers in the ancient world. The monarchy of David and Solomon is seen as escaping the outside imperial control which has been a constant feature of the history of Palestine from the Bronze Age to the present day, that wider reality of imperial power and domination which has sought to control and *define* Palestine throughout its history. Yet the proponents of an imagined past of a Davidic empire have failed to take into account the structural features of empire. This is not to suggest that all empires are structurally identical; there are clear differences between such organizations both in the past and in the present. However, we can see similarities and make comparisons between different periods of imperial control. The discourse of biblical studies has failed to ask a series of important questions. Why has Palestine been the subject of constant imperial control? How has this affected its economy, settlement patterns, and demography? Are there common features that accompany the rise or decline of empire in relation to the region? How are periods of an imperial power-vacuum, if they exist, to be explained? It has been noted that Palestine can hardly be defined as a unity: the geographical and climatic differences have meant that we are forced to talk of the many diverse Palestines that go to make up the singular entity Palestine. The consideration of a major state power in Palestine cannot be understood in isolation from a consideration of these wider structural features and questions.

The important study of the rise and fall of great powers by Kennedy (1988) reveals a very important correlation between economy and power which challenges the perpetuation of an imagined past of a Davidic super-power in the ancient world. The kinds of questions raised by Kennedy are an area of study which has been neglected in the consideration of the involvement of imperial powers in Palestine in antiquity. Kennedy (1988: xxiv–xxvii) outlines a number of important principles in the study of world empires, or what he terms 'the Great Powers'. Although his study is concerned with the modern period, the sixteenth century to the present, his findings are also germane to any consideration of power shifts in the ancient world. Most importantly, he detects a causal relationship between shifts in the general economic and productive balances and the position of individual powers in the international system. In particular, he highlights the move in trade from the Mediterranean to the Atlantic and north-west Europe from the sixteenth century onwards, and the redistribution in the shares of world manufacturing output away from Western Europe in the decades after 1890. These economic shifts were followed by the rise of new great powers which altered the military and territorial order. The historical record shows a very clear connection *in the long run* between an individual great power's economic rise and fall and its growth and decline as an important military power (or world empire). The correlation is reasonably straightforward in that economic resources are necessary to support large-scale military establishments. However, a further important principle, which again is not surprising in itself, is that wealth and power are always relative. Kennedy found that a nation's relative economic and military power did not rise and fall in parallel. Very often there was a noticeable time-lag between the trajectory of a state's relative economic strength and the trajectory of its military and territorial influence. A power with an expanding economy might well decide to become richer rather than invest significantly in military power. But priorities change over time and Kennedy suggests that a half-century or so later the burden of overseas obligations brought about by the economic expansion, the necessity of and dependence on foreign markets and raw materials, bases and colonies, means that the power has to invest in armaments to protect its markets, trade routes, and raw materials against other competing and expanding powers. He concludes that in conflicts between great powers victory invariably goes to the power with the more flourishing productive base. A good example is that of the decline of Spain in the seventeenth century. Spanish agriculture suffered from extortionate rents, the actions of the Mesta, and military service, which were exacerbated by a series of plagues that depopulated the countryside around the beginning of the seventeenth century. It was at such a point that American silver was brought back to Spain and caused price inflation which severely damaged the Spanish economy. 'The flood of precious metals from the Indies, it was said, was to Spain as water on a roof – it poured on and then was drained away' (Kennedy 1988: 70). The result of all this was the eventual decline of Spanish military power, which did not manifest itself until the 1640s, but whose causes Kennedy (1988: 70) has identified as existing decades before.

The conclusions which Kennedy draws from his magisterial analysis of the last five centuries of the modern era are instructive for any study of the shifts in power in the ancient world and worth quoting at length:

> The argument in this book has been that there exists a dynamic for change, driven chiefly by economic and technological developments, which then impact upon social structures, political systems, military power, and the position of individual states and empires. The speed of this global economic change has not been a uniform one, simply because the pace of technological innovation and economic growth is itself irregular, conditioned by the circumstance of the individual inventor and entrepreneur as well as by climate, disease, wars, geography, the social framework, and so on. In the same way, different regions and societies across the globe have experienced a faster *or* slower rate of growth, depending not only upon the shifting patterns of technology, production, and trade, but also upon their receptivity to the new modes of increasing output and wealth. As some areas of the world have risen, others have fallen behind – relatively (or sometimes) absolutely. None of this is surprising. Because of man's innate drive to improve his condition, the world has never stood still. And the intellectual breakthroughs from the time of the Renaissance onward, boosted by the coming of the 'exact sciences' during the Enlightenment and Industrial Revolution, simply meant that the dynamics of change would be increasingly more powerful and self-sustaining than before.
>
> (Kennedy 1988: 566)

It is important in the light of this study to consider the impact of economic and technological developments upon the relative shifts in power in the ancient world and the ways in which these affect Palestine in relation to 'world economies'. It will help to explain why Palestine has been rarely, if ever, a regional power in its own right and certainly calls into question the standard assertion that the Davidic–Solomonic state was a leading world power in the Iron Age.

Furthermore, the second major conclusion of Kennedy's (1988: 566) study that the relative military power and strategical position of states is dependent upon the uneven pace of economic growth is also important for our consideration of ancient empires. It might seem obvious that military power, the ability to finance and equip an effective army, is dependent upon 'a flourishing productive base' and technological development. Yet many of the standard treatments of the reign of David and Solomon and other periods of Israelite history seem to ignore the obvious. It is the case that

> all of the major shifts in the world's *military-power* balances have followed alterations in the *productive* balances; and further, that the rising and falling of the various empires and states in the international system has been confirmed by the outcomes of the major Great Power wars, where victory has always gone to the side with the greatest material resources.
>
> (Kennedy 1988: 567)

Kennedy's study confirms the dynamics of world power from 1500 CE to the present day. The technological advances of antiquity or the shifts in productive base may not have happened with the rapidity and frequency of the modern period, but none the less the history of Palestine and the rise and fall of 'world empires' from the Late Bronze Age to the Roman period illustrates that it is a dynamic that was just as important in the ancient world. A consideration of some of the factors highlighted by Kennedy in relation to Palestine's position in the geopolitics of the ancient world will help to explain why it was part of a succession of empires: a dynamic of world power in which a number of regions fell behind in absolute terms to such an extent that they could no longer retain their position in this nexus of power.

The three essential characteristics of empire are control, land, and profit. We are not here concerned with the theological, that is, ideological justification of empire but with its practical effects upon the region. These three factors, control, land, and profit, coincided in the case of Palestine in order to explain why empire has been such an enduring reality throughout its history. In order to understand this constant factor of imperial presence it would be necessary to examine some of the key elements in the dynamics of world power identified by Kennedy: productive base, geography, economics, and technology. Coote and Whitelam (1987: 64) stress that the infrastructural inferiority of Palestine in comparison with its neighbouring riverine civilizations has been a constant factor in its dominance by outside powers. Agricultural production was always labour intensive in ancient agrarian economies, a situation that continued into the present in many regions. This has meant that regions with the greatest local agricultural resource and largest labour pool had the greatest production and possessed a vital natural advantage. Palestine simply could not compete with the far superior riverine agrarian economies and demographic base of Egypt and Mesopotamia. Later it would be the natural advantages of the Anatolian and Persian plateaux, and eventually Europe, in the form of the Greek and Roman powers, which would come to dominate Palestine. A region with the infrastructural inferiority of Palestine could not compete with contemporary military powers while agricultural production and demography remained such key factors in the dynamics of world power. The imagined past of a Davidic empire needs to be examined in light of this fundamental reality.

Our demographic data are so imprecise and limited that it is impossible to provide precise population figures. However, it is the order of magnitude that is important when comparing the demographic and production base of Palestine with that of its imperial neighbours. McEvedy and Jones (1978: 226) have estimated that the population of Egypt during the New Kingdom period was approximately 3 million compared with no more than 250,000 in Palestine. A demographic peak of roughly 5 million was achieved in the first millennium BCE which was not to be surpassed until the modern period.[37] Furthermore, even on their lowest estimate (1978: 149), the area of modern-day Iraq during the second millennium BCE possessed a demographic base that was three to four times greater than Palestine at around 750,000 and 1 million with an increase to 1 million–1.25 million. The Assyrian Empire witnessed a significant increase in population rising to around 2 million in the seventh century BCE. Similarly, they estimate (1978: 152) that the area of modern-day Iran had a population of 2 million by the Late Bronze Age (c. 1000 BCE). It is interesting to note that this rose to 2.5 million–4 million during the Persian period. Recent archaeological survey data from both Palestine and elsewhere in the ancient Near East would allow a slightly more accurate picture to be produced. The important point, however, is the order of magnitude in comparing the size of population of one region with another. It is an issue that has been ignored by most biblical historians when discussing regional power in Palestine vis-à-vis its ancient context. Palestine lacked the demographic and economic base to compete with the major powers of the ancient world.[38]

CONCLUSION: FREEING PALESTINIAN
HISTORY

The convergence of a variety of factors – changes in approaches to the text of the Hebrew Bible, the lack of archaeological evidence, and the infrastructural inferiority of Palestine in comparison with the great riverine civilizations and other powers of the ancient world – undermines the claim of biblical studies to have discovered a Davidic empire which was a major power in the Iron Age. The recognition of the mirage of the Davidic empire, an Israelite state which has dominated the Palestinian past, means that Palestinian history is freed from the control of an imagined past which has been claimed for Israel alone.

The situation described above illustrates the power of such a discourse to obstruct alternative claims on the past despite the lack of unambiguous evidence to confirm the dominant construction. Yet biblical scholarship has remained strangely reticent in its attempts to account for the silence of the archaeological record on this glorious empire, seeking instead to exploit the silence by projecting a construction of the past predicated upon biblical traditions. It might be countered that the challenge to the dominant construction is simply a convenient argument from silence. But the silence is overwhelming! The irony is that we are presented with the paradox of an imperial control and definition of the past: an imagined Israelite state or empire which has successfully subdued any alternative understanding of the past. 'Imperialism', in the words of Said (1993: 271), 'after all is an act of geographical violence through which virtually every space in the world is explored, charted, and finally brought under control.' Biblical studies has participated in this act of imperialism by contributing to a construction of the past which has denied any alternative claims. This understanding of the past has had profound political implications by confirming and supporting modern Israel's claims to the land against Palestinian claims to the past or the land. The dominant discourse of biblical studies has been involved in this act of dispossession through its continued reiteration of a series of claims which tie the past to the present: the claim to the land through 'historic right' on the basis of prior state formation and possession of the land, the stress on the corruption or incompetence and failure of indigenous political structures to reach the pinnacle of (Western) civilization, the need for external influx in order to realize the potential of the land, the notion of a 'defensive' empire, and the notion of 'Greater Israel'. The insistence on the continuum between past and present has been couched only in terms of a continuum between Davidic Israel and the modern state of Israel. There is no corresponding notion of any continuum between the indigenous Palestinian population of the past and the present. Once the mirage of the Davidic empire is admitted, then this raises the question of how we are to investigate and conceive of the history of Iron Age Palestine. Any alternative construction of the past would need to be part of the continuum with the Late Bronze–Iron Age transition: it would need to examine the growing archaeological data and surveys, freed from the assumptions of 'Israelite' settlement, in trying to account for the settlement and demographic shifts in the region in the context of the shifts in imperial power in the ancient world. It would form part of the investigation of the transformation and realignment of Palestine society, of which Israel is a part but not the dominant part, which excludes all other voices. The discussion will then turn to the question of the processes at work in settlement shift and the extension of settlement in Iron I, as with the discussion of the Late Bronze–Iron Age transition, rather than relying upon an agenda which is set by and dominated by the Hebrew Bible. It will need to give greater emphasis to the regional variation and the wider political and social realities than has been customary in our standard 'biblical histories'.

5

THE CONTINUING
SEARCH

INTRODUCTION

The mid- to late 1980s witnessed the development of what we might term the 'new search' for ancient Israel. This new search is represented by a series of publications (Lemche 1985; Ahlström 1986; Coote and Whitelam 1987; Finkelstein 1988) which have been understood as a major challenge to the dominant constructions considered in chapter 3, contributing to a significant shift in perceptions as to the nature or existence of early Israel in the Late Bronze–Iron Age transition. These are the revisionist, or 'deconstructionist', histories which Rainey believes can *safely* be ignored by all those *seriously* interested in the history of Israel. In effect, these works, independently of one another, focused upon the failure of the three earlier models associated with Albright–Bright, Alt–Noth, and Mendenhall–Gottwald to deal with the growing body of archaeological data from the region and the shifts in literary approaches to the Hebrew Bible. The work of Finkelstein is distinctive and important for the direction of future discussions, being the publication and analysis of new and vital survey data by a professional archaeologist. The three works which preceded this were all by biblical specialists who had become dissatisfied with the standard histories of ancient Israel and were trying to respond to the significant changes which were taking place in the discipline. They have been followed by a 'new' history of Israel (Lemche 1988), a synthesis of recent research on early Israel (Coote 1990), a detailed study of Israelite and Judaean history (Thompson 1992a), and the posthumous study of Palestinian history by Ahlström (1993), along with numerous articles in specialist journals.[1] Davies (1992) has attempted to draw together the implications of the shifts in the discipline and various points made by Ahlström, Lemche, Coote and Whitelam, Finkelstein, and Thompson, among others, about the study of the history of early Israel.

These works, and the debate generated by them, have contributed to a reassessment of the early periods of Israelite history. The most profound challenge has been to the long-held, and continuing, assumption that the biblical traditions provide the best or the only source for the history of the period. The significance of the challenge can be seen in the shape of the volume by Miller and Hayes (1986) on Israelite and Judaean history which provides a very guarded treatment of the pre-state periods concentrating upon the difficulties of construction in light of the nature of the biblical sources. Most of the recent works cited above question the usefulness of the biblical traditions for understanding the emergence or origins of Israel, emphasizing that these traditions in their current forms are late and are more applicable to understanding the monarchic and second Temple periods than Israel of the Late Bronze–Iron Age transition. The other distinctive feature is that they build upon the critiques of Mendenhall and Gottwald in emphasizing the indigenous nature of Israel in the Late Bronze–Iron Age transition. They reject the notion of a peasant revolt but accept that current archaeological evidence points to early Israel as indigenous to ancient Palestine. A number, notably Ahlström (1993), Thompson (1992a; 1992b) and Whitelam (1991; 1994; 1995b), have also argued, more explicitly, for the study of ancient Palestinian history.

Their challenge to the dominant discourse of biblical studies, the questioning of fundamental presuppositions and consensus positions about the emergence of Israel, has contributed to a climate of confusion in the discipline leading to claims of a major paradigm shift in biblical studies (Davies 1992: 12–16; Thompson 1992a; Whitelam 1994: 58; Lemche 1994: 167).[2] However, the effects of the debate, despite the professed intentions by some to pursue Palestinian history, have been to reinforce the continued search for ancient Israel thereby obscuring the claim to a Palestinian past which is worthy of study. Coote's (1990: viii) claim that recent research on early Israel has led to 'a new understanding', 'a new horizon', stressing the set of shared assumptions rather than the differences between the different positions, is only part of the story. It is questionable what this new horizon really represents and how far it has managed to escape from the discourse which has dominated historical research throughout this century. Fundamental to these 'shared assumptions' of Coote's new horizon is the continued identification of Israel with the settlement shift which took place in the Palestinian hill country during the Late Bronze–Iron Age transition. Thompson (1992a) has pointed out that virtually all research since Alt and Albright has taken this correlation for granted. Although these new studies argue that the Israel of this Late Bronze–Iron Age transition settlement shift is indigenous rather than external, they remain constrained by the dominant discourse of biblical studies. The conclusion that Israel was indigenous to Palestine rests upon the interpretation of the material culture of the rural sites in the central hill country and margins. But the prior conclusion that the inhabitants of these sites are 'Israelite' is not determined from a reading of the archaeological evidence but from a controlling assumption drawn from the Hebrew Bible that Israel during this period inhabited particular areas of Palestine, namely the central hill country.

It is the discourse of biblical studies that has determined that these settlements are to be identified with Israel and Israel alone. It is the power of this discourse which continues to define the 'horizon' and what might be found once the horizon is reached. The controlling nature of this 'shared assumption' is evident in the titles of these monographs – *Early Israel: Anthropological and Historical Studies in the Israelite Society before the Monarchy, Who Were the Israelites, The Emergence of Early Israel in Historical Perspective*, and *The Archaeology of the Israelite Settlement*. The titles reveal that it is Israel which is the focus of attention, the object of the 'new' search. They are locked into the dominant discourse, bound by a powerful circular argument which continues to shape research strategies and findings. All of these works, despite their appearance of radical critique, have continued the search for ancient Israel. Rather than representing a 'new horizon', they represent the end point of the classic search for ancient Israel, a search which only now, at least in some quarters, is being seen as having failed. Only after the biblically inspired assumption, which identifies the settlement shift of the Late Bronze–Iron Age transition with Israel, has been removed can the discussion proceed to explore the possibilities of giving voice to alternative, Palestinian claims to the past. Before the task of pursuing the study of the history of the region can be defined outwith the confines of the traditional biblically inspired approach, it remains to consider why the new search has failed.

The critiques by Ahlström, Lemche, Coote and Whitelam, and Thompson, all biblical specialists rather than archaeologists, are dependent upon interpretations of growing archaeological data from the region. It is necessary to consider the archaeology of ancient Israel in order to understand the effect of the constraints inherent in their works which has effectively blocked the realization of Palestinian history. The English publication of Finkelstein's (1988) study of Israelite settlement, containing important new survey and excavation data, is usually seen as advancing the study of Israelite origins by providing data which are important for the assessment of the hypotheses of Ahlström, Lemche, and Coote and Whitelam. However, his monograph is equally bound by the discourse of biblical studies perpetuating fundamental assumptions of the archaeology of Israel which have determined the search. The archaeological search, an essential component of the biblical search since the work of Albright, brings together a powerful set of shared theological and political assumptions. The theological quest, embodied most noticeably in the Biblical Theology movement, relied upon the archaeological quest for physical confirmation of the actions of the deity in history. This has been complemented and extended by the Zionist search for Israel in the past, intensified since the founding of the modern state of Israel in 1948, in order to confirm current claims to the land. Evangelical and conservative Christianity has been allied with political and religious Zionism in the quest for the physical reality of ancient Israel. A consideration of the archaeology of ancient Israel, or at least some representative examples of the assumptions embodied in recent work, will help to explain why the critiques of Ahlström, Lemche, Coote and Whitelam, and Thompson have failed to break free from the discourse which has determined the research strategies and results of the study of the history of the region for the Late Bronze and Iron Ages. It is a discourse in which the search for ancient Israel has been paramount and in which the concern for Palestinian history has been marginalized and effectively silenced.

THE ARCHAEOLOGY OF EARLY ISRAEL

It is not an exaggeration to say that the prospect of the study of Palestinian history for these periods, as a subject in its own right, has been made possible, however unwittingly, by a marked shift in the nature of archaeological investigations in the region in recent years. It has been made possible by the switch of focus by archaeologists from an almost exclusive interest in urban tells at the beginnings of archaeological research in the region to a more balanced interest in regional surveys in conjunction with the excavation of larger urban and smaller, often single-period rural sites. The reasons for an earlier preoccupation with urban tells has been well documented elsewhere and is entirely understandable in the context of the need for spectacular results in order to continue funding for these expensive projects. However, such an approach also coincided with the interests of 'biblical archaeology' which sought to illuminate the biblical traditions by tying it to the material realities of the past. The biblical texts often mention major urban centres, their conquest and destruction, therefore it was only natural that 'biblical archaeologists' should concentrate on such tells in order to confirm the events of the past and reveal the realities of ancient Israel and the Bible. Furthermore, since ancient Israel was conceived of as a nation state, or incipient nation state, it was natural to look for confirmatory evidence at the major urban centres – the obvious markers, it was believed, for such a state.

However, the vital switch from single-site excavation to regional surveys has begun to provide settlement data which allow the observation of the patterns and rhythms of Palestinian life over centuries.[3] Such an approach allows the historian to try to account for the differences and similarities in these rhythms over time. As Renfrew and Wagstaff (1982: 1) remind us, 'the spatial and temporal patterns of human culture are never stationary, particularly when viewed in a long-term perspective. Changes may be discovered: cultures emerge, flourish and decay.' The slow, often imperceptible, patterns and changes of settlement when viewed over a few decades might suggest a static society. However, the rhythms of change often only become apparent when viewed over centuries. On other occasions, of course, there are dramatic bursts of activity with sudden declines or expansions or changes in regional settlement. The historian needs to be aware of the different levels of time in settlement history and needs to analyse, compare, and contrast the different phases of settlement in order to try to understand the forces and processes at work in the history of the region.[4] Snodgrass's expression of the importance of archaeological surveys to Greek archaeology could equally be applied to Palestinian history:

> It enables them to contribute substantially to a different branch of historical study from the traditional, event-oriented political one, and to do this on the scale not of a simple, restricted locality, the site, but of a *region*. It explores the rural sector of

ancient Greek life on which our ancient Greek sources are most
defective, and corrects the urban bias of the past century and
more of excavation in Greece. It generates relatively little in the
way of preserved finds, but an almost endlessly exploitable
store of new knowledge.

(Snodgrass 1987: 99)

Yet once again, although survey and excavation data are fundamental
for the study of Palestinian settlement, unfortunately but inevitably
we are faced with a series of partial texts. They are partial partly
because not all subregions have been surveyed to the same level of
intensity and partly because the new data generated by this switch
in strategies from tell-centred archaeology is only just beginning to
be exploited in historical syntheses and the generation of new
hypotheses. More importantly, however, the partiality is governed
by political and theological assumptions which determine the design
or interpretation of such projects. Even so, this trend is the most
promising development for the historian desperate to understand the
settlement, organization, and economy of ancient Palestinian society.
The body of data is growing at a considerable rate; but it remains the
case, of course, that the historian will always be faced with partial
data, however extensive the archaeological work might be.

Snodgrass (1987: 102–3) raises the important question of the
differences in survey techniques: intensive and extensive surveys.
Intensive survey is obviously more labour intensive and expensive in
proportion to the size of area that can be surveyed. He opted for the
former on the basis of the discovery that intensive surveys in Greece
had revealed a density of sites that was significantly higher, by a
factor of fifty times or more, than extensive surveys. As he notes, this
raises the serious question that a great deal of information is likely
to be missed by extensive surveys. This is a serious hindrance to the
study of settlement patterns and changes in Palestinian history since
the historian is forced to work with data that can only allow large
generalizations about demographic, economic, or settlement trends
in a region. Even though we are dealing with an expanding database,
it is none the less the case that practical and financial difficulties will
severely hinder the completion of intensive surveys for the whole
region. The best that can be hoped for is a mixture of intensive and
extensive surveys so that the data can be compared and modified
where necessary.

Snodgrass points to another important limitation:

in the task of understanding and explaining the classical past, survey offers an entirely fresh and potentially valuable dimension. It is a dimension that brings out very clearly another relationship, emphasized in some recent nonclassical work, but previously much neglected: I mean the relationship of the archaeological record to the present day. 'The archaeological record,' writes Lewis Binford, 'is here with us in the present ... and the observations we make about it are in the here and now'; they are 'not "historical" statements.' The truth of this observation is perhaps more apparent to the surveyor, painfully conscious of the vulnerability of his raw data to the effects of seasonal, even ephemeral, modern activity, than it is to the excavator; for we all share to some degree the illusion that a progress downwards into the earth is a journey backwards into the past. It is not: the stratified deposits uncovered by the excavator all began their existence as surface deposits, for however fleeting a period, and were thus subject to some of the processes of degradation, displacement, and dispersal for which the data of surface survey are often criticized; not to mention the multifarious effects of 'post-depositional' factors once these deposits disappeared from sight.

(Snodgrass 1987: 130–1)

Yet there is a more important connection with the present day which Snodgrass does not go on to develop. In the case of Greek archaeology and history, although it has been subject to the same Eurocentric representation, it has not suffered from the search for 'ancient Israel'. The utilization of the new store of knowledge pertaining to the ancient Palestinian past has been dictated and hindered by the powerful political and theological assumptions which have guided the search for ancient Israel. The irony of the situation is that the new possibilities for the study and development of Palestinian history, which have been opened up by these surveys, have been masked by the all-consuming search for ancient Israel. The new store of knowledge has been exploited by the very same research strategies which have invented and located Israel in the Late Bronze–Iron Age transition and early Iron Age.

The theological and political assumptions inherent in the search for ancient Israel, in defining research strategies, have determined the nature and utilization of the results. This is not an objective search that provides objective data for the historian simply to arrange into a narrative which reflects a trustworthy account of the past. The historian is faced with partial texts in every sense of the term. Again, it is the fascination with Israel which has dominated biblical archaeology so that the focus has often been upon those sites, subregions, or periods which are thought to illuminate the emergence and development of Israel. The obsession with the 'emergence of Israel' has meant that vast scholarly resources have been focused upon the Late Bronze–Iron Age transition and Iron I in terms of survey and excavation where it is believed that Israel is to be located. It is noticeable that the most intensive survey work has been carried out in the central hill country of Palestine because it was assumed from the time of Alt and Albright onwards that this was the location of 'Israelite' settlements. The Land of Israel Survey has continued to carry out vital work in different areas, adding to the valuable data, while regional surveys in Jordan have begun to provide vital information about areas that until recently were archaeologically little known. Yet the coastal area of Palestine, so vital in the history of the region, has not been surveyed to the same extent. Therefore it is simply not possible to make comparisons between some, often very important, subregions. Israel Finkelstein, who has contributed so much to providing the new body of survey and archaeological data, states that 'Canaanite' urban centres had nothing to tell us of the processes of 'Israelite settlement' (1988: 22–3).[5] Similarly, Finkelstein (1985a: 123) defined the goals of the Shiloh excavation as 'elucidation of the history of the site prior to Iron Age I and the circumstances of its development into an important Israelite religious, economic and political centre; determination of its character during Iron Age I and its position in the overall settlement pattern and social system of the period; a better understanding of the material culture of the central hill country in the Middle Bronze, Late Bronze and Iron Age I periods'. Once again it is Israel which dominates the agenda and forms the assumptions of archaeological and historical investigation. The initial investment of precious resources in excavations and regional surveys has been heavily influenced by biblical scholarship and the all-consuming search for 'ancient Israel'.[6]

This partiality is manifested in the regions where extensive surveys have been carried out, since in a number of cases, where results have been published, the focus has been upon the Iron Age, the period of the essential Israel. The principal interest in the results has been to quantify and qualify Israelite settlement or the development of the monarchy. Earlier and later periods are less well served, either in terms of the publication of results or the detailed analysis of the data.[7] The patterns and rhythms of settlement need to be studied, compared and contrasted, in the long term. It is vital to try to understand how any one period fits into the settlement history by comparing it with earlier and later periods from the Stone Age to the present. Such a task will not be possible until all regions are surveyed with an equal intensity and, equally importantly, the data for all periods, not just those thought to be of interest to biblical archaeologists and historians whose special interest is the emergence and development of Israel, are published. The task of the latter is not well served by the partial surveys or the partial publication of data since it denies important comparisons over *la longue durée*.

Finkelstein has described the developments in archaeology since Albright's excavations at Tell el-Ful as a 'a veritable revolution' in research on 'Israelite Settlement' (1988: 20). He has made a major contribution to research through the timely publication of data from his own Land of Israel Survey and his excavations at 'Izbet Sartah and Shiloh. Yet his revolution, like Coote's new horizon, is more apparent than real. It is a term that might be used to qualify the rapid increase in the quality and quantity of data since the heyday of Albright's work in the field. However, the essential assumptions which underlie the archaeological investigation of the region for the period of the Late Bronze and early Iron Ages have not changed significantly. If anything, the political search for the reality of ancient Israel has grown stronger since 1948, supplementing and strengthening the theological motivations which informed Albright and a host of other biblical archaeologists. This so-called revolution suffers from the very same distractions of the search for and invention of ancient Israel, the problems of trying to free historical research of the region from the constraints imposed by the Hebrew Bible and the discourse of biblical studies, which historical research has encountered throughout the century. The switch from site excavation to regional survey, or a combination of these, has succeeded in intensifying rather than diminishing the search for ancient Israel. The way data, which are vital to the realization of Palestinian history in its own right, are utilized to continue the search for Israel and to silence Palestinian history is illustrated in the opening pages of Finkelstein's monograph. His assumptions, shaped by the dominant discourse, mean that the past belongs to Israel, effectively silencing any alternative construction:

The Settlement of the Israelites in the 12th and 11th centuries BCE, and their transformation from a society of isolated tribes into an organized kingdom, is one of the most exciting, inspiring, and at the same time controversial chapters in the history of the Land of Israel.

(Finkelstein 1988: 15)

The terminology, partly explained in a footnote (1988: 15 n. 1), is significant. He uses 'Settlement' to refer to Israelite settlement, while the same term in lower case, 'settlement', 'is used with its regular meaning'. This suggests from the very outset that there is something special about Israelite settlement whereas the settlement of other groups is not particularly noteworthy or at least is not to be demarcated in any special way. Furthermore, this is the 'Land of Israel'. The denial of any Palestinian claim to this space is completed by the manipulation of time: 'The historical concept "Settlement period" or "period of the Settlement and Judges" is synonymous with the term "Early Israelite period" and the archaeological definitions "Iron I" and "Early Iron Age"' (Finkelstein 1988: 15 n. 1). He then adds that this is equivalent to the period from the end of the Late Bronze Age to the beginning of the Israelite monarchy, 'whatever the label'. The last comment suggests a matter-of-fact reporting which assures the reader that there is nothing contentious here. But, as we have seen, the label is crucial. The terms are not neutral: they imply claims to the land and the past denying other competing claims. The reference to the 'period of Settlement and Judges' already indicates the influence of the periodization of the Hebrew Bible, and alerts the reader to the possibility that the biblical traditions have played a much greater role in the interpretation of the archaeological data than is at first apparent. The aside that 'Iron I' and 'early Iron Age' are synonymous with the 'early Israelite period' drives home the notion that this is Israel's past. However, before turning to this issue, the way in which recent surveys have determined the conceptualization and control of the ancient past needs to be considered.

The surveys which have been carried out embody a paradox: they are vital to the pursuit of Palestinian history but they are also an expression of a claim to the land by the mapping and conceptualization of that land. Thus Israeli scholars have recently conducted surveys in Manasseh (Zertal), Ephraim (Finkelstein), Judah (Ofer), Western Galilee (Frankel) and Lower Galilee (Gal). Again the terminology is significant since the claim that these are surveys of 'tribal areas', embodied in the names Manasseh, Ephraim, and Judah, reinforces both the search for ancient Israel and the belief that this is the land of Israel. The concentration of effort on the occupied West Bank underlines the search for Israel as conceived in the biblical traditions. It is an expression of a claim to the land by naming and mapping that land. One of the early surveys conducted by Kochavi in the central hill country and the Golan was entitled *Judaea, Samaria, and the Golan: Archaeological Survey 1967–1968*. This is the 'Judaea and Samaria' of Begin, which in modern political parlance embodies the claim through historic right to inhabit the land of 'biblical Israel'. The discovery of 'Israelite' sites in this politically sensitive region is bound to have considerable political consequences for the present. Significantly, those areas which are thought to have been 'Canaanite', particularly in the coastal lowlands, have not been subjected to such intensive research. Finkelstein (1988: 22–3) acknowledges the selective use of archaeological data in his analysis: 'We have already expressed the opinion that however much the evidence for the large Canaanite mounds may contribute to the understanding of various phenomena at the end of the Late Bronze period, it can do little to advance the study of the process of Israelite Settlement.' It is the occupation of the land of Israel which is important; other occupants of the land or their claims to the land are not of significance. They are not designated by capitalization (Settlement) nor are they relevant for understanding Israelite settlement. The partiality of archaeological research is determined by which sites are excavated or which areas are surveyed: what is searched for determines to a large extent what is found. It is a process which confers legitimacy on some aspects of the past and not on others: a process which is concerned with the location of ancient Israel and not with the explication of Palestinian history in general.

The identification of 'Israelite' sites and 'Israelite' material culture is a fundamental part, whether consciously or otherwise, of the politics of archaeology. This search for and location of the material realities of the past in many parts of the globe, as we have seen, is a crucial factor in the construction and confirmation of social identity. The discovery of the past provides a cohesive factor which helps to confirm the present (cf. Rowlands 1994: 130; Elon 1994). As Rowlands (1994: 133) has noted, 'nations without pasts are contradictions in terms and archaeology has been one of the principle suppliers of the raw material for constructing pasts in modern struggles for nationhood'. Elon (1994: 14) points out, for example, that virtually all the major Israeli national symbols, the State seal, medals, coins, and postage stamps, are derived from archaeology. It is not just the sense of identity which the construction of the archaeology reinforces and confirms but the material presence and right to the land. This has been an important aspect of the invention of ancient Israel from the inception of biblical archaeology but has become of even more vital concern since the growth of Zionist immigration in the 1920s and particularly the foundation of the modern state in 1948. Elon (1994: 14) relates the story of the discovery of a synagogue mosaic at Beit-Alpha in 1928 during the construction of an irrigation system. The inhabitants of the commune, members of the socialist *Hashomer Hatzair* (the Young Guard), debated whether or not to cover it up as an irrelevant religious symbol. It was eventually decided to preserve it as a political, Zionist monument revealing the Jewish presence in the land and confirming 'the legitimacy of the Zionist claim'.[8] In the 1950s and 1960s archaeology became more than an amateur pastime, it was a national obsession (Elon 1994: 16; Silberman 1989: 87–136). But it was an obsession with the search for ancient Israel which cemented their claim to the land and helped to forge a sense of shared identity among a disparate population. The archaeological investigation of the Late Bronze–Iron Age transition and Iron I in recent years is in reality a narrative about possessing the past. It has been couched in terms of objectivity and scientific investigation which mask the power of representation (see, for example, Bond and Gilliam 1994). The theologically motivated search of Western biblical studies, the search for confirmation of divine action within history, has articulated well with and been enhanced by the politically motivated search of the modern state of Israel. The development of archaeology in the service of the present has probably been more advanced in Israel than any other area of the modern world. It reflects the need of the nation state to legitimize its possession of the present by discovering itself in the past.

The search for ancient Israel has been given reality through the very materiality of the archaeological process. Thus the real irony of the claim is that it is the switch to survey work which has provided the prospect of progress in the realization and articulation of Palestinian history, whereas the practical effect has been to establish the presence of ancient Israel in the past, thereby creating a *real* presence in terms of its 'historic right' to the land. The recent intensive surveys have added an impressive catalogue of sites which has reinforced the 'reality' of Israel. How could it be dismissed as an imagined past when the material reality of presence and possession is so evident in the surveys of Finkelstein, Gal, Zertal, Frankel, and Ofer? The cataloguing of hundreds of Iron I sites and their identification as Israelite, particularly in the hill country, modern Israeli 'Judaea and Samaria', have only emphasized Israel's claim to the land both past and present. The archaeology of ancient Israel has effectively confirmed, for most scholars, that the past belongs to Israel.

It is only with the recognition of the essential circularity of reasoning that it becomes clear that the interpretation of excavation and survey data has resulted in an imagined past. This can be illustrated from the first major survey of southern Upper Galilee conducted by Aharoni in the 1950s. He discovered a number of small sites in close proximity and assigned them to the Late Bronze–Iron Age transition on the basis of the pottery assemblage at Khirbet el-Tuleil (Horvat Harashim). He was then able to conclude that 'this wave of settlement from the beginning of the Iron Age is Israelite' (1957: 149). Notice that he refers to a wave of settlement echoing the domain assumption, common at the time, that social change was the result of waves of Semitic nomads coming from outside. However, the crucial point here is that this conclusion, drawn from a reading of the biblical traditions rather than the archaeological evidence alone, follows in the tradition of Alt and Albright that such early Iron Age sites must be Israelite. It contains an essentially circular form of reasoning in order to sustain the notion of identity and land: the definition of Israelite culture and sites has been determined archaeologically; the Hebrew Bible indicates which areas were Israelite during the Late Bronze and early Iron Ages; those sites which fall within these areas are Israelite; Israelite material culture is defined as the material culture at the sites in areas designated by the Hebrew Bible to be Israelite; the discovery of these Israelite sites confirms the essential historicity of the biblical narratives. The debate in archaeology has not concerned the identity of the inhabitants; this was taken for granted as self-evident until recently. The concern has focused on the dating of particular sites and the direction of settlement.[9] It is only once the circularity of argument is admitted that the full implications of recent archaeological data become apparent. Yet it is the power of the discourse of biblical studies which has helped to mask the circularity.

The numerous reports on site excavations and surveys of Iron I settlements have stressed, with varying degrees of emphasis, the continuity between Late Bronze Age material culture, particularly ceramic assemblages, and finds at these sites. Any alternative constructions which might try to make sense of all relevant data, particularly the anomalies which do not fit with dominant constructions, have remained unthinkable or marginalized within the discipline. It has taken a long time for significant numbers of scholars to come to the conclusion that the evidence points to indigenous development. The discourse of biblical studies, the network of associations and assumptions that have grown up reinforced by religious and political beliefs, is so strong that the prevailing belief has been that these sites are to be identified with Israel. The heat of the debate over the various 'models' of Israelite origins and the initial hostile reception to the suggestion of indigenous origins in the form of a peasant revolt only succeeded in masking the more crucial issue of the far-reaching implications of recently published archaeological data.

The grip of the discourse of biblical studies in controlling the interpretation, in preventing scholars escaping from dominant models and domain assumptions, is evident in a wide variety of archaeological publications. It is instructive to begin with Finkelstein's major publication (1988) of the results of his Land of Israel Survey and accompanying excavations at Izbet Sartah and Shiloh. This is now generally recognized as the most complete review and interpretation of archaeological evidence pertaining to the emergence of Israel which will be fundamental to future research in this area. He appears at first sight to escape the methodological bind of the Hebrew Bible which has coloured previous scholarship. He rejects the failures of 'traditional biblical archaeology' to reconstruct 'the process of Israelite Settlement'. Although he acknowledges the importance of the Hebrew Bible for the study of the history of Israel, he believes that the book of Joshua, 'the primary biblical source', redacted centuries later, presents an understanding of Israelite settlement at the end of the period of the monarchy rather than as a contemporary record of the Late Bronze–Iron Age transition (1988: 22; see also 1991: 56). Thus he appears to give methodological priority to the interpretation of archaeological data: the implications of this data for an understanding of the biblical narratives can only follow as a secondary step in the research strategy.

The real test of this strategy is provided in his discussion of 'Israelite identity' and the precise meaning of the term 'Israel' in archaeological terms. Finkelstein (1988: 27) believes the formation of

Israelite identity to have been 'a long, intricate and complex process' which was not completed until the beginning of the monarchy. Yet his definition of Israelite identity precedes his review and analysis of excavation and survey data from all regions of the country. The professed research strategy is effectively reversed and undermined:

> An important intermediate phase of this crystallization is connected with the establishment of supratribal sacral centers during the period of the Judges. The most important of these centers was the one at Shiloh, whose special role at the time is elucidated in 1 Samuel – *a historical work, as all agree*
>
> (Finkelstein 1988: 27; emphasis added)

The archaeological evidence, presented in his preliminary report on the excavations at Shiloh (1988: 205–34), does not support his bold conclusion that Shiloh was a 'supratribal sacral center' or that this site, therefore, played a crucial role in the crystallization of Israelite identity. His evidence for a sanctuary is the terraced structures in area C which he believes 'hint at the physical character of the sanctuary itself' (1988: 234; cf. also 1985a: 168–70). He thinks that these structures are 'no ordinary houses' and represent the only public buildings found at an 'Israelite' settlement site. Dever (1991: 82) rejects this claim as 'nothing but wishful thinking, hardly worthy of the hard-headed realism Finkelstein exhibits elsewhere'. The attempt to discover the archaeological remains of a sanctuary at Shiloh is governed by his acceptance of its status in the Samuel traditions. Yet the archaeological evidence is extremely flimsy, as Dever points out. Finkelstein, none the less, believes that this is not just a sanctuary but a 'supratribal sacred center'. What is it in the archaeological record which would point to such a conclusion or what evidence would an excavator have to find in order to justify such an assertion? It is clear the biblical traditions have methodological priority in his research strategy. Finkelstein, in accepting the status given to Shiloh in the books of Samuel, is predisposed to see the terraced structures in area C as the remains of this sanctuary. Furthermore, his acceptance that Israel is a tribal organization is shaped by the biblical traditions rather than the archaeological data. This claim clearly embodies an explicit assumption that 'Israel' was some form of tribal organization and religious unity. His assertion that 'all agree' that 1 Samuel is a 'historical work' hardly reflects the newer literary approaches to this text over the last decade and a half.[10] The stranglehold of the discourse of biblical studies is clearly evident in this series of assumptions which control, have methodological priority over, his interpretation of the archaeological data. It is evident in his use of the biblically derived chronological period-ization, 'the period of the Judges'. To label the period in such a way is to assert Israel's claims to the past: it prevents an examination of the archaeological data for understanding the processes at work in the settlement shifts taking place in Palestinian society of the Late Bronze and early Iron Ages.

The interpretation of Gal's preliminary findings from the Land of Israel Survey are also bound by the network of assumptions em-bodied in the discourse of biblical studies. He refers to the settlement of Issachar, thereby immediately tying his interpretation of the archaeological data to a reading of the biblical traditions: the naming of the land in terms of a biblically derived tribal designation is an expression of Israel's claim to the past. His final report, which includes survey data for the Chalcolithic through the Persian periods, still focuses upon the settlement in those areas 'relating to the tribes to whom Galilee is allotted' (Gal 1992: viii). Since it is not made explicit it can only be assumed that this is an assertion of Israel's right to the land on appeal to divine fiat. Gal opens the earlier preliminary report with a brief review of the biblical material, mentioning Issachar in the context of his survey of 'the region of Ramoth Issachar, covering the area from the Harod Valley in the south to the Jabneel Valley in the north, from the Jezreel Valley in the west to the Jordan Valley in the east' (1982: 80). Already the biblical traditions and their claims are pre-eminent. Gal reports that there were 'no sites here that could be dated to the settlement period – nor even to the Late Bronze Age'. The term 'settlement' does not need capitalization, as in Finkelstein's work, since the controlling assumption is that any settlement in this period must be 'Israelite settlement'.[11] The absence of settlement is a problem for Gal: his expectation, that because this is the land of Issachar, Israel's possession ought to be manifest in the material remains of the past, is not confirmed. He is then forced to try to make sense of the biblical traditions in the light of this silence:

> The absence of Israelite sites of the settlement period in the basalt heights is undoubtedly linked to the fate of the cities in the valleys below. Presumably, if these cities had come under Israelite control in the 12th or early 11th century, Ramoth Issachar would have become Israelite territory as well. Since our survey proves that Israelites had not yet settled the heights

at this time, it would be logical to assume that they had not yet settled in the valleys either.

(Gal 1982: 80)

However, his reasoning is not logical. It is driven by the domain assumption, derived from the biblical traditions, that any settlement at this time, in this region, would have to be Israelite. He presumes that if the Israelites had been in control of the cities they would have settled in the highlands above the cities. His reasoning illustrates clearly the way in which Palestinian history is effectively silenced: he never asks the question as to why the non-Israelite Palestinian inhabitants of the cities do not expand into the highlands. It is a question which can be posed only about Israel. The latter situation is not a puzzle for Gal: Palestinian history is not allowed any voice.

Gal tries to justify his conclusions with a brief review of the sites in the valleys, which stresses that they were not occupied by Israelites. The consistency and logic of his interpretation of the evidence is interesting. In the case of Megiddo, he concludes that despite the discovery of collared-rim ware in Stratum VI this is not 'sufficient to determine that this stratum represents an Israelite village, particularly when other features attest to the continuity of the Canaanite tradition' (Gal 1982: 80). However, the 'conspicuous' absence of collared-rim ware in Stratum IIIA at Affulleh, along with a pottery repertoire 'typical to that prevailing at the end of the Canaanite period' confirms that it cannot be Israelite (Gal 1982: 81). The absence of collared-rim ware at one site confirms that it is not Israelite but its presence at another is not enough to confirm that it is Israelite. How much collared-rim ware needs to be present in order to confirm the presence of Israelites? In the case of other sites in the valley such as Tel Kedesh, Tel Qiri, Tel Qishion, and Tel Menorah, the controlling factor in determining the ethnicity of the inhabitants is the continuity of pottery repertoires with the Late Bronze Age. Gal then tries to correlate the findings from his survey with a re-examination of the biblical traditions about Issachar. Thus the failure to mention Issachar in the story of Gideon's pursuit of the Midianites or the battle of Deborah (Judges 4) is seen as confirming that Issachar was absent from the land assigned to it. He does not puzzle over why a territory named after the tribe is empty of that tribe. Instead, references to Issachar's tenuous connection with the Samarian hills (1 Chronicles 7: 1; 1 Kings. 15: 27) results in the claim that 'in the light of this archaeological and biblical evidence, we may conclude that Issachar settled together with Manasseh within the latter's territory in the northern Samarian hills' (Gal 1982: 83). Only after the destruction of the Canaanite cities at the beginning of the tenth century BCE did some of the clans of Issachar move to the basalt heights of eastern Lower Galilee (Gal 1982: 83) – seemingly, moving to a territory which according to Gal was already named after them! It is his understanding of the biblical traditions and not the archaeological evidence which governs his assumptions about the location of Israel or particular tribes. There is nothing in the archaeological data which would allow particular sites to be identified with Issachar or Israel for that matter: the presence or absence of particular pottery types seems to have no effect upon the decision. The findings of the survey, in particular the absence of early Iron I sites in this region, ought to lead to questions about the process of settlement and the factors which affect it. Are the sites indigenous, do they show clear signs of material continuity, and, if so, why did sites appear here in the early Iron Age? But instead the concern is with trying to correlate this with the biblical traditions. Despite all the problems inherent in interpretation of the archaeological data, no thought is given to the possible relevance of this material for the pursuit of Palestinian history.

The circularity of reasoning which stems from the central problem of the discourse of biblical studies in the quest for this imagined past of ancient Israel is evident in a number of other influential and representative reports and monographs on the archaeology of early Israelite settlement. The excavation and publication of the small rural site of Giloh on a high ridge to the south-west of Jerusalem with Bethlehem on the south-east provides a case in point (Mazar 1981: 1–36; 1982: 167–78). Mazar asserts that 'it is the only site in the northern part of Judah which can be related *with much certainty* to the earliest Israelite settlers in this area' (Mazar 1981: 2; emphasis added). The certainty is dependent, however, on an understanding of the material finds at the site read in conjunction with the traditions of the Hebrew Bible. Thus, he points to sites 'which can be attributed to the early Israelite settlers' (1981: 4), such as Tell el-Ful, Khirbet Raddanah, and Khirbet Umm et-Tala which are located in similarly remote places.[12] But this is all part of the circular argument as is demonstrated by his explanation of the material culture and identification of the inhabitants of this site. He notes that the four-room house type, found at Giloh, is known in 'non-Israelite regions of the country' (1981: 10), as at Tel Qasile, Tel Sera, and Megiddo Stratum

VIB, but still insists that because it is also found at Khirbet Raddanah, Izbet Sartah, and Tel Masos 'it has become clear that this plan was common in Israelite sites of the Iron Age I' (1981: 10). The recognition that this architectural form is 'widely distributed in all parts of Palestine' (1981: 11) does not lead him to question the identity of the inhabitants of Giloh.[13] Similarly, his publication of the pottery assemblage from Giloh stresses the continuity in ceramic forms with the Late Bronze Age. He notes the problems of accepting collared-rim ware as a marker of Israelite settlement given that it is found at Sahab in Jordan, sites such as Tel Megiddo and Tell Keisan, and is absent from sites in the northern Negev. Yet he still concludes that 'the fact remains, however, that in the central mountain sites which can be related *with confidence* to the Israelite settlers, these pithoi were not only popular, but indeed the most common pottery type' (1981: 30; emphasis added). His confidence is not drawn from the archaeological data, however, since these sites can only be regarded as Israelite if one accepts the picture presented in the biblical traditions. Mazar (1981: 30) notes the socio-economic importance of collared-rim pithoi for storage at such sites but fails to expand upon this observation because the search for ancient Israel, rather than an explanation of the archaeological data, is all-consuming.

Giloh is described as a 'fortified herdsmen's village' (1981: 32) which adds to our understanding of 'the complex process of Israelite conquest and settlement' (1981: 36). What is interesting about his presentation is that, despite a number of guarded comments about the problems of interpretation or the significance of the data, he is able to present the archaeological evidence as though it is this that points to the conclusion that ancient Israel has been revealed. This is exacerbated in his more popular presentation of his findings (1982: 167–78) where he refers to the house form as reminiscent of the houses which became common during the 'period of the Judges' (1982: 169). The problematic distribution of ceramic or architectural types is overcome when the reader is informed that 'the identification of the settlers with the earliest families of Judah who settled in this region suggests itself naturally' (1982: 170). But why is it such a natural conclusion? Suddenly we move from qualified statements concerning material features used to identify particular groups to the reality of ancient Israel in control of the land: 'The architecture of the excavated private house, apparently an early example of typical Israelite private architecture, reinforces this conclusion; the site at Giloh effectively illustrates the process of Israelite settlement in the central hill country' (1982: 170). Yet the ambiguous archaeological data cannot confirm any such conclusion. Such an assertion is dependent upon factors external to the archaeological data, namely the biblically inspired idea that Israel is to be found in the Palestinian hill country.

We find similar problems in the interpretation of a small Iron I site on a ridge in the northern part of the central hill country. Mazar (1982: 27) describes this site, in the opening paragraph of his report, as 'an open cult place situated on a hill in the Land of Manasseh and dated to the period of the Judges'. Palestinian history is silenced before it can have a chance to speak: the labels used emphasize that this time and this space belong to Israel. He concentrates on the bronze figurine found at the site, which despite its obvious connections with indigenous Palestinian religious iconography and imagery is thought to be in the possession of Israelites:

> The use of a sophisticated bronze figurine by Israelite settlers of the 12th century B.C. . . . can be explained in the light of our knowledge of the continuation of Canaanite metallurgy during the Iron I, as evidenced from the finds at Megiddo, Beth-shan, and Tell es-Saidiyeh.
>
> (Mazar 1982: 32)

It seems they either obtained this by trade or, less plausibly, through manufacture by an Israelite craftsman inspired by Canaanite traditions. Again the pottery finds are said to show continuity with the Late Bronze Age. Whereas for Gal such a continuity confirmed that sites in 'the land of Issachar' were not Israelite, it does not seem to deter Mazar from seeing this site as Israelite. However, we rapidly move from this to discover the reality of ancient Israel. The site is said to be located in the midst of a cluster of Iron I sites which should 'probably be related to the settlement process of the Israelite tribes in the area' (1982: 37).[14] The so-called bull site is then considered to be 'a central ritual place for the group of settlements' (1982: 37–8), a conclusion which then leads to a further conclusion that 'Israelites, probably of the tribe of Manasseh, were builders of our site' (1982: 38). Thus a chain of 'probabilities', based on assumptions drawn from the biblical traditions, concludes with the discovery of Israel. Here is Israel located in the land, located in the past. This imagined past, however, has blocked any attempt, however tentative, to explore alternative constructions of the past based upon the archaeological evidence freed from the straitjacket of the Hebrew Bible.

Mazar's (1990) recent general review of the archaeology of 'the land of the Bible' shows a growing awareness of the problems of interpretation which have governed this search. He makes a conscious attempt to use the term 'Palestine' rather than 'land of Israel' or 'Eretz Israel' to refer to the region. However, the qualification of the term 'Palestine' with the phrase 'the land of the Bible' (1990: 33 n. 1) indicates that the region has little intrinsic value on its own except as the backdrop for understanding the Bible. The volume is designed 'to illuminate the *realia* of the biblical narrative' (1990: xv) which means that it is Israelite rather than Palestinian history in general which is bound to be the focus of attention. Mazar is still able to refer to the 'Israelite Conquest' despite the fact that most commentators have accepted that the growing body of new archaeological data from the region has fatally undermined Albright's proposals. He adds that 'in examining the archaeological aspect of the conquest of Canaan, we shall concentrate on the *factual content* at the various sites which are related to the conquest by biblical tradition' (1990: 329; emphasis added). He urges due caution in trying to distinguish different ethnic groups at various sites but once again is able to conclude that the newer surveys and excavations enable a better understanding of 'the settlement process of the Israelite tribes' (1990: 329). Thus he uses the rhetorical device, which we have met on several occasions, whereby the reader is alerted to difficulties and problems of interpretation, before advancing to a much more certain conclusion. The device serves to convince the reader that due objectivity is observed but at the end of the process of cross-examination a trustworthy verdict can be announced:

> Consequently, defining a distinctively "Israelite" material culture is a difficult venture. Our departure point in this issue should be sites which according to biblical traditions are Israelite during the period of the Judges, such as Shiloh, Mizpah, Dan, and Beersheba; settlements with similar material culture in the same region can be defined as Israelite.
>
> (Mazar 1990: 353)

The problem of ethnic identification is overcome once again by appeal to the biblical traditions. It is the biblical text which has methodological priority rather than the archaeological evidence; for, as Mazar admits, there is nothing in the archaeological record alone which would allow the attribution of particular sites in the Late Bronze–Iron Age transition to different ethnic groups. He is still able to refer to Israel during this period as 'a new national entity' (1990: 334) while his conscious attempt to use the term 'Palestine' is forgotten in favour of references to 'the tribal territories of Manasseh and Ephraim in the central hill country of Palestine' (1990: 335). The continuing power of the discourse of biblical studies is able to hold together this interlocking network of ideas despite the profound challenges to its central assumption that Israel is to be located in the Late Bronze–Iron Age transition. The pursuit of Palestinian history is hindered by the failure to accept that the term 'Israelite' has no archaeological meaning but is imposed upon the evidence by the claims of the biblical text.

The most noteworthy attempt to deal with the problem of ethnicity and 'Israelite identity' has come from Finkelstein who believes distinctions between ethnic groups at that time were 'apparently still vague' (1988: 27). The reader is not informed as to the nature of the evidence which forms the basis for his understanding of the self-definition of various groups. In an apparent disagreement with Mazar, he states that it is doubtful whether a twelfth century BCE inhabitant of Giloh would have described herself or himself as an 'Israelite'. Finkelstein employs the rhetorical device of measured caution before moving to a much firmer conclusion: 'Nonetheless, we refer to this site and its material culture as "Israelite"' (1988: 27). It does not matter if the inhabitants' own self-identity is different since the search for and location of ancient Israel is all-important. Israel is able to claim possession of the land in retrospect:

> an Israelite during the Iron I period was anyone whose descendants – as early as the days of Shiloh (first half of the 11th century BCE) or as late as the beginning of the Monarchy – described themselves as Israelites.
>
> (Finkelstein 1988: 27)

This is a stronger, more encompassing definition of 'Israelite' identity than we have encountered elsewhere. It is a label which is used to claim the past of the inhabitants of sites which are to be located in the biblically defined territory of the Israelite monarchy. They are 'Israelites', regardless of their own self-understanding, because this is the land of Israel; their territory and their past belongs to Israel. Once again the controlling factor in all this, as we have already noted, is an acceptance of the essential historicity of the narratives in 1 Samuel (see Miller 1991a: 97–9).

The conceptualization and control of the past inherent in Finkelstein's definition is drawn into sharp relief by the problem of Galilee, as he is aware (1988: 28). Here is a region of Palestine which is not considered to be part of the territorial jurisdiction of the early monarchy. It does not therefore qualify as Israelite under the terms of his definition. Furthermore, he argues, against Aharoni, that Iron I settlement in the area was later than previously thought, belonging to a later or secondary phase rather than as part of the first phase of settlement (1988: 323–30). As is well known, these settlements are not characterized by the collared-rim ware common in the central hill country and other areas of Palestine. Yet none of these seemingly fatal objections prevents him from insisting that it is 'Israelite'. It then becomes part of his definition of what it is to be 'Israelite':

> Israelites in the Iron I are those people who were in a process of sedentarization in those parts of the country that were part of Saul's monarchy, and in Galilee. The term 'Israelite' is used therefore in this book, when discussing the Iron I period, as no more than a *terminus technicus* for 'hill country people in the process of settling down'.
>
> (Finkelstein 1988: 28)

The definition is so wide that it encompasses all inhabitants of those areas which have been designated as Israelite.[15] The definition is not dependent upon archaeological evidence but stems from a reading of the Samuel narrative in the Hebrew Bible. Finkelstein has realized the inherent problems of such a definition by his admission that he would consider omitting the term 'Israelite' from the discussion of Iron I settlement and refer instead to 'hill country settlers' until the period of the monarchy (1991: 52). The concession is significant since it confirms the growing recognition that the archaeological evidence from recent surveys and excavations cannot be used to differentiate Israelite and indigenous material culture. The reluctance of Finkelstein or Mazar, for instance, to accept the full implications of this conclusion illustrates the difficulties of overcoming and breaking away from a dominant discourse. Finkelstein might be willing to omit the term Israelite and substitute a circumlocution, 'hill country settlers', but is unable to talk of indigenous Palestinian settlement. In fact, these caveats have little practical effect upon his subsequent discussion since he continues to talk of 'Israelite Settlement'. The concession is important, however, because once the label 'Israelite' is removed the debate is freed from the control of the Hebrew Bible and its conceptualization and control of the past. Instead it can become a discussion of the processes involved in and the factors affecting Palestinian settlement during the Late Bronze–Iron Age transition and later. It allows a comparison, or encourages strategies designed to elucidate a comparison, of regional variations in settlement throughout Palestine and neighbouring regions. This requires intensive survey of all areas of Palestine, not just those deemed by the discourse of biblical studies to be Israelite.

Yet it is not a set of shared assumptions that is likely to be overturned easily. The unease which is engendered as the implications of this change slowly seep through is expressed in the plaintive cry of Shanks:

> The settlement of the central hill-country of Canaan in the Iron Age I is of special interest because these settlements are thought to be Israelite. People want to know what happened here and what it meant to be Israelite. If these people were not Israelites, they have as much interest to us as Early Bronze Age IV people. That does not mean we are uninterested, but it does mean considerably less interest than if they were Israelites. In short, we want to know what all this evidence – and there is a great deal of it – can plausibly tell us about early Israel. Caution certainly is in order, but isn't there something affirmative to say, even within the limits imposed by caution?
>
> (Shanks 1991: 66)[16]

Thus we discover that these settlements are of 'special interest' because they are *thought* to be Israelite. Interestingly the inhabitants of settlements which are not Israelite or from other archaeological periods, said to be of 'interest', remain anonymous. They are 'Early Bronze Age IV people' not Palestinians. Despite the profession of interest, it is clear that Palestinian history is of no concern at all. It is the search for ancient Israel which is important: Shanks's message is that scholars should concern themselves with this even though it is only 'thought', not demonstrated, that these are Israelite settlements. Where does this thought come from? It can only come from an acceptance that the biblical claims in Joshua and Judges are to be accepted as historically viable. Yet it is a thought that is fundamental to the theological and political assumptions which have helped to shape and sustain the discourse of biblical studies.

What we have seen with the sample of discussions above, and this could easily have been expanded considerably, is that the existence or lack of existence of particular material features is used differently in order to locate Israel in the central hill country, Galilee, and Negev. At some sites, we are told that particular features of the material culture, principally collared-rim ware or the four-room house, are important indicators of Israelite presence but that at other sites their absence is not significant. At all these sites it is acknowledged that features of the material culture have continuity with the Late Bronze Age, but the explanation for this seems to be that Israelites have borrowed techniques and styles from the indigenous population, usually a population they are at war with or from which they are isolated. It is clear in these comparisons that it is the biblical text and not the archaeological data which determines the definition. The reader is often left wondering how much collared-rim ware needs to be present or absent in order to confirm or deny the presence of Israelites. Finkelstein has tried to address some of these issues by concentrating upon geographical location, site size, settlement pattern, architecture, and site layout (1988: 29–33) in order to sharpen his discussion. However, in each of these cases the principal value of the evidence is in helping to determine the socio-economic and environmental factors affecting regional settlement in Palestine. The implication of this observation is continually inhibited by his search for ancient Israel as conceived through his reading of the biblical traditions:

> we again note that the historical biblical text, *being the only available source*, provides the basis for identifying the principal regions of Israelite Settlement, and at the Iron I sites in these regions, researchers have discovered a material culture with distinctive features, some of which are appropriate for a poor isolated society in the incipient phase of sedentarization and organization.
>
> (Finkelstein 1988: 29–30)

However, there is no logical connection between the two parts of this sentence. It is clear that it is not the archaeological features of these sites which are determinative of the label 'Israelite Settlement'. This just continues the circularity of the discourse of biblical studies as illustrated in his assertion that 'Israelite cultural traits must therefore be deduced from the Iron I sites in the central hill country, especially the southern sector, *where the identity of the population is not disputed*' (1988: 28; emphasis added). Yet, like so many other archaeologists, he notes that all these material features have precedents or connections with features at 'non-Israelite' sites or previous periods and that they are probably determined by topographic and economic considerations. The last point is vital to the pursuit of Palestinian history but its implications are denied by the search for ancient Israel. This is evident in his subsequent presentation of survey and site information of which the discussion of the 'territory of Benjamin' is typical:

> The accumulated archaeological data for Benjamin, *combined with the biblical descriptions of the days of Samuel and Saul,* indicate that the main Israelite activity in Benjamin in Iron I was concentrated in the eastern part of the ridge and the desert fringe.... The territory of Benjamin was thus divided along ethnic lines. The Hivites settled in the west and the Israelites in the east. In any case, *we are unable to single out differences in material culture between these two ethnic entities living in the territory of Benjamin at the beginning of Iron I.*
> (Finkelstein 1988: 65; emphasis added)

It is abundantly clear that despite the sophisticated use of percentage counts of pottery types or the comparison of other material features, there is nothing in the archaeological record which allows one site to be labelled 'Israelite' or another 'Hivite'. Finkelstein does not even attempt to discuss Hivite identity: it is a label which is taken over from the Hebrew Bible. He admits that he does not know how the Hivites came to be in the region or how the cities came to be Israelite. This ethnic differentiation is drawn on the basis of the biblical traditions despite the fact that there is nothing to confirm this in the archaeological data.

As we have seen throughout, the puzzle for archaeologists is that they have assumed that ancient Israel inhabited particular areas of the country and therefore it ought to be possible to distinguish Israelite occupation. Even after it became clear that particular ceramic and architectural forms were found in diverse parts of Palestine or in areas which the Bible does not reckon to be Israelite, the drive to find Israel continued. It is the discourse of biblical studies which has encouraged this blinkered pursuit of an imagined past – a situation which has been reinforced by the political needs of the modern state of Israel to find itself in the past. Despite the fact that the increasing body of archaeological data and the undermining of historical-critical approaches to the biblical texts have effectively shattered the dominant paradigm, it has such a hold on the conceptions and consciousness of Western and Israeli scholars that it has clung on tenaciously in the face of such overwhelming dissonance. This is one of the best illustrations of the power of the discourse of biblical studies to silence Palestinian history and obstruct any alternative construction or claim to the past.

The politics of archaeology, evident in so many different regions of the world, has been raised to a fine art in biblical studies. Anderson (1991: 183) notes that archaeology is such a profoundly political enterprise that the personnel of a colonial state are unlikely to be aware of the fact. This deeply political shaping of archaeology has rarely been acknowledged in the discourse of biblical studies. It is not as if this is a matter that has not been recognized by political commentators such as Elon:

> In the political culture of Israel, the symbolic role of archaeology is immediately evident. Israeli archaeologists, professionals and amateurs, are not merely digging for knowledge and objects, but for the reassurance of roots, which they find in the ancient Israelite remains scattered throughout the country.
>
> (Elon 1983: 280)

He also refers to the treatment of the discovery of the Dead Sea Scrolls as assuming 'a hallowed air', considered by many to be 'almost titles of real estate, like deeds of possession to a contested country' (1983: 285). Yet the discourse of biblical studies has tried to present the search for these roots, the excavation and mapping of various sites, as the objective search for knowledge. The critical issue which Elon identifies, the implications of archaeology or the constructions of the past for contemporary struggles over a contested land, is ignored or denied in the discourse of biblical studies. The stranglehold of this discourse, its ability to disguise the political shaping of the past, is revealed ironically and unexpectedly in Silberman's (1992) review of recent scholarship. Silberman remains strangely silent on the politics of this new archaeology of Israel. In reporting the results of Finkelstein's survey, he refers without comment to 'Israelite settlements' and says:

> Thus the founding fathers of the Israelite nation can now be seen as scattered groups of pastoralists living in small family groups and grazing their flocks on hilltops and isolated valleys in the hill country, reacting in their own way to the far-reaching social and economic changes that swept over the entire eastern Mediterranean world.
>
> (Silberman 1992: 30)

The archaeology of Israel, with all its hidden assumptions, has exerted a subtle influence on the new search for ancient Israel.

THE RECENT SEARCH FOR ANCIENT ISRAEL

The switch in research strategies to a greater emphasis on intensive regional survey, at a time when biblical studies has been exposed to various movements in the humanities and social sciences which have undermined its notions of text, has helped to undermine some of the classic constructions of Israel's imagined past. However, the search for ancient Israel has continued unabated. The critiques of aspects of the dominant discourse emanating from Ahlström, Lemche, Coote and Whitelam, Davies, Thompson, and others, have added to the fracturing of these models. However, they also embody an inherent confusion. While their critiques focus upon the temporal location of ancient Israel, whether it is to be found in the early or later Iron Age, the Persian or Hellenistic periods, the tentative attempts to articulate the need to divorce the historical study of the region from biblical studies have not been clearly worked out. It is a confusion which has contributed to the silencing of Palestinian history.[17] They have been involved in a 'new' search for ancient Israel. It is only with the failure of the search that the implications for the study of the history of the region, the need to reformulate and rethink the task, have become clearer. The debate has centred around three important and closely related areas: the date of the biblical traditions and their relevance for historical construction, the significance of the Merneptah stele, and the interpretation of newer archaeological evidence in the search for ancient Israel or the pursuit of Palestinian history.

There is a widespread perception that one of the major shared assumptions of the recent search for ancient Israel, part of Coote's 'new horizon', is the rejection of the biblical traditions for historical construction of the Late Bronze and early Iron Ages. There are clearly underlying connections but by no means unanimity on the understanding and dating of the relevant biblical materials. Ahlström's view that the biblical text is a product of faith which was not meant to report on or preserve historical facts (1986: 2) would meet with general agreement, whereas his ideological explanation of the Exodus traditions (1986: 45–55) would not. Furthermore, while he claims that the book of Judges is of little use for historical construction (1986: 75), his understanding of the monarchy, and his construction of the Late Bronze–Iron Age transition, is tied to the biblical traditions.

Ahlström's methodology is one where he appears able to pick out relevant and trustworthy historical data, although the reader is not supplied with clear criteria which explain these choices (1986: 57–83). Thus, although the primary aim of the biblical text, for Ahlström, was not to preserve historical data, his approach to the texts is not radically different from many standard histories of ancient Israel. For example, he claims that 'any reconstruction of the central hill country for the period between Merneptah's mention of Israel and the emergence of the Israelite kingdom under Saul' (1986: 74) must take into account the biblical traditions. It has to be analysed carefully 'to sort historical data from theological fiction'. He acknowledges that the Hebrew Bible as the product of faith 'represents theological reflections of later periods about earlier events' (1986: 74), yet he is able to distinguish reliable historical data which pertain to the Late Bronze–Iron Age transition. This means that, in effect, Ahlström has been locked into the search for ancient Israel, despite the production of his massive volume on the history of ancient Palestine. It is Israel, or the search for this entity, which dominates his narrative of the Late Bronze–Iron Age transition and early Iron Ages. It is a focus of attention which obscures and hinders his own attempts to formulate a strategy for the pursuit of Palestinian history. Palestinian history becomes, in effect, confined to those periods or areas where Israel is not located rather than the overarching object of study.

One of the most striking aspects of the recent search for ancient Israel, reflecting a growing trend in the discipline as a whole, is the attempt to push the date of the biblical traditions ever later. Whitelam, for instance, has argued that the biblical traditions regarding the pre-monarchic period, as conceived by biblical writers, were not reflections of historical reality but rather reflections of perceptions of the past by the later writers. The social production of the biblical traditions, particularly as products of the second Temple communities, has become of increasing concern over recent years.[18] The traditions of Israel's origins as external to Palestine, as presented in the Deuteronomistic History, are in conflict with traditions contained in the books of Chronicles which present Israel as indigenous to the land (Whitelam 1989). Whitelam interprets this as a reflection of competing factional disputes over the land between those returning from exile in Babylonia and the indigenous population around Jerusalem and its environs. Lemche, Thompson, and Davies have been among the most vociferous in arguing for a late dating of the biblical traditions in the Persian or Hellenistic periods. Most of those involved in the new search would accept Lemche's underlying principle that *'the gap between written fixation and the "underlying events" is too great to permit us to accept the tradition as a primary source for our reconstruction of the past'* (1985: 377–8; his emphasis).[19] He concludes that the preconditions for the concept of Israel as a unity did not arise before the monarchy and that a 'pan-Israelite' historical writing could not be any earlier than the Exile (Lemche 1985: 384).

This would appear to free the study of Palestinian history for the Late Bronze–Iron Age transition and early Iron Age from the stranglehold of the biblical traditions. Yet the discussion has been concerned with the possibilities of writing a history of ancient Israel effectively overshadowing any concern with Palestinian history. The attacks upon text-based approaches to the history of ancient Israel, the challenge to source-critical analyses in the light of newer literary approaches, helped to undermine the confident production of a whole series of volumes on Israelite history in the 1970s and 1980s. This at least gave pause for thought as to the nature of the enterprise.[20] However, attempts to redefine the nature of the historiographic task by appealing to the growing body of archaeological data for the region were still locked into the search for ancient Israel (Whitelam 1989; Thompson 1987: 13–40). Davies (1985: 169–70) had urged that if there were no reliable *written* sources for the period, then it was not possible to write a history. The debates focused upon the type of history which was possible, a move from the event-centred, personality-dominated narratives of traditional biblical histories to a Braudelian-inspired concern with social history in its broadest terms (Coote and Whitelam 1987; Whitelam 1989). But, at the point when some were arguing that the study of the Late Bronze–Iron Age transition and early Iron Age had been freed from the constraints of the periodization and characterization of the biblical traditions, the new search remained in the grip of the powerful assumptions of the discourse of biblical studies. It remained a search for ancient Israel rather than a pursuit of Palestinian history.[21]

The central confusion between the relationship of Israelite to Palestinian history remained the stumbling block to a realization of the far-reaching implications of the shifts which were taking place in biblical studies and related disciplines. Thompson's vision of an 'independent history' is couched in terms of the history of Israel rather than of Palestine. The independence sought is from the control of the biblical text to define the nature of Israelite history, its periodization, and major concerns, as has been the case with standard 'biblical histories'. But it has struggled to break free from a series of domain assumptions informing the discourse of biblical studies which has shaped the search for Israel for over a century. Although Thompson talks of a 'new historiographical paradigm' (1992b: 2), the full implications of the series of shifts he identifies under this label remain obscured by Israel's control of the past. The talk is still of researching 'Israel's origins' (1992a: 107) as 'methodologically apart from the late Judaean historiography about its past' (1992a: 108). The effect of the concern with the late, ideological construction of the past has been to push the starting point of the history of Israel to later periods, producing essentially a history of the gaps. For Soggin and Miller and Hayes the starting point has to be delayed until the period of the Davidic monarchy, whereas for Lemche, Thompson, and Davies the focus of attention switches to the Persian and Hellenistic periods. The effect is that as preceding periods become devoid of history the focus on Israel and its past is so all-consuming that the gaps become of little intrinsic interest as the gaze follows the temporal movement of ancient Israel. Lemche, Ahlström, Coote, Thompson, and Whitelam refer to the desire to pursue a wider regional history of Palestine but it is rarely clearly demarcated from the search for ancient Israel. Thompson, for instance, can state that 'the issue of whether a history of Israel can be written at all must take central stage in all future discussions' (1992a: 110). Yet the logic of his argument, as with others involved in the new search, is not prosecuted with sufficient vigour in order to articulate the priority of the study of the history of ancient Palestine divorced from the concerns and control of biblical studies. The recent search has shown how difficult it is to escape from the limits of a particular discourse which shapes academic research in ways of which the participants are often unaware. The full implications of the increasing location of biblical traditions in the Persian and Hellenistic periods or their relationship to historical reality have not been worked out in freeing the past from the control of Israel or of the biblical traditions. The challenge to the dominant discourse, the attempts to offer alternative constructions of the past, have remained bound by other of the domain assumptions which have shaped historical research in biblical studies helping to marginalize and silence the study of the history of ancient Palestine.

The Merneptah stele, first discovered in 1896, containing the first mention of Israel in an extrabiblical text, has begun to assume an importance in recent discussions similar to that of the Tel Dan inscription in the defence of the biblical traditions of David. The well-known, yet tantalizing reference to Israel's defeat at the hands of Pharaoh Merneptah, 'Israel is laid waste, his seed is not', which appears on the obverse of a victory hymn over the Libyans has become a centre of focus in defence of 'biblical Israel' against the revisionism of the new search. Bimson (1991) provides a spirited defence of the biblically inspired imagined past of Israel based on his interpretation of the stele. He is adamant that 'there is no reason at all to doubt that the Israel of the stela is biblical Israel of the pre-monarchic period' (1991: 14), arguing that 'it is quite unreasonable' to deny this correlation. The appeal to what is reasonable is part of the rhetoric of objectivity in order to support the dominant con-struction of Israel's past within the discourse of biblical studies. Any opposing views are by definition unreasonable and to be rejected. However, the reasonableness of Bimson's conclusion is not immediately apparent. He does not elaborate on the nature of 'biblical Israel' in terms of whether or not it is a picture drawn from the Pentateuch, the Deuteronomistic History, Joshua, Judges, Chronicles, or an amalgam of all these and other biblical materials. He acknowledge that the stele does not provide information on the social organization of this entity Israel but he remains 'reasonably sure that Merneptah's Israel was a tribal confederation, such as we find reflected in the Song of Deborah' (1991: 14). It is difficult to see what is reasonable about this conclusion. The notion that Israel was a tribal organization is drawn from his understanding of biblical traditions.[22] It is only reasonable if one accepts his reading of the traditions and the assumption that these traditions in some way reflect the historical reality of the Late Bronze–Iron Age transition. It still remains to make a clear and unequivocal connection between the entity mentioned in the stele and Bimson's biblical Israel.[23] The only clear information provided by the inscription is that some entity called Israel was encountered in the region by the Pharaoh's troops towards the end of the thirteenth century BCE: it does not confirm or deny whether this was a tribal organization or 'geographically extensive'.

The stele has also played a central role for some of those involved in the new search. Ahlström's distinctive contribution to the discus-sion has been to insist that the term 'Israel' was originally a territorial designation for the central hill country of Palestine. He asserts this on the basis of his proposal that the final lines of the stele have a distinctive ring structure which equates different elements. Thus Hurru is composed of Canaan and Israel where Canaan refers to the more densely populated coastal lowlands and Israel designates the hill country. He traces the development of the use of the term Israel from a territorial term, to a political term designating the state in the central hill country established by Saul, to its later restriction to the northern kingdom until 722 BCE. It later became a religious term to designate the people of Yahweh, was then restricted to the returnees under Ezra's law, before eventually becoming an ideological term for Judaism (Ahlström 1986: 118). On the basis of his understanding of its origins as a geographical term, he goes on to argue that 'it was with the emergence of Saul's kingdom that the name Israel came to signify a political entity' (Ahlström 1986: 40). Ahlström was one of the first scholars to question the common application of ethnic labels to Iron I sites supposedly on the basis of the archaeological evidence. He was also a pioneer in articulating the need for the study of Palestinian history, a long-term project which was seemingly realized with his posthumous volume (1993). Paradoxically, however, he has perpetuated the search for ancient Israel and its claim to the past. His focus is clearly upon Israel and Israelite self-definition marginalizing any Palestinian perspective. The territorial label of the central hill country as Israel, the modern occupied West Bank, reinforces, however unwittingly, the claim of Israel to its possession through historic right.

The Merneptah stele has also figured prominently in Coote's exploration of the 'new horizon' which he perceives as resulting from the new search. His description of Israel as 'a Palestinian tribe or tribal confederation' is based upon a reading of the Merneptah stele and anthropological studies of tribal societies (1990: 71–93). The discussion of tribal organization, social relations, and settlement provide a valuable basis for the study of Palestinian history in general. However, like Bimson, he draws a series of far-reaching conclusions which can hardly be supported by an appeal to the ambiguous reference provided by Merneptah's scribes. Israel, for Coote, was a political entity, in his words 'a name for a structure of power' (Coote 1991: 40), a tribal organization, which imperial Egypt was forced to confront and then sustain in order to bolster its empire against the Sea Peoples and the Hittites to the north (see also 1991: 45). His valuable discussion of political and social relations in the Late Bronze and Early Iron Ages is undermined by the distraction of his search for ancient Israel. His appeal to anthropological parallels in understanding the nature of tribal society – Israel was not 'a single religious group, family, nation, race, nor ethnic group' (1990: 71) – is governed by a concern to find Israel. Palestinian history remains muted and marginalized. Coote is able to assert that 'the origin of Israel, while indeterminate, is not, in my view, a mystery' (1990: viii). While recognizing that the entity referred to as Israel by Merneptah's scribes pre-dates the shift to highland settlement (1990: 72), he still makes a direct link between this entity and the inhabitants of the settlements, continuing the assumption which has dominated the discourse of biblical studies and shaped the archaeology of ancient Israel: 'In the twelfth and eleventh centuries, people named Israel inhabited recently founded villages in the highland' (1990: 72). The appeal to social anthropology and historical parallels has failed to free the study of the history of ancient Palestine from Israel's dominance of the past. This dominance is so complete that Coote is able to state that 'the political integrity of much of Palestine depended upon Israel's viability' (1990: 75).

The Merneptah stele is very similar to the Tel Dan inscription in that it offers very little unambiguous evidence about the nature and location of ancient Israel or its connection with the picture presented in different parts of the Hebrew Bible. The problem turns on the significance and meaning of the determinative which has been applied by the Egyptian scribes to Israel compared with other entities or locations mentioned in the same context. Israel appears to be distinguished from the place names Ashkelon, Gezer, and Yano'am by a determinative which is used elsewhere to designate 'people' or 'foreign people'. This fact has been used to support the imagined pasts of Albright and Alt that Israel was external to Palestine, indicating a nomadic group possibly in the process of sedentarization, as well as the recent constructions by Ahlström and Coote proposing that Israel was indigenous. There clearly appears to be some differentiation intended, but the wide-ranging, often competing conclusions which have been proposed on the basis of this tantalizing reference move way beyond the available evidence. The most that the inscription reveals is that Israel was in existence in the region at this time and that it may have been of *relative* significance. It can hardly be used to support the elaborate theories and extravagant claims that have been made on its behalf. This is, after all, a royal inscription and subject to all the caveats that accompany royal propaganda: the Egyptian scribes in mentioning victory over these entities are hardly likely to claim the defeat of non-entities. The stele represents a particular perception of the past embodying important ideological and political claims on behalf of the Egyptian Pharaoh.

Many of the constructions of this past have focused upon a supposed geographical arrangement of this section of the stele. This supposed south–north arrangement has been used to support a northern location for Israel and, as we have seen, underlies Coote's claim that Israel was a Palestinian tribal organization used by the Pharaoh as a buffer against the Hittite threat from the north.[24] Yet this is hardly conclusive since this perceived arrangement is dependent upon the mention of two or three towns and a further unidentified site. The location of Yano'am is unknown and disputed, which means that attempts to draw wide-ranging conclusions about the geographical arrangement of the text and the location of Israel move way beyond the evidence.[25] The ring structure of the text is equally questionable since it appears to be restricted to this short section at the end of the inscription immediately preceding the usual list of Pharaonic titles. Even if there is a formal literary structure, as Ahlström, Edelman, and Bimson suggest, it is difficult to be sure that this then reflects a geographical arrangement given the small number of sites mentioned. It certainly provides no information on the social organization or geographical extent of the entity Israel. Yet the reading of the Merneptah stele comes to form part of the interlocking network of assumptions which inform the archaeology of ancient Israel: Israel is to be connected with the settlement shift to the highlands of Palestine in the Late Bronze–Iron Age transition, therefore Merneptah's Israel must be located in the hill country. The circularity is self-confirming since the reference in the stele is then appealed to, as we have seen with Bimson, to confirm the archaeological connection which then has been used to justify the picture of 'biblical Israel' in Joshua and Judges. The entity Israel, one of a number of different entities which the Pharaoh claims to have defeated, is no longer an aspect or participant in Palestinian history; it dominates the whole of Palestinian history preventing the construction of any alternative claim to the past.

The other characteristic feature of the new search has been a self-conscious attempt to question the biblically inspired constructions of the past in the light of social anthropology and the interpretation of archaeological data from the region. Lemche's massive tome on early Israel began as a critique of Mendenhall and Gottwald, incorporating a wealth of anthropological detail on the nature of social relationships in ancient Palestine. He acknowledges that the discussion of current anthropological work takes up a disproportionate amount of space (1985: xiv). Yet he provides one of the most comprehensive treatments of anthropological theory and data as part of a critique of what he terms 'the revolution hypothesis' and the earlier constructions of the past by Alt–Noth and Albright–Bright. Similarly, Coote and Whitelam (1987), Coote (1991), and Thompson (1992a) rely heavily upon social anthropology in trying to understand the nature of social relations in Palestine in the Late Bronze and early Iron Ages. Yet throughout these works it is the distraction of the label Israel, the distraction of the search for ancient Israel and the power of Israel's imagined past presented by the biblical writers, which continues to hinder and confuse the pursuit of Palestinian history.

Ahlström (1986) is less explicit in his use of anthropological parallels but was one of the first to question the veracity of ethnic labels used to differentiate Iron I sites. He was well aware that archaeology alone reveals nothing about the origins of Israel but provides information on the settlement patterns and cultural traits of the population of Palestine 'during the period in which Israel appeared in history' (1986: 2; 1991a: 19). He notes that the interpretation of archaeological data has been guided by a pan-Israelite ideology (1991a: 24).[26] This increase in settlements in the sparsely populated hills in the thirteenth to twelfth centuries BCE is understood by Ahlström as motivated by a desire to escape from the wars and upheavals of the period (see also Callaway, Coote and Whitelam). He appeals to the Amarna letters to show that it is possible to deduce that social unrest and discontent were primary forces which prompted the movement of population groups from all directions (Ahlström 1986: 18–19). However, the material evidence for the central hill country of the fourteenth to thirteenth centuries BCE was Canaanite, as was the material culture of the Negev for the period c. 1200 BCE: this is evident in the house types and the pottery (1986: 27–8).[27] His summary (1986: 83) of the period as showing a material and religious cultural continuum from the Late Bronze Age to the Iron I period is echoed in the works of Lemche (1985), Coote and Whitelam (1987), Coote (1991), and Thompson (1992a).

All this would appear to point to a clear articulation of the broad features of Palestinian history in the Late Bronze–Iron Age transition. Ahlström makes clear that the settlement shift is indigenous to Palestine and explainable in terms of social and political processes at work throughout the region. However, this construction of the past, the further probing of Palestinian history from this perspective, is hindered because of his continued fascination with the search for ancient Israel. Thus he describes his study as principally an attempt 'to situate the Israelites in history' (1986: 1). Despite his questioning of many domain assumptions of standard reconstructions of the period, he is bound by biblically based reconstructions of the pre-monarchic and monarchic periods of Israelite history. Thus he argues that the increase in cultivation in the highlands led to bigger clans and villages and eventually to centralization and to 'the formation of an extensive political unit, the territorial state' (Ahlström 1986: 20). Israel again emerges to dominate and effectively silence the Palestinian past.[28]

Lemche complains of the circularity of interpretation common within biblical studies, pointing out that the period around 1200 BCE is hardly ever described as an archaeological phase rather than a historical period:

> The reason for this seems to be the fact that some archaeologists appear to find it more fascinating to hunt for 'proof' of the presence of Israel, since even the most minute changes in architecture, pottery, town lay-out, and so forth, have been taken to show the presence of new (foreign) elements among the existing population at this time.
>
> (Lemche 1985: 386)

He calls for a description of the Late Bronze–Iron Age transition in Palestine from an 'international perspective' along similar lines to the archaeologically based historical surveys of the Mediterranean, particularly for Greece.[29] He points out that merely to note settlement change, like Alt, does not confirm that this is the result of external immigration. What is needed is a clear understanding as to the continuity, or discontinuity, of material culture, which accompanies such settlement shifts. This, he notes, was not possible for Alt since his conclusions were based on available textual material, and he did not have access to current archaeological information. This led to an important conclusion which has resonance with others involved in the new search:

> Our conclusion is therefore unambiguous: archaeology and text may not be subsumed under a single formula. Thus it was correct to dismiss the importance of the Settlement traditions

in the OT and to see them instead as expressions of a very late
view of the nation's origins which arose in the last part of the
monarchical period and particularly in the period after the loss
of national independence. The consequences of this fact ought
to be taken seriously. It is no longer legitimate to attempt to
'save the appearances' of certain portions of the Settlement
narratives. Rather, it is the very idea of Settlement, as it appears
in the OT, which must be done away with, for historical
reasons. In one's reconstruction of the course of events towards
the close of the second millennium one ought at least in the first
instance to ignore completely the OT traditions, and instead
attempt to reconstruct the archaeological history of the period
without considering whether it was Israelites or Canaanites
who were active at one site or another. If an archaeological
description of the culture of Iron Age Palestine shows that
there was continuity between this period and the culture of the
Late Bronze Age, then we ought simply to avoid speaking of
any concentrated Israelite immigration into the country in the
13th–12th centuries. By 'concentrated' I mean the idea of a
collected Israelite invasion as well as the notion of an unco-
ordinated mass immigration of Israelite nomads into the
country.

(Lemche 1985: 391)

This appears to free the discussion from the constraints of the
Hebrew Bible and from the search for ancient Israel. Here is an
expression, although he does not make this explicit, of the need to
investigate the history of the region devoid of the constraining ethnic
labels which have thus far dominated and misdirected the discussions. Again his conclusions on settlement patterns and social change
illustrate the set of shared assumptions which Coote identified as part
of his 'new horizon': the materially poorer culture following the
destruction of various urban centres during the Late Bronze–Iron
Age transition is not 'synonymous with a new culture but a result of
the far less favourable conditions which characterized the Iron Age
societies' (Lemche 1985: 400). The dramatic events in the region are
not connected with Israelite immigration. There is nothing in the
archaeological record alone which indicates anything about an entity
called Israel since the evaluation of Israel as a political phenomenon
depends upon the use of the biblical traditions. Interestingly he states
that 'our most important duty is to acknowledge our ignorance

(Lemche 1985: 414; his emphasis). These are important observations which are broadly shared by an increasing number of scholars. It appears to signal the end of the search for ancient Israel in the Late Bronze–Iron Age transition in contrast to the positive statements and constructions of imagined pasts of those who deplore the negativity of the new search. Lemche rightly points out that

> The result has invariably been an account of the pre-monarchical history of Israel which has continually had to be modified as soon as new archaeological data or new sociological insights have arrived on the scene. In practice this has entailed the creation of a picture of Israel's earliest history from which scholars have gradually retreated after lengthy debates which have showed the picture in question to be based on positions which could not be sustained in the light of new information.
>
> (Lemche 1985: 414–15)

What Lemche is proposing is an investigation of the social, economic, cultural, and political history of Palestine. But the problem, as with all these discussions, is that it proves impossible to escape from the confines of Israel's past. This becomes clear in Lemche's response (1991) to the others involved in the new search where his focus on the origins or emergence of Israel obscures the need to pursue these proposals further. The concern for Palestinian history becomes lost in the continuing search for ancient Israel in whatever period it is to be located.

The joint volume by Coote and Whitelam (1987) provides a further illustration of the problem of extricating the pursuit of Palestinian history from the dominant discourse and its overriding concern with Israel's imagined past. Their discussion of the emergence of early Israel is set in the context of an understanding of a broad regional history of Palestine covering settlement patterns from the Early Bronze Age to the present, along with social relations and geography in the history of the region. Again, like Lemche, they articulate a concern with the demographic, economic, social, and political history of ancient Palestine. However, the impulse remains to discover 'how the emergence of Israel in the early Iron Age fits into the march of time' (Coote and Whitelam 1987: 8). After a consideration of historiographical principles and a treatment of Palestinian history from the perspective of Braudel's *la longue durée*, the focus is firmly on 'The Emergence of Israel: Iron I

Transformation in Palestine' and 'The Formation of the Davidic State'. The authors' purpose is defined as 'an attempt to provide a new synthesis of the history of early Israel by bringing together insights drawn from many disciplines as well as recent biblical studies . . . we seek to advocate a particular reconstruction of the emergence of Israel and to indicate how that reconstruction bears on the ways in which later ideas of Israel developed and functioned in the communities of faith' (Coote and Whitelam 1987: 16). The discussion may be set in the context of the 'kaleidoscopic history of Palestine' but its focus upon 'the emergence of Israel' means that it remains firmly in the context of the search for ancient Israel as conducted by the discourse of biblical studies.

The history of Palestine in reality forms little more than a backdrop to Israel's past. It is Israel which claims this landscape and this past. At the heart of this and the monographs of Ahlström and Lemche is an essential difficulty as to the task at hand. They have been struggling to articulate a conception of the history of Palestine as a subject in its own right while all the time constrained by the power of a discourse which has insisted on Israel's claim to the past. It has been unthinkable that little or nothing could be known of Israel in the Late Bronze–Iron Age transition or Late Bronze Age or that it should play a secondary role to a consideration of trying to investigate and articulate a history of Palestine. Thus Coote and Whitelam are able to say in the opening chapter that 'we are interested in describing less the cause of the emergence of Israel – though that is not in itself an invalid subject – than the set of conditions and circumstances within which Israel emerged' (Coote and Whitelam 1987: 24). The confusion remains that, although they investigate the processes which led to the settlement shift during the Late Bronze–Iron Age transition and compare these with settlement shifts throughout Palestinian history, they have made the fundamental assumption that this shift concerns Israel and Israel alone. Thus the confusion helps to contribute to the silencing of Palestinian history. They have produced an attempt to analyse 'the patterns and processes of Palestinian history' (1987: 27) both in terms of social relations and settlement patterns. But this is overshadowed, almost silenced, by their assumption that 'the most commonly agreed datum to mark the emergence of Israel is the extension of village and agricultural settlement in the central highlands of Palestine from the thirteenth to the eleventh centuries BCE' (1987: 27–8). Their examination of the material culture of published sites for this period is in line with many other scholars in arguing that all the indications are for a continuity in material culture from the Late Bronze Age through the Iron I period. They question the use of the ethnic label 'Israelite' to describe the inhabitants of many of these sites but still claim to be dealing with the emergence of Israel. They develop an explanation for this settlement shift in terms of the economic disruption of the whole of the eastern Mediterranean at the end of the Late Bronze Age which is an important facet of understanding the processes affecting Palestinian settlement shifts during this and subsequent periods. However, they have clouded the issue by claiming that 'the settlement into villages in the hinterland was given political and incipient ethnic form in the loosely federated people calling themselves Israel' (Coote and Whitelam 1987: 136). The power of the discourse of biblical studies, the search for ancient Israel, has hindered a clear understanding of the implications of the essential points of their research. It has proven impossible to escape from the accepted rhetoric of the discourse of biblical studies even where that discourse has seemingly been fundamentally challenged. They discuss (1987: 167–77) the reasons why biblical scholarship from the early nineteenth century onwards has perpetuated the biblical picture of the origins and unity of early Israel without realizing that they have contributed to that perpetuation.

The understanding of Israel as indigenous is a common thread running through all these works; at the time it was considered radical, building on and challenging the work of Mendenhall and Gottwald. Yet its very radicality obscured a much more important conclusion which was hinted at throughout; namely, the attempt to articulate the study of Palestinian history in its own right, to offer an alternative construction of the past which challenged the dominant under-standing of the present in which both past and present belonged to Israel. Coote and Whitelam (1987: 167) hint at the problem but are never able to articulate it clearly: 'Our assumption, shared by many historians and archaeologists, that the emergence of numerous rural sites in the highlands and margins of Palestine during the transition from the Late Bronze to the early Iron Age is to be identified with a single people, "Israel", itself begs the question.' They ask why the traditions obscure the nature of the emergence of Israel but do not ask about the much greater act of obscuration, the silencing of Palestinian history. Similarly, in a footnote to the introduction (Coote and Whitelam 1987: 179 n. 3), they claim that 'we do not assume that by referring to the early Iron Age highland settlement

as "Israel" that we have said anything qualitative about "early Israel".
We focus our history of "Israel" on this highland settlement because
it is the clearest archaeological datum that precedes the eventual
emergence of the kingdoms of Israel and Judah.' The use of quotation
marks betrays an unease with the term Israel but it has little practical
effect in freeing the discussion of the history of the region from the
domination of biblical studies.[30]

It is now becoming clear that once the label 'Israel' is removed
from the discussions, these authors are describing or trying to
account for the political and social factors which affect the transformation and realignment of Palestinian society. Coote's (1990)
later attempt to articulate his understanding of the common trends
in the new search is a case in point. The title of the work, *Early
Israel: A New Horizon*, makes it clear where the focus and concern
really lies. He notes that the Merneptah stele and the spread of
settlement have been known for a long time and insists that 'these
new settlements housed much of the population called Israel in
early scriptural texts'. The controlling assumption in reading the
Merneptah stele and the archaeological evidence is his understanding
of the production of many of the biblical materials at the court of
David. It is part of the stranglehold of the discourse of biblical studies
which has imagined a past from which biblical scholars and archaeologists have struggled but failed to free themselves. This is illustrated in Coote's elaboration of the new horizon which, while
recognizing that the inhabitants of the settlements are largely indigenous, claims that '*Israel was a strong tribal confederacy developed by
Egypt and Palestinian chiefs*' (1990: 5) or that '*The population of these
new settlements enlarged the tribes of Israel, whose chiefs were
increasingly regarded by Western Palestinians as the legitimate
alternative to European and Anatolian rule*' (1990: 5). He recognizes
that Israel and the highland settlement are not coterminous and tries
to explain this:

> Nevertheless, the spread of settlement and the origin of Israel
> were not the same thing. The extent of the settlement was not
> coterminous with Israel, Israel was a tribal force before the
> reversal of settlement trends, and settlement spread in many
> areas other than those that became Israelite. Before the spread
> of villages in the highlands, Israelites had contacts there,
> but most Israelites were located elsewhere, in the northern
> lowlands and the outlying settlements. Moreover, there was

nothing unique about the spread of settlement that produced highland Israel. Like its people, highland Israelite society was an extension of Palestinian Israel in the thirteenth century. The highland settlement had everything to do with the age-long survival of the name Israel, but nothing to do with its origin.

(Coote 1990: 115; re-emphasized in 1991: 45)

The problem here remains the distraction of the label 'Israel' and claims to knowledge about the nature and social organization of this entity on the basis of the Merneptah stele and the biblical traditions. No evidence is offered to support the claim that Israel had contacts in the highlands before the settlement shift. The previous assumption that the settlement shift was to be equated with the emergence of Israel has been replaced by an assumption that this was an extension of tribal Israel. Thus Israel remains the focal and dominating point of all Palestinian history. He moves away from the conclusion of Coote and Whitelam, that the settlement shift was related to the economic disruption of the eastern Mediterranean, to stress that it was due to a change in political circumstances in which 'tribal Israel was the political entity in the best position to oversee the spread of settlement and agriculture in the areas that later became highland Israel, the political change must have involved them' (Coote 1990: 116; 1991: 44). This, he concludes, led to a shift from a tribal confederation in the northern lowland and frontier Palestine which was tied to Egypt, to a tribal confederation located mainly in the central highlands at first tied to Egypt and then freed from it after the decline of the New Kingdom. It was this latter entity which was involved in a struggle for supremacy with the lowland Philistine power. Many aspects of his synthesis point to the kinds of issue, the processes of settlement shift, economic and political organization which ought to be the focus of a regional Palestinian history of the period. However, once again, Palestinian history has been effectively silenced by the failure to escape from the all-pervading search for ancient Israel which comes to dominate the past by blocking and obscuring alternative constructions of the Late Bronze–Iron Age transition. What he terms 'the basics of the revolution' (1990: 7) are not a revolution in our understanding of early Israel except as an illustration of Lemche's plea for an acknowledgement of ignorance. The significance of Coote's discussion of tribal society, minus the label 'Israel', lies less in the search for early Israel than in the pursuit of Palestinian history freed from the domination of this imagined past constructed by biblical studies from its understanding of the European nation state and the emergence of Zionism in the nineteenth century.

The continued confusion and failure to escape the search for ancient Israel, to step outside the discourse of biblical studies, is illustrated by T.L. Thompson's (1992a) *The Early History of the Israelite People: From the Written and Archaeological Sources*. This is an extensive critique of biblical historiography which has many points of contact, as well as very significant differences, with the works of Ahlström, Coote, Lemche, and Whitelam.[31] In trying to describe what he terms 'the search for a new paradigm for the history of Israel' (1992a: 105), Thompson refers to the 'historiographical crisis created by the rapid deconstruction of "biblical history"' from the 1970s onward. Yet, like most other works, it is bound by the distraction and confusion of the search for ancient Israel as the title suggests. Thus he describes the current situation in the following terms:

> These recent studies, since the mid-1980s, take a new direction which today seems most promising and takes us away from an historiography based on the fragile syntheses of biblical and archaeological research that had been overly dependent on issues of historicity and a biblical perspective, in the direction of an independently conceived history of Israel's origins.
>
> (Thompson 1992a: 107)

In commending Finkelstein's study, within a larger critique, he concludes that 'his book establishes a firm foundation for all of us to begin building an accurate, detailed, and methodologically sound history of Israel' (1992a: 161). But how can it, if the label 'Israelite' is removed from the interpretation of the data, if it is agreed that there is no distinction between this and other forms of material culture indigenous to Palestine from the Late Bronze through the early Iron Age? It establishes no such foundation. It provides instead important data for studying the Late Bronze–Iron Age transition in Palestine as part of a history of the region freed from the discourse of biblical studies and the search for ancient Israel. Thompson actually outlines such an enterprise, or at least one version of such an enterprise, a few pages later (1992a: 162–4) but the force of his argument is lost because it forms a subtheme to his concern for an 'independent history of Israel and Judah'. The concern for Palestinian history becomes even more muted in light of the claim that 'recent publications show clearly that a history of Israel's origins can now be written, in a relatively objective, descriptive manner, once issues relating to the historicity and relevance of later biblical tradition are bracketed' (Thompson 1992a: 168–9). But history writing should not be merely descriptive nor is it objective, as we have seen. The implications of the vast archaeological data which he reviews bear testimony to the fact that we know nothing of the origins of Israel. Nevertheless, Thompson believes that recent scholarship has been 'building a foundation for a new history of Israel' (Thompson 1992a: 169). He recognizes that Israelite history, of whatever period, forms part of the history of Palestine. Thus he observes that 'the focus of this book has been on the implications of interdisciplinary historical research in *Palestine* in the hope of developing an understanding of the history of "Israel" within the context of a comprehensive regional and historical geography of *Palestine*' (1992a: 402; his emphasis). Yet the problem inherent in this and other works associated with the new search is that such sentiments have little practical effect upon the realization of a history of ancient Palestine. They are all limited by their failure to break free from the inherent confusion involved in their attempts to construct alternative pasts. This failure to escape from the constraints of the dominant discourse ensures Israel's control and domination of the past.

CONCLUSION

The history of ancient Palestine has been dominated by a single entity, 'ancient Israel'. Possibly the most remarkable aspect of this domination is that it has not been achieved by a powerful political or geographically extensive entity. Palestinian history has been silenced by an entity which in literary terms is extremely small. The sections of the various works associated with the new search from the mid-1980s onward which offer positive constructions of Israel in the Late Bronze–Iron Age transition are strikingly brief (see Coote 1991: 42). In Lemche's case, of a work which is nearly five hundred pages long only twenty-four pages are devoted to his alternative explanation of Israel's origins which he terms 'evolutionary Israel'. This would rise to forty-nine pages if his discussion of the archaeological evidence was included. Similarly, Coote and Whitelam (1987: 117–38) only devote twenty-one pages to the 'emergence of Israel' out of 188. Thompson (1992a) is more difficult to quantify because his proposals are dispersed throughout a wide-ranging review of scholarly discussions and archaeological data, although again it is a tiny percentage of a massive study. The bulk of these works is not given over to the exploration of Palestinian history but to the analysis of anthropological and historical parallels, the results of excavations and surveys, and reviews of previous scholarship. Yet in all this the focus is firmly on the search for ancient Israel while the idea of a Palestinian history remains confined in the background.

The welcome reassessment of the Persian and Hellenistic periods as the temporal locus for the development and crystallization of much of the biblical material has also opened up a consideration of the ideologies which have shaped these narratives. What has been ignored, to a large extent, is the ideological shaping of the history of the region by contemporary political and religious ideologies. The cross-examination of ancient sources to determine their trust-worthiness has been unaware of or chosen to ignore the political, economic, and theological factors which have shaped contemporary scholarship. Thompson rightly acknowledges the importance of understanding Israelite and Palestinian history as part of the general cultural heritage, particularly in the context of 'current political developments'. This, I think, encapsulates the problem which has been the central concern of this book: the problem that con-temporary struggles for land and national identity between Israel and the Palestinians remain unspoken in biblical studies, or at the most, as in Thompson's concluding statement, raised in muted tones. These 'current political developments' remain unspecified. Biblical scholar-ship has refused to acknowledge or face the problem of the Palestin-ian struggle for self-determination. The question of the modern state of Israel and its treatment of the Palestinians has been too delicate an issue to be raised in the discourse of biblical studies. It threatens at times to surface but each time it is successfully prevented. The enterprise which has been begun in the last few years to revise understandings of the history of ancient Israel and to develop Palestinian history as a subject in its own right freed from biblical studies will not be achieved unless this crucial issue of the political nature of the past and the Orientalist nature of the discourse of biblical studies is addressed explicitly.

Davies, however, is attuned to some of the ideological aspects of the construction of the past and their implications:

> Exporting a literary construct and dumping it into Iron Age Palestine has succeeded in creating a 'history of ancient Israel'.

But it has also interfered with the real history of Palestine, which now has a cuckoo in the nest. For of course, as I remarked earlier, there *was* a population of Iron Age Palestine, including a kingdom called Israel, and real people lived there, real kings ruled, real wars took place and real transportations, in and out, were practised by conquering armies and sovereigns. *These* are the people and societies whose relics archaeologists discover when they dig for 'ancient Israel'. If it is clear that biblical scholars are not writing *their* history, who will write it? Who will write the history of a people whose real character has been obliterated by a literary construct? If what I am saying is right, biblical scholarship is guilty of retrojective imperialism, which displaces an otherwise unknown and uncared-for population in the interests of an ideological construct.

(Davies 1992: 31)

Biblical scholarship is not just involved in 'retrojective imperialism', it has collaborated in an act of dispossession, or at the very least, to use Said's phrase, 'passive collaboration' in that act of dispossession. The construction of the literary entity 'ancient Israel', to which Davies refers, has silenced the history of the indigenous peoples of Palestine in the early Iron Age. He points out how biblical scholars have long assumed that there is no difference between 'ancient Israel' and the population of Iron Age central Palestine: 'Certainly, no biblical scholar has ever explicated that distinction' (1992: 32). It is the explication of that distinction which needs to be undertaken if the idea of a history of ancient Palestine is to be achieved. But it cannot be undertaken until the ideological influences which are inherent in all historical narratives are acknowledged and confronted. The failure to make this distinction clear, the failure to acknowledge that the constructions of the past which have dominated the discourse of biblical studies for the past century or more are shaped by political and social locations, has ensured the silencing of Palestinian history.

6

RECLAIMING
PALESTINIAN HISTORY

REPRESENTING THE HISTORY OF PALESTINE

The right to represent the history of ancient Palestine for the Late Bronze and early Iron Ages, along with many other periods, has been claimed by Theology and Religion through the discourse of biblical studies. It is the continuation of a right claimed by European travellers during the eighteenth and nineteenth centuries. For the last two centuries, Palestinian history has become one of the many 'excluded' histories as a result of the stranglehold on the study of Palestine and the ancient Near East which biblical specialists, historians, and archaeologists, have exerted (see Bowerstock 1988: 164). The consequence of this has been that Palestinian history has been denied a place in Western academic discourse. Europe's strategic concern with Palestine coincided with its quest for the roots of its own civilization as identified with ancient Israel and the Bible. Biblical scholars accepting, in broad outline, the construction of the past offered by biblical traditions began the search for Israel's physical presence among the monuments and ruins of the land. What they found, or were predisposed to find, was an Israel which resembled their own nation states: Israel was presented as an incipient nation state in search of a national homeland in which to express its national consciousness. Throughout the present century, this projection of ancient Israel has come to dominate and control the Late Bronze and Iron Ages. It is a representation of the past which was given added urgency and authority with the rise of the Zionist movement, an essentially European enterprise, whose own history was seen to mirror ancient Israel's conquest of the land followed by the founding of a nation state which soon dominated the region. Here in broad outline is a master narrative whose essential outline, part of the 'assured results' of biblical studies, remained unchallenged until the 1970s, despite the reformulation of various details. There might be questions as to the nature of ancient Israel, the manner in which it acquired the land, but for the discourse of biblical studies there was no question that this was Israel's past and Israel's land. The right of the indigenous population to the land or its own history was not a meaningful question in the context.

The presentation of this past, through its constant repetition by the major figures in the field and in academic and popular handbooks, assumed a reality that was difficult to question. This reality was manifested for countless undergraduate and graduate students, professional academics, and interested lay readers in the 'massed histories', to adapt Said's phrase (1994b: 26), which culminated in the publishing frenzy of the 1970s and 1980s. Most of these 'biblical histories' of ancient Israel repeated or paraphrased the accounts in the Hebrew Bible. They were in the words of Davies (1991: 14) 'an essentially midrashic historiography, in which rationalistic glosses are introduced into a paraphrase of the biblical story'. Yet the growing unease with the viability of such projects, represented in the criticisms of Davies, coincided with this publishing boom in new and revised histories. The fracturing of the contexts in which these narratives had been constructed (Sasson 1981), along with other shifts taking place in the discipline, helped to expose the extent to which this imagined past had been constructed on the basis of models of contemporary experience. The break-up of the Soviet Union, the debates on the future and unity of Europe, and, particularly, the Palestinian intifada have all contributed to the continued fracturing of perspectives which had been influential in the construction of this dominant narrative.

The growth of post-colonialist histories, however, has had remarkably little effect upon the historiographic enterprise of biblical studies. The stranglehold on the past achieved by European scholarship has been maintained by American and Israeli scholarship in the latter part of the century in projecting this as the period of Israel's emergence and dominance as a major state in the region. Said (1992: xvi) has pointed out the extent to which modern Israel, since its founding in 1948, has enjoyed an astonishing dominance in scholarship, as well as many other areas. The investment of vast resources, intellectual and financial, in the search for ancient Israel has no counterpart in the pursuit of Palestinian history for the same or any subsequent periods. The theological and political motivations behind the search in the West and in Israel have combined to deny the claims of the indigenous population to representation in history. The history of ancient Palestine is a subject that has been excluded by Theology and ignored by History. The pursuit of post-colonialist history, the attempt to give voice to the many histories that have been deemed not to be part of officially sanctioned narratives, is not just a case of 'kicking the dead dragon of colonialism', as Gellner (1992: 47) claims. Colonialism is not dead while the assumptions of superiority and the right of force which inspired it are inscribed in the rhetoric of the discourse of biblical studies, a rhetoric which has been taken up and reinforced in Israeli scholarship after 1948. It is this rhetoric which has been allowed to shape the imagined past of Late Bronze–Iron Age Palestine. It has produced and continues to defend a construction of the past which devalues indigenous cultures and histories. The rhetoric of biblical studies, just like the rhetoric of modern Zionism, refuses to acknowledge the inherent value of indigenous culture and its right to its own history.

The struggle for 'the permission to narrate' (Said 1994a: 247–68) a modern Palestinian narrative, a struggle carried on by Antonius, Muslih, Tibawi, Khalidi, Abu-Lughod, and Said, among many others, has failed to retrieve the ancient past from the stranglehold of the West and Israel. This is epitomized in Bowerstock's (1988: 184) assessment that the Roman and Byzantine periods have enjoyed a resurgence of interest in the region in an attempt to restore part of this excluded history. He characterizes this as the era from the end of the 'Biblical period' to the coming of Mohammed. Noticeably the Palestinian past of the 'biblical period', the period prior to the Roman and Byzantine era, has been abandoned to Israel and the West. The invented Israel of the Late Bronze and early Iron Ages has cast its shadow of influence backwards to claim previous periods as its 'prehistory'. It is part of the elaborate evolutionary scheme, whether temporal, political, or religious, which has informed and aided the displacement of ancient Palestinian history. Said's complaint about the contemporary situation is equally applicable to the construction and representation of the ancient past:

> Thus Israel can make claims for its historical presence based on its timeless attachment to a place, and supports its universalism by absolutely rejecting, with tangible military force, any other historical or temporal (in this case Arab Palestinian) counter-claims.
>
> (Said 1994a: 17)

Biblical studies has formed part of the complex arrangement of scholarly, economic, and military power by which Palestinians have been denied a contemporary presence or history. As we have seen, countless scholars have referred to the area in the Late Bronze and Iron Ages as Palestine, including a 'Palestinian economy', 'Palestinian highlands', or 'Palestinian coastline', but the population have remained anonymous or described by some ethnic label which reinforces the evolutionary assumption that they have been supplanted and surpassed by Israel. Said complains that one of the greatest successes of Zionism has been 'the absence of a major history of Arab Palestine and its people. It is as if the Zionist web of detail and its drama choked off the Palestinians, screening them not only from the world but from themselves as well' (Said 1994a: 35). However, the silence of history is even more profound than Said appears to appreciate. His concern is with the modern history of Palestine as a counter-narrative to Zionist or Zionist-influenced histories dealing with the eighteenth century to the present. But Europe's search for itself, taken up and reinforced by Zionism seeking to legitimize its roots in the past, has removed the Palestinian claim to the Late Bronze and Iron Ages. This removal is so thorough that the idea of a history of ancient Palestine is not even contemplated by contemporary writers concerned with countering Zionist histories of the present. The oppressive weight of silence pervades the whole of biblical studies. Any recognition of the context in which biblical historians and archaeologists work, the contemporary struggle for land and self-determination, is absent. When it does appear it is couched in the form of regret or anguish for this troubled land and a hope for peace for its peoples. Yet it is a recognition of the realities and implications of the political struggle between Israel and the Palestinians which is not allowed to impinge upon the presentation of (objective) academic discourse. The implications of the construction of Israelite history for the contemporary struggle remain largely unarticulated, except for a few notable exceptions. It is epitomized in Silberman's (1989; 1992) recognition of the political implications of Albright's or Yadin's work but his failure to address the same issues in reviewing more recent hypotheses of Israelite origins (Silberman 1992).[1]

The power of the discourse of biblical studies to mask these problems has been illustrated in the failure of recent revisionist scholarship to break free of this control of the past. The paradox inherent in the work of Mendenhall and Gottwald is that it promises to give voice to the Palestinian peasantry only for this to be stifled by insisting that the essential nature of Israel is derived from a revolutionary religion or social organization brought from outside allowing Israel to transcend the failure of indigenous social, political, and religious organization. Similarly, faltering attempts to articulate a history of ancient Palestine by Ahlström, Lemche, Coote, Thompson, Weippert, and Whitelam are distracted by their continued search for ancient Israel. It is only slowly and begrudgingly recognized that the 'virtual self-evidence' (Foucault) of the network of ideas and assumptions that have sustained the discourse of biblical studies is the product of self-interest and subjectivity. The problems of trying to escape from a dominant discourse, the problem of trying to adopt a different perspective in order to imagine a counter-narrative have been highlighted by Mannheim:

> ruling groups can in their thinking become so intensely interest-bound to a situation that they are simply no longer able to see certain facts which would undermine their sense of domination ... the collective unconscious of certain groups obscure the real conditions of society both to itself and to others.
>
> (Mannheim 1985: 40)

The painfully slow, but perceptible, shift towards a regional history of Palestine has been obstructed by the lack of an appropriate rhetoric with which to represent this alternative past. The only rhetoric available has been that of a biblical studies in search of ancient Israel. The theological paradigm of biblical history has been maintained by the consent of biblical specialists located in faculties of theology and seminaries who have contributed to and accepted its claim to the truth (Davies 1992: 15–16). There has been no rhetoric available by which to articulate and pursue the history of ancient Palestine.

The heated reaction to the revisionism of the late 1980s and early 1990s signals that the consensus is beginning to fracture, the master narrative is becoming increasingly difficult to maintain and defend. The trend from the 1980s onwards towards slimmer and slimmer volumes or sections of volumes on the history of ancient Israel and Judah, often prefaced by longer prolegomena, indicates that a critical point in the representation of the history of the region has now been reached. In order to give voice to an alternative Palestinian past, to a post-colonial, contrapuntal reading of the ancient Palestinian past, it is vital to construct a rhetoric of Palestinian history.

RECLAIMING PALESTINIAN HISTORY

The earlier discussion of the new search for ancient Israel revealed that a growing number of scholars were questioning the biblically inspired interpretation of archaeological data from surveys and excavations. The domain assumption, since the time of Alt and Albright, that the growth of Palestinian highland settlements was to be identified with Israel had been qualified by the increasing recognition that the inhabitants of these settlements were indigenous. The term 'Israelite' when applied to these settlements has become meaningless; as Thompson (1992a: 310) suggests, it is 'misleading to speak of the term "Israelite" in an archaeological context of Iron I *Palestine*'. The archaeological data covering the Late Bronze–Iron Age transition and the early Iron Age provide valuable information on the demography, settlement, economy, and social organization of Palestinian society. They say nothing directly of an entity called Israel, even though the Merneptah stele reveals that some entity by that name was in the region. However, Finkelstein's (1991: 53) concession that he is willing to replace the term 'Israelite' with a broader term such as 'hill country settlers' is little more than a rhetorical device which continues to deny Palestinian history. It is noticeable that he does not label these sites as 'Palestinian'; the inhabitants are now anonymous settlers in the highlands. The lack of an appropriate rhetoric with which to articulate a history of ancient Palestine means that the settlement shift has not been understood as part of a general transformation and realignment of Palestinian society which took place at the end of the Late Bronze Age and had far-reaching effects well into the Iron Age.

The search for ancient Israel predisposed historians and archaeologists to emphasize disruptions in material culture as evidence for cultural and ethnic discontinuity. This articulated well with the view that the cultural and ethnic break which had been brought about first by European colonialism and later through Zionist immigration was mirrored in the ancient past. The representation of the Late Bronze Age as a period of dramatic urban collapse and cultural decline to be replaced by a radically new culture which was to give birth to monotheism and the Hebrew Bible appeared to confirm and mirror what was happening in the early decades of the twentieth century. Yet the significance of continuities in material culture, which had long been known by archaeologists working in the region, were ignored or underplayed. The notion of a dramatic break in culture around 1200 BCE further emphasized the understanding of history as the study of discrete events and clearly demarcated temporal units (cf. Bloch, 1954: 183–4). The steadily accumulating weight of evidence illustrating the continuities in material culture between Late Bronze and Early Iron Age sites, coupled with a growing unease over the lack of precision of ceramic dating (Fritz, 1987: 86–9), has revealed that the settlement shift of the Late Bronze–Iron Age transition was part of a protracted process which needs to be understood in the context of the complex events and forces affecting the whole of the eastern Mediterranean over a century or more. H. Weippert (1988) has drawn attention to the crucial problems of dating in Palestinian archaeology which undermine the discrete periodization of biblically based constructions of this period. Her insistence that different areas of Palestine probably experienced considerably different rates of development (Weippert 1988: 26–7) has been confirmed by T. Dothan's (1989: 1–14) recent reassessment of the initial appearance and settlement of the Philistines and other Sea Peoples in Palestine. Her findings suggest that the transition period from Late Bronze–Iron I Age was not uniform or simultaneous throughout the country but was characterized by a complex process in which indigenous, Egyptian, and Philistine cultures overlapped for certain periods.

The realignment and transformation of Late Bronze–Iron I society was clearly a very complex process, as we would expect. Since the eastern Mediterranean was a closely interlocking network of different power groups and spatial entities, any structural alterations on such a widespread scale were bound to influence Palestinian society. The disruption of a vast area throughout the eastern Mediterranean at the end of the Late Bronze Age was bound to effect all levels of social and political activity in Palestine as well. Palestine has occupied a strategic place in the world trade axis, a complex of trade networks which in antiquity linked the Mediterranean, Red Sea, Persian Gulf, and Indian Ocean, throughout history.[2] Yet its position on the transit routes has meant that it has been particularly sensitive to any disruption or decline. The existence of such a closely integrated world economy, in particular in the eastern Mediterranean during the Late Bronze Age, also meant that any disruption to part of the trade network influenced other areas. Palestine invariably played a dependent role in trade, since it provided the land bridge, and hub of the waterways, to the infrastructurally more important economies of the major continents. Palestinian urban centres were therefore sensitive and vulnerable to trade cycles and suffered severely from the disruption of the Mycenaean world, whatever the causes may have been.[3] It is not possible, then, to concentrate attention on settlement shifts in the highlands of Palestine at the beginning of the Iron I period without taking adequate account of the structural alterations brought about by changes in the wider network. The decline of trade and economy, along with the many circumstances that attended it, were integral to the transformation of economic, political, and social relations in Palestine.

The growth of highland settlements is the most evident result of the realignment of Palestinian society but it can hardly be described as unique or the result of the intrusion of a new ethnic group. Similar settlement shifts were experienced elsewhere in the eastern Mediterranean (Desborough 1972: 19–20; 29; 41; 82; 88; Snodgrass 1971: 34; 40) and have been part of the centuries-long cycle of growth, stagnation, decline, and regeneration in the history of Palestine (Coote and Whitelam, 1987: 27–8; Braudel 1972: 34; 53). A central feature of the study of Palestinian history for the period ought to be the investigation of the socio-environmental and economic features of settlements throughout the region. The appearance and use of pillared buildings, silos, cisterns, terracing, and pottery forms such as collared-rim ware are explicable in terms of the topographical and environmental conditions facing the inhabitants of highland and marginal settlements in the context of the disruption of local and regional economies (see also Dever 1991: 83–4). The technological solutions and expertise displayed in the use of cisterns, terracing, or the construction of pillared buildings militate against the view that the population of these sites were nomads in the process of sedentarization (Coote and Whitelam 1987: 123–4). The evidence put forward by Finkelstein, when stripped of the distractions of putative ethnic labels, provides further support for the view that the settlement shift at the end of the Late Bronze Age and beginning of the Iron I period was a reaction to economic disruption which had an impact on all aspects and levels of Palestinian society rather than being the direct result of social conflict brought about by class struggle or external invasion or infiltration.

Historians must await the results of further archaeological research, particularly comprehensive surveys of the lowlands and coastal areas along with comparative excavations of sites of differing sizes in these areas in order to produce a more complete regional picture of the settlement patterns. The lack of comprehensive surveys of all regions of Palestine, and particularly of the lowlands, is a major obstacle in trying to understand the processes at work in the Late Bronze–Iron Age transition. London (1989: 42) makes the point that 'until now archaeologists have been comparing rural sites in the hill country with urban sites in the lowlands and then attributing the differences to Israelite versus Canaanite communities. The differences may be more indicative of rural versus urban lifestyles.'[4] The existence of villages on the exposed edge of the highlands, or other villages with or without outer defences, indicates that social conflict was only part of the processes which explain the shift in settlement. Progress in this field is now even more dependent upon the continued publication and judgements of archaeologists, so that historians can interpret the material in a comparative interdisciplinary context. Yet an important part of the investigation must include the exposure of the particularity of the data, the motives and interests which have informed the scholarly enterprise, both its design of research strategies and the subsequent presentation and interpretation of the data.

The same type of investigation also needs to be undertaken for subsequent periods of the Iron Age in order to free the study of the region from the stranglehold of biblical historiography. The so-called period of the united monarchy needs to be fundamentally reassessed. The mirage of the Davidic 'empire', the retrojection of the modern state of Israel into the Iron Age, has completely distorted the representation of the history of the region. The spread of settlement in the Iron Age ought to be viewed as part of a continuum with the transformation and realignment of Palestinian society resulting from the dislocations of the Late Bronze–Iron Age transition. Historians have failed to investigate the processes involved in this settlement shift, with its accompanying destruction, abandonment, or fortification of sites. They have rarely been concerned to investigate what evidence there is to suggest centralization or the existence of a major state in the region. Instead the monopolistic claims of the Hebrew Bible have been allowed to dictate any construction of the past. There has been an indecent haste to correlate archaeological findings with the biblical traditions, to identify a destruction level with some battle mentioned in the Bible, or to associate the fortification of a site with the building programme of some Judaean or Israelite king who is given a few verses in the Deuteronomistic History. Socio-environmental factors, the fluctuations in economic cycles, have been ignored in favour of the seemingly easy option of accepting, or supplementing, the construction of the past offered by writers of the Hebrew Bible.

What is fascinating about the Hebrew Bible is that it appears to contain competing conceptions of the past, particularly in the Deuteronomistic History and Chronicles, which suggest competing presents. Yet, above all, it gives access to the privileged conception of reality of a literate stratum of society revealing little or nothing of what Hobsbawm terms the 'sub-literate culture' or the deep-seated movements of history. As such, its value as a source for the historian is not so much in terms of the past it purports to describe but as an insight into the perception or self-perception of the literate stratum of society, mainly in the Persian and Hellenistic periods. It is important, therefore, as much for what it chooses to leave out as for what it includes. If as historians we choose to accept the testimony of this version of the past, then we participate in helping to silence other past realities. We know, for instance, that the pastoral–nomadic element has been a constant in the social continuum of the region. Yet this element of society does not form part of the self-perception of those responsible for the development of the traditions. While nomads may have been a constant in the history of the region, their part in the past, and so the present, has been silenced by the literate elite of the second Temple period, or whoever is responsible for this construction of this past. Furthermore, these traditions tell us little or nothing of how Israel and Judah or the region in general was linked to the wider economy, whether Egyptian, Assyrian, Babylonian, Achaemenid, Hellenistic, or Roman. Nor is it informative of demography, settlement patterns, or economic trends, the best indicators of the deep-seated movements of history which provide the wider perspective from which to view the short-term trends that are the inevitable focus of our literary deposits. This will be misunderstood or misrepresented as the denial of Israelite history, as the fierce debate on the Tel Dan stele already indicates. Yet it is not a denial of the existence of Israelite and Judaean monarchies: it is an attempt to redress the balance whereby Israelite and Judaean history has been presented as *the* history of the region rather than as a part of a history of ancient Palestine.

The same process needs to be applied to later Persian and Hellenistic periods, where, for example, the claims to the past of the tiny province of Yehud have been allowed to silence virtually all other competing claims (Davies 1992: 58). The danger inherent in the reassessment of the Persian and Hellenistic periods is that the methodological mistakes of the past will simply be repeated here. There is a danger that as the starting point of Israelite history is pushed back even further, the Persian period will come to represent one more (temporary) plug to fill the gap. The location of the biblical traditions in the Persian and Hellenistic periods, rather than in the periods of emergence or monarchy, allows the discourse of biblical studies to continue to claim the past for Israel. The insistence of this discourse that written texts form the basis for writing history means that the methodological circularity of the earlier search for Israel is likely to be transferred to the Persian period. The literary construct that is 'ancient Israel', which has obscured the history of ancient Palestine in the Late Bronze and Iron Ages, will be allowed to achieve the same objective for later periods. The tiny province of Yehud (Ahlström 1993: 843–4) has been allowed to monopolize and dominate discussions of the period. It is a period desperately in need of reassessment in order to free Palestinian history from the tyranny of the discourse of biblical studies.

A rhetoric of Palestinian history would also provide a much more positive appreciation of the material and cultural achievements of the inhabitants of the region as a whole. The evolutionary scheme which has presupposed the replacement of Canaanite by Israelite culture has detracted from the aesthetic and cultural qualities exhibited in the rich deposits of ceramics, faience, glass, jewellery, etc., evidenced throughout Palestine. The discovery of female figurines and statuettes in the different levels at many Palestinian sites is invariably presented as evidence of a widespread fertility cult.[5] The implication is that the degenerate and immoral indigenous religions have been replaced by a monotheism: a monotheism which is conceived as the basis of Western civilization. In the same way, Israel has replaced the indigenous population, the Canaanites. Little thought is given to the aesthetic qualities of the representation and modelling of the human form or what that might reveal about the values or achievements of the artist or the society of which she or he was a part. The positive elements of indigenous religious systems, the concern for the marginalized and underprivileged or the notion of harmony, are masked by the representation of a static and degenerate culture which must inevitably be replaced. The lack of an appropriate rhetoric to represent indigenous cultural achievements has meant that the only rhetoric available has been adopted: a rhetoric which is designed to denigrate any cultural achievement which is not thought to have been derived from Israelite religion which formed the basis of later Judaism and Christianity.

We have concentrated on the two defining moments for biblical studies because it is these two periods which have represented Israel's control of the past. The 'first moment of true civilization', as Dharwadker (1993: 175) has pointed out, takes on a crucial significance in the history of any people. It is historically and historiographically the key moment which, if understood in its totality, provides the basis for understanding all subsequent history. The periods of the 'emergence' of Israel in Palestine and the development of an Israelite state have been accorded that status in biblical studies. They define the essential nature of Israel, its sense of national identity, which is portrayed as unchanging throughout subsequent periods of history connecting the past with the present. The construction of the past, then, is a struggle over the definition of historical and social identity. If we can alter the perspective from which these are viewed to show that the discourse of biblical studies has invented a past, often mirroring its many presents, then it will be possible to free Palestinian history and progress toward a rhetoric which will allow alternative constructions of the past. It will also free previous and subsequent periods of the region from control by Israel's past.

LOCATING PALESTINIAN HISTORY

The production of a 'master story' of ancient Israel has formed part of a theological enterprise conducted mainly in faculties of theology and divinity in the West. Said makes a very telling point about the audience of scholarship: 'None of the Orientalists I write about seems ever to have intended an Oriental as reader. The discourse of Orientalism, its internal consistency and rigorous procedures, were all designed for readers and consumers in the metropolitan West' (Said 1995: 4). This is equally true of the intended and actual audiences of the outpouring of works on the history of ancient Israel, those works reviewed in chapters 2, 3, 4, and 5. They are not addressed to a Palestinian or non-Western, non-Israeli audience. The audience furthermore is principally Christian and Jewish. 'Orientalism was', in the words of Prakash (1990: 384), 'a European enterprise from the very beginning.' Biblical studies has been part of, and in many ways an extension of, Orientalist discourse. At no point is the intended reader shown to be Palestinian or any other non-Western reader; they are European, American, and Israeli. These histories are couched in the language of reasonableness, of a profaned detached objectivity. Yet as part of that wider interlocking discourse of Orientalism they are implicated in the politics of representation. The indigenous cultures of Palestine are represented as incapable of unified action, national consciousness, or outright immorality. They are often anonymous, rarely named as Palestinians, the opposite of the sophisticated, rational, objective Westerners who have a clear notion of their own national identity. This has been reinforced during this century in the growth of Israeli scholarship which continues the theme of Israel as set apart from its environment, bringing civilization and progress to the region, and achieving a level of political development of which the indigenous groups were incapable. Biblical studies, as a discipline, has evolved a rhetoric of representation which has been passed down without examination, which has dispossessed Palestinians of a land and a past. It is a discourse of power; seen from a non-Western, and particularly Palestinian, perspective, this discourse has excluded the vast majority of the population of the region in a search for Europe's and, latterly, modern Israel's roots in the past. It is also a discourse which through its location in faculties of Theology and Divinity has been given the full weight and authority of Western universities.

The question remains, however, as to where such a history of ancient Palestine, and with it the histories of Israel and Judah, will be located. If it is no longer to be excluded from the discourse of history, if it is to form part of the contested versions of the past, it has to have a location from which it can be pursued. The location of alternative narratives of the past is crucial, therefore, since it is an acknowledgement of the permission to narrate. If Palestinian history is to be freed from the tyranny of the discourse of biblical studies, it must be freed from the theological constraints which have governed the history of the region. This means that an alternative location, outside the confines of biblical studies, will need to be found. Palestinian history has to be recognized as a subject in its own right, as part of the study of history and 'cultural studies discourse', if it is to be given a voice of its own to challenge the invention of ancient Israel and to contest the past of the Late Bronze and Early Iron Ages.

Liberation movements of the twentieth century have given voice to the marginalized and underprivileged of society and history. One of the ironies of Said's *Orientalism* is that, though it focuses upon the

Middle East, its greatest success in terms of reclaiming the past has been achieved by Indian historiography. Yet there is no body of comparable material which offers a critique of the Orientalist assumptions of the discourse of biblical studies or ancient Near Eastern history, for instance, even though Said himself acknowledges that biblical studies is part of the Orientalist enterprise (1985: 17, 18, 51). Whereas the past has become a contested territory in so many other fields of study, in so many other areas of history, this has not been the case in biblical studies. The struggle for the Palestinian past is only just beginning. For it to succeed, it will be necessary to expose the political and religious interests which have motivated the invention of ancient Israel within the discourse of biblical studies. It will also need to create its own space, in order to produce its own contested narrative of the past, thereby helping to restore the voice of an indigenous population which has been silenced by the invention of ancient Israel.

The Subaltern project has been successful in challenging dominant models of Indian historiography, drawn from its colonial past, because it has been able to claim an academic context from which to work and from which to subvert 'official' narratives. It has also created a forum, *Subaltern Studies: Writings on South Asian History and Society*, to present and develop its research strategies and findings. The scholars involved in this movement have been located, to a large extent, in departments of History. They have been contesting both an ancient and a modern space. By contrast, attempts to articulate a history of ancient Palestine, to challenge the dominant narratives of ancient Israelite history, have come from biblical specialists located in departments of Biblical Studies. If Palestinian history is to be freed from the constraints of biblical studies, which it must if it is to have a voice, it will need to create its own space or contest the current spaces available. It is not clear where this space might reside which will allow the permission to narrate ancient Palestinian history. To begin with, the contest will take place within current academic locations, within departments of Biblical Studies and its cognate subjects, which means by and large within departments and faculties of Theology. The reason for this is because the most immediate task is the need for self-reflection of its practitioners on the development of biblical studies in the context of the colonial enterprise. The task is to demonstrate the politics of biblical scholarship and its construction of the past. It will require an investigation of the archival materials which exist in order to allow a complete reappraisal of the motives and interests which have been masked in the public writings of the discipline.

Only after that task has been undertaken with sufficient rigour will it be possible to prise ancient Palestinian history from the grasp of the vested interests which have helped to silence it for so long. Yet the question of its location remains crucial. There is no forum within the discipline, comparable with *Subaltern Studies*, which permits the narration of this history. Nor is it granted permission to narrate within departments of History. In order for the idea to be realized, it will be necessary to break free from the confines of biblical studies and try to claim its rightful location within the academic discourse of history which has ignored it as part of the biblically based history of ancient Israel. The principal challenge, however, still remains to (re)discover the rich cultural heritage of ancient Palestine which testifies, through its written texts and traditions (including the Hebrew Bible), ceramics and artifacts, monuments and material remains, to the achievements of its many peoples. It is, surely, an idea worth pursuing.

NOTES

INTRODUCTION

1 Prakash (1990: 401) states that 'rather than seeing these events as important because they were well regarded in the past, it interrogates the past's self-evaluation . . . The purpose of such disclosures is to write those histories that history and historiography have excluded.'

2 See Dever (1985; 1992) for the background to the debate and relevant literature. He has claimed of late that 'Syro–Palestinian archaeology' has come of age (Dever 1993).

3 A search of recent titles in *International Dissertation Abstracts* reveals than an increasing number of Ph.D. theses within biblical studies and cognate areas now contain the word 'Palestine' in their titles compared with Israel or ancient Israel. It is not clear whether this signals a radical shift in approach or not. The use of the terms 'Palestine' or 'Palestinian' is no guarantee that Palestinian history has been given a voice. Chapter 2 will deal with the ways in which these terms have often been emptied of meaning thereby denying the notion of Palestinian history.

4 See Whitelam (1995b) for a consideration of this shift and the ways in which the so-called 'sociological approach' to Israelite history has helped in exposing the need for the pursuit of Palestinian history.

5 Thompson (1992b) sees a strong influence from Chicago and Tübingen. However, he rightly sees this as a convergence of different scholars drawn from biblical studies, archaeology, and semitics rather than a separate approach. For the view that it has emerged particularly in a European context in association with European scholars and those who have close connections with Europe, see Whitelam (1995b).

6 See chapter 1 for the importance of the concept of 'deep time'. Viewed from this perspective, ancient Israel represents but a moment in the larger context of Palestinian history.

7 This is not to privilege 'third world' nationalist traditions but rather to suggest that it is important to have competing formulations of history from all perspectives. Said points out that:

> But only recently have Westerners become aware that what they have to say about the history and the cultures of 'subordinate'

peoples is challengeable by the people themselves, people who a few years back were simply incorporated, culture, land, history, and all, into the great Western empires, and their disciplinary discourses.

(Said 1993: 235)

Prakash (1990: 399) illustrates that 'national origin is not a necessary requirement for the formulation of a post-Orientalist position' by pointing out that almost all those involved in the Subaltern project are located in India, Britain, and Australia and have had first-world academic training or experience.

8 See the various volumes of *Subaltern Studies*, edited by Guha, along with selected essays in Guha and Spivak (1988).

9 Said (1992: xii–xiii) notes that 'one of the features of a small non-European people is that it is not wealthy in documents, or in histories, autobiographies, chronicles and the like. This is true of the Palestinians, and it accounts for the lack of a major authoritative text on Palestinian history.' He talks of restoring history to the Palestinians (Said 1988: 17) but still appears to be thinking in terms of modern rather than ancient history. The ancient past also needs to be reclaimed and given voice. It has been obstructed by a scholarship which has constructed a powerful narrative which retains the past for Israel.

10 Claims to write a 'new history' are, of course, relative as references to such enterprises in the 1920s show (see Fogel 1983: 16–17). However, the crucial problem in talking of a new history is not, so much, that of relativism. The question which needs to be answered is that posed by Robert Young (1990: 119): 'But how to write a new history? When, as Césaire (1972: 54) observed, the only history is white?'

11 Young (1990: 10) points out that Said has criticized world history as practised by Braudel, Wallerstein, Anderson, and Wolf as still derived from the enterprise of Orientalism and its colluding companion anthropology, which has refused to encounter and interrogate its own relationship as a discipline to European imperialism. For Said (1984: 22), the problem is the failure to evaluate the relationship between imperialism and its representation of other cultures resulting in an historicism and 'the universalism and self-validating that has been endemic to it'.

1 PARTIAL TEXTS AND FRACTURED HISTORIES

1 Wickham (1990: 4–8) refers to the response of some historians to Aboriginal objections to the Australian bicentennial celebrations as 'a fascist act of intellectual terrorism'. He points out that this illustrates how historical knowledge of Australia is part of the 'History of the Pastness of Australia': this history is untouchable. He argues that such a reaction is in fact hiding behind the past to protect a political objective of a particular 'official' historical knowledge from being contested: this political objective is the promotion of certain knowledges at the expense of others. Similarly, Said (1993: 378), in talking about *Subaltern Studies*, Samuel (1989), and Bernal (1987), makes the point that: 'The idea behind

these works is that orthodox, authoritatively national and institutional versions of history tend principally to freeze provisional and highly contestable versions of history into official identities.' Similarly, the standard histories of ancient Israel produced within biblical studies, themselves highly contestable versions of history, have taken on the authority of officially sanctioned constructions of the past.

2 Long (n.d.) made this point in a paper read at the SBL Annual Meeting in San Francisco, November 1992.

3 He goes on to say:

> Such attitudes surely underlie Mendenhall's recent and vehement disavowal of connection to Gottwald's *magnum opus*, which so clearly identified its Marxist orientation and modern social concerns – the issue here is not so much differences of historical interpretation as such (if such an abstraction can ever exist) but rather the polemic in which interpretation is couched and the consequences it bears for religious and political attitudes today.
>
> (Eden 1989: 291)

4 The Gaza–Jericho First accord, recently signed by the PLO and the Israeli government, has led to the setting up of a fledgling Palestinian antiquities authority. However, it will be a considerable time before there can be the substantial financial support for a national archaeology to rival other nation states in the region.

5 Trigger (1984: 368) is undecided as to the most appropriate label for Israeli archaeology since it contains elements of both 'nationalist' and 'colonial' archaeology. He notes that 'Israelis claim substantial historical roots in the land they are occupying'. The implications of this claim for biblical scholarship will be examined in the rest of this study.

6 Silberman describes the importance of Masada in the following terms:

> For modern Israelis, deeply concerned with issues of sovereignty and independence, the finds at Masada had long offered a tangible link between the present and the past. The fact that after nearly two thousand years of exile Jews returned to reveal the splendour and the tragedy of an earlier national existence at that remote mountain in the Judaean Desert made Masada a powerful political metaphor.
>
> (Silberman 1989: 87)

Yadin's interpretation of archaeological evidence and his use of Josephus's account have come in for considerable criticism (see, for example, Silberman 1989: 95–9; Cohen 1982).

7 Zerubavel shows how problematic aspects of the account, such as the mass suicide, were ignored or later reinterpreted as a 'patriotic death'. She also notes the development of counter-narratives. See also Schwartz, Zerubavel, and Barnett (1986) on the changing nature of the story in Israeli society.

8 Zerubavel (1994: 85) suggests that 'Israeli memory thus reconstructs a coherent temporal continuum between Masada and contemporary Israel:

the end of Antiquity symbolically opens up, leading into the beginning of the modern Zionist revival.'

9 He subsequently revised this view (1991: 48–9), recognizing that comprehensive surveys of the lowlands need to be conducted in order to match the work already carried out in the hill country. The dichotomy between 'Israel' and 'Canaan' and the ways in which one supplants the other will be discussed below. This provides an important link between the European appropriation of the Israelite past as the root of its own cultural heritage and Israeli nationalist history. Most 'imperialist archaeology', in Trigger's study (1984: 363–8), emphasizes the primitive and static nature of other cultures in comparison with the rapid development of its own, in this case European, culture. It is Canaanite culture which is presented as static only to be replaced in European and Israeli scholarship by the dynamism of 'ancient Israel'. Trigger notes that the achievements of ancient Near Eastern civilizations were appropriated for Western Europe by claiming that Western Europeans rather than the people who lived in the Near East today were their true spiritual heirs. Israel, as the representative of the European nation state, is presented as replacing the static culture of Canaan in just the same way that European civilization had replaced the static cultures of the Middle East.

10 The literature on the growth of nationalism is immense. See the classic studies by Anderson (1991) and Hobsbawm (1990) for a discussion of the complex issues. Braudel (citing Lestocquoy 1968: 14) says, in the context of his discussion of the development of the unity of France, that:

> And yet the *modern* notion of *la patrie*, the fatherland, had scarcely appeared in the sixteenth century; the nation took on its first explosive form with the Revolution: and the word *nationalism* appeared only from the pen of Balzac – when everything was still to be played for.
>
> (Braudel 1990: 18)

11 His observation that there are undoubted historical connections between the new and old Israels is particularly problematic. It is even questionable that there is a direct connection between the entity called Israel in the Merneptah stele at the end of the Late Bronze Age and the monarchic state or later entities in the second Temple period (Whitelam 1994). The widespread belief in a direct continuum between the past of ancient Israel and the modern state is an important rhetorical device which has played a crucial role in silencing Palestinian history.

12 Chakrabarty (1992: 19) asks the intriguing question as to why history is a compulsory part of modern education in all countries including those who did quite comfortably without it until as late as the eighteenth century. He argues that the reason lies in the combination of European imperialism and third-world nationalisms which has resulted in the universalization of the nation state as the most desirable form of political community:

> Nation states have the capacity to enforce their truth games, and universities, their critical distance notwithstanding, are part of the battery of institutions compliant in this process. 'Economics' and

'history' are the knowledge forms that correspond to the two major institutions that the rise (and later universalization) of the bourgeois order has given to the world – the capitalist mode of production and the nation state.

(Chakrabarty 1992: 19)

13 Clements (1989: 3; 1983: 122 ff.) and Iggers (1980) also discuss the development of German historiography.
14 We should also remember Ernest Gellner's (1964: 169) well-known dictum that 'nationalism is not the awakening of nations to self-consciousness: it *invents* nations where they do not exist'.
15 Thus a history of Palestine must deal with those people, in Said's words (1993: 75), 'on whom the economy and polity sustained by empire depend, but whose reality has not historically and culturally required attention'.
16 Chakrabarty states that a critical historian has to negotiate this knowledge and therefore needs to understand the way in which the state is justified through narrative. He adds that:

Since these themes will always take us back to the universalist propositions of 'modern' (European) political philosophy – even the 'practical' science of economics that now seems 'natural' to our constructions of world systems is (thus relatively) rooted in the ideas of ethics in eighteenth-century Europe – a third world historian is condemned to knowing 'Europe' as the original home of the 'modern' whereas the 'European' historian does not share a comparable predicament with regard to the pasts of the majority of humankind.

(Chakrabarty 1992: 19)

17 Davies (1992: 13) points out that attempts to understand the past, usually couched in story form, are never 'an innocent representation of the outside world'. The critical question remains as to why the story is being told.
18 Levinson (1989: 3) remarks that 'a reading of the past which is not also and integrally a reflected operation on the present betrays its received historicist premises'. Similarly Davies (1992: 13) emphasizes that historiography, as a branch of literature, is an ideologically motivated form of persuasion which conveys its author.
19 The discussion in the wake of Said's *Orientalism* has sharpened awareness of the supposed objectivity of Western scholarship. This is a major issue that has not been addressed in biblical studies. Literary critics, who have focused upon the biblical materials, have only addressed questions of subjectivity and authority in the reading of the Bible. However, what remains to be exposed is the role of biblical studies in the colonial enterprise.

Pollock (1993: 85–6) argues that it is the separation of 'fact' from 'value', resulting in the decontextualization and dehistoricization of scholarship, which has allowed 'some of the most deformed scholarship in history to come into existence'. He goes on to make the interesting point about the crisis within Indology which may be relevant to the current crisis in biblical studies:

> In other words, if Indological knowledge has historically been coexistent with vanished institutions of coercive power, then the production of such knowledge no longer serves its primary and defining purpose. Our obsession with Orientalism over the past decade might suggest that Indologists, who have begun to realize their historical implication in domination only now that it has ended, no longer know why they are doing what they do.
>
> (Pollock 1993: 111)

This might also help to explain the crisis of confidence in constructing the history of Israel which has emerged in Western biblical scholarship compared with the strong sense of certainty and 'impartiality' in Israeli historical scholarship: Western biblical scholarship has become unsure of its role and function as the West has progressively lost its colonial role compared with Israeli scholarship which is still involved in the colonial experience.

20 It should be noted that Halpern (1988: 3–13) acknowledges that history writing is selective and fictional. The crucial distinction for Halpern is whether or not the author tried to represent the past to the best of his or her ability rather than knowingly trying to deceive the reader about the past. 'History, in sum, *is* subject to falsification, to argument as to the accuracy of its particulars and the assessment of their interrelation' (1988: 10). The criteria he adduces are as follows: 'But when a stripped-down text does not trade *primarily* in metaphoric language . . . it deserves to be examined as history. Economy, in a political-historical narrative, is one sign of historiographic intentionality' (1988: 13). He believes that although it does not prove what the author intended to write, it does produce evidence of those intentions. Thus he defends Noth's Deuteronomistic Historian as 'a thinker emboldened by honest conviction to impose a meaningful order on his nation's past' (1988: 31) in contrast with van Seters's presentation of 'a rogue and a fraud' (1988: 31).

21 However, note Elton's denial of this analogy with the court of law in his dispute with Fogel on method:

> Nor do we examine or cross-examine our evidence as we would deal with a witness, if only because the bulk of our evidence is not provided by people concerned to produce testimony in support of a truth or falsehood: it is produced by people doing things, not observing them or commenting on them. At best, therefore, the legal model covers only a small part of the traditional historian's area of operations, and even at its best it is a poor representation of what actually goes on when an historian evaluates his evidence and seeks to prove his case.
>
> (Elton 1983: 92)

22 Samuel and Thompson (1990: 4), following Tonkin's (1990) analysis, note the 'failure to recognize rationalistic realism as the special myth of Western culture'.

23 I owe this point to Burke Long (n.d.) who made the observation in a paper read to the SBL Annual Meeting in San Francisco, November 1992.

24 It is highly questionable that a few scattered inscriptions and graffiti testify to widespread literacy in ancient Israel, as some have claimed. Harris (1989) focuses on Greek and Roman literacy, raising important questions about general literacy levels in antiquity. As is well known from a variety of studies (Goody 1968; Cipolla 1969; Ong 1982), widespread literacy is dependent upon a complex set of interrelationships backed by very significant centralized or government investment, as in Japan after the Meiji Restoration or in Cuba and Nicaragua (Harris 1989: 11–12). Harris notes that major historiographical works do not emerge in the Greek world until the fifth century BCE. This is to be contrasted with a general assumption in biblical studies that major historiographical works appeared at the court of David in the tenth century BCE. The role of urban centres in the spread of literacy and the development of historiographical works needs to be considered more carefully. The work of Harris (1989) points to the importance of the Persian and Hellenistic periods for exploring the development of biblical historiography as van Seters, Davies, Lemche, and Thompson have been arguing.

25 This was part of a published interview in *Woman's Own* (October 1987).

26 Gould (1987: 2) discusses the significance of McPhee's (1980) term for geological research.

27 Bohannan (1967: 327–9) points out that the Tiv of Nigeria do not by and large correlate events or a period of time beyond a generation or two. There is no desire to indicate time in the distant past with any greater accuracy than for the future. Pocock (1967: 304) examines the problem when people know that they have changed and continue, nevertheless, to live in a world whose values depend upon immutability: 'Here we have a choice: either we credit these people with an immense capacity for self-deception, an ability to live in permanent contradiction with their experience, or we must re-examine the assumptions in the light of which these facts constitute a problem.' The critical issue, however, is the anthropological use of time. See Fabian (1983) for a critique of the ideological use of time in social anthropology. Chapter 2 will deal with this problem in relation to Palestinian history.

28 Lord (1965: 29) reminds us that 'the picture that emerges is not really one of a conflict between preserver of tradition and creative artist, it is rather one of the preservation of tradition by the constant recreation of it'.

29 As Tonkin (1990: 25) notes: 'Myth is a representation of the past which historians recognize, but generally not as an alternative to proper history. I think we should dissolve this dichotomy.' Myth is often understood as a story about the gods or a story-like representation of the past to illustrate an important if unverifiable truth. See, for instance, Hughes (1990: 3) who complains that many biblical scholars refuse to use the term 'myth' in relation to the Bible because it is commonly defined as stories about gods whereas the Hebrew Bible is presented as non-

mythical and monotheistic. He argues that the biblical chronology is essentially mythical in that 'it uses historical fiction to express ideological beliefs'. Anyone who has tried to define the term 'myth' will be aware of the problems involved. Rogerson (1974: 174) emphasizes the 'multi-dimensional nature' of myth and advises following Lévi-Strauss in not offering a formal definition. However, the problem remains the continued use of the term in opposition to history, implying that history is objective and value free by contrast to the ideologically generated myths of ancient societies.

30 They go on to add:

> In the same spirit, we can re-examine just how collective myths claim and reshape the past for themselves. We need as historians to consider myth and memory, not only as special clues to the past, but equally as windows on the making and remaking of individual collective consciousness in which both fact and fantasy, past and present, each has its part. They admit us a rare view of these crucial processes, which we have so far neglected: to the possibility of a better understanding of a continuing struggle over the past which goes forward, always with uncertain outcome, into the future.
>
> (Samuel and Thompson 1990: 21)

31 See Whitelam (1989) for a study of the different origin traditions in the Hebrew Bible as representations of factional disputes over the right to the land in the second Temple period.

32 See Whitelam (1995b) for a discussion of the labels 'sociological approach' and 'sociological school' in recent biblical scholarship as misnomers.

33 Garbini (1988: 51) argues that without the use of external documentation it is impossible to identify where the biblical narratives are sound. Thus, without adequate extrabiblical sources, it is impossible to write a history of Israel. However, Garbini does not appear to appreciate the significant difference that recent literary study has made to the discipline and the difficulties of using the texts for historical reconstruction.

34 The phrase ought to be reserved for discussions concerning the historical development of the biblical texts themselves rather than as a label for the discussion of the history of the communities which gave rise to the literature.

35 Chakrabarty (1992: 1) points out the ambivalence in any such exercise:

> It is that insofar as the academic discourse of history – that is, 'history' as a discourse produced at the institutional site of the university – is concerned, 'Europe' remains the sovereign, theoretical subject of all histories, including the ones we call 'Indian', 'Chinese', 'Kenyan', and so on. There is a peculiar way in which all these other histories tend to become variations on a master narrative that could be called 'the history of Europe'. In this sense, 'Indian' history itself is in a position of subalternity; one can only articulate subaltern subject positions in the name of this history.
>
> (Chakrabarty 1992: 1)

2 DENYING SPACE AND TIME TO PALESTINIAN HISTORY

1 Said (1994a: 413–20) provides a critique of the Gaza–Jericho agreement which leaves the Palestinians without sovereignty or freedom.

2 Davies (1992: 23 n. 2) argues for the use of the term 'Palestine' while rejecting the common alternative 'land of Israel' on the basis that the former has been in use since the Assyrian period and the latter is unsuitable because only a small part of the region was occupied for a short time by a state of 'Israel'. He goes on to add that he disclaims 'interest in any political argument in this book'. However, the present work hopes to show that scholarship cannot disclaim such interest since the choice of terminology carries very important political implications.

3 The collection of essays edited by Miller, Hanson, and McBride (1987) indicates the re-evaluation of Israelite religion which is now taking place. Dever (1987) and Coogan (1987) illustrate the crucial links between Israelite and 'Canaanite', i.e. indigenous Palestinian, religion. Lemche (1984; 1988) has emphasized the religion of Israel as an indigenous phenomenon.

4 Inden (1986: 405; 1990: 50) points out how Western Europe saw the Semitic Near East and Aryan Persia as monotheistic and individualistic cultures similar to the West in contrast to the Far East of India, China and Japan. He cites Campbell (1962) as a classic example of the belief that the civilizations of the ancient Near East were culturally continuous with the West. This cultural continuity does not extend, however, to ancient Palestinian culture.

5 This is a frequent representation and justification of the modern state of Israel. Reifenberg (1955) presents a classic example of the view that it is the modern state which restores an ancient civilization following the supposed decline during the Ottoman period. There are numerous critiques of views which have ignored the size and role of the indigenous population in Palestine prior to and after the Zionist movement and subsequent establishment of the modern state of Israel (Khalidi 1984; Abu-Lughob 1987; Said 1992: 7–9). Hutteröth and Abdulfattah (1977) provide a more positive assessment of the Ottoman period.

6 Similarly, Edelman (1991: 3–6) uses the term 'Cisjordan' in an attempt to find neutral terminology to describe the region. As we have seen, however, no terminology which defines space can be said to be neutral.

7 Baly (1984) discusses the relationship of geography to history in the Persian period in a volume in the *Cambridge History of Judaism* series. Although the article was published in 1984, it was completed by 1973. He refers to 'Palestine proper, that is, the area of effective Jewish settlement' (1984: 2) as stretching from Dan to Beersheba and Joppa to Jordan. He contrasts this with the whole 'Palestine area' which ranges from Dan to Ezion-geber and Jaffa to Philadelphia (modern Amman).

8 The use of terminology to define time has profound implications for any understanding of Palestinian history. This will be treated in the following section.

9 The same phrase was also used in the government White Paper of 1939

(Laqueur and Rabin 1981: 68). A similar phrase, a 'natural home in the ancestral land', appears in the Zionist reaction to the White Paper in a statement prepared by the Jewish Agency for Palestine in 1939 (Laqueur and Rabin 1981: 76–7).

10 It is noticeable that the various respondents at the conference chose to ignore the arguments advanced by Dothan, concentrating instead on a presentation by Redford on Egyptian influence on the region. This tends to suggest that this is an issue that is usually seen as too sensitive to address: the problem of the political implications of the discourse of biblical studies for contemporary disputes over the land is a problem that remains unspoken. Seger (1985: 158) was a noticeable exception in rejecting Dothan's terminology on the grounds that 'these changes emphasize ethnic associations which are archaeologically the most difficult to adequately identify and assess'.

11 It should be noted that Baly refers to 'Palestinian communities' (1984: 2) and 'the Palestine population' (1984: 20) in his discussion of the Persian period.

12 This has been cited by Said (1992: 79) and taken from an unpublished dissertation by Miriam Rosen, 'The Last Crusade: British Archaeology in Palestine'. I have been unable to obtain a copy of her work.

13 Golda Meir's famous denial in 1969 of the existence of Palestinians (Said 1992: 4–5) is echoed in Peters's (1984) attempts to remove them from history.

14 Ackroyd (1987: 248) has remarked on the misleading and inaccurate uses of such terms as 'Exile' and 'Restoration'. The term 'Exile', as he points out, is tendentious and encourages assumptions based on a dangerously simple reading of the biblical texts. Such terms perpetuate a biblically based view of the region in which the vast majority of the inhabitants are ignored.

15 For the presentation of Indian history as static, see Inden (1986: 423).

16 The *Annalistes* conception of history as related to the problem of re-creating the history of early Israel has been outlined by Whitelam (1986: 45–70). Miller (1987: 57 n. 3) believes that this is an overly optimistic enterprise which sets out an unrealistic agenda.

17 Braudel borrowed this concept from Wolfram Eberhard (1965: 13).

18 Foucault (1984: 87) criticizes the notion of 'total history' as claiming to be able to present the past as a completed development which can be grasped as a whole while standing outside history itself.

19 He does make the important point that much of the independence of the state which existed in the region for roughly ten per cent of the time under review was illusory (1984: 2). The question of an independent Israelite state in ancient Palestine will be examined in chapter 4.

20 Iggers (1979: 10) notes that it has been the ambition of the *Annales* historians to lay the foundations of a 'global/total' history of a region of larger geographical whole such as the Mediterranean. It is the underlying material forces of the interactions between the population and economic factors which provided the unifying elements of such a study rather than politics or ideology. McNeill (1961: 30; 45; 1982: 75–89) is a proponent of 'world history' which offers a panoramic

view by which to discover rhythms and patterns which are not discernible from a detailed study of the different segments of history. However, the criticisms of Said and Foucault need to be borne in mind in order not to divest Palestine of inherent value thereby continuing its exclusion from historical discourse.

21 Davies believes that Miller and Hayes (1986) represents the pinnacle of *biblical histories* since it is unlikely that this particular kind of history can be written much better. He goes on to add:

> The way forward – if it exists – would seem to lie with the (combined) methods of the social sciences: sociology, anthropology and archaeology. The results will invert the status of the biblical literature: instead of asking how the history can be explained from the literature, we must ask how the literature can be explained from the history. If *literary* study is turning its face away from history, concentrating on what is *in*, not *behind*, the text, there yet remains a legitimate task for the *historian*, but this task will be increasingly divorced from literary criticism.
>
> (Davies 1987: 4)

Gunn also believes that the study of history will proceed in a similar manner. He predicts that 'The results will be nothing like a what-happened-next history, its periodization will be broad, and it will depend upon literary criticism (including structuralist criticism) for its appropriation of texts' (Gunn 1987: 67).

3 INVENTING ANCIENT ISRAEL

1 Asad (1975: 274; see also Said 1994a: 85) criticizes A. Cohen's study of *Arab Border-Villages in Israel* for its use of the *hamula* to emphasize that Arab villages in Israel were only collections of village clans incapable of national identity. Cohen (1965: 149) argues that a number of factors prevented the development of a united Arab political front particularly as 'the Arabs in Israel do not constitute a united, integrated, community'. This representation of contemporary political organization, or lack of it, is mirrored within the discourse of biblical studies.

2 This body of archaeological data and its implications for the realization of a history of ancient Palestine will be considered in the next chapter

3 The collection of articles in *Biblical Archaeologist* (1993) provides an overview of the conscious design behind the propagation of Albright's ideas. I have also had access to Burke Long's unpublished research on Albright and the Biblical Colloquium.

4 Alcalay (1993: 35–52) describes how the indigenous Jewish population of Palestine and the Levant was deprived of its cultural heritage after Zionist immigration and dominance in the region. He reveals a rich Arab and Jewish cultural heritage which existed throughout the Levant prior to the modern period.

5 The major reassessment can be found in Running and Freedman (1975), van Beek (1989), and *Biblical Archaeologist* (1993).

6 Freedman (1989: 33), in his assessment of Albright as a historian, makes it quite clear that he was 'an apologist for a somewhat traditional, even archaic outlook'. His underlying philosophy of history was a Christian synthesis which relied upon Aquinas, Augustine, and Calvin.

7 This influence is extensive, with many of his students dominating American biblical scholarship through their appointment and promotion to senior academic positions. Their publications and the training of subsequent generations of students have meant that Albright's views and scholarship have left an indelible mark on the field. Burke Long has explored the mechanisms of how Albright's views were propagated in some of his, as yet, unpublished work. The creation and maintenance of this network is also a major factor in the problem of where the study of ancient Palestinian history might be located in the future as it breaks free from the control of biblical studies.

8 Running and Freedman (1975: 377–8) provide further information on Albright's political opinions which sheds valuable light on the political views which clearly informed his construction of the past. Professor Aviram is quoted as reporting that Albright advised the audience at a dinner in his honour at the home of the President of Israel in March 1969 not to give up any land captured in the Six Day War. Revealingly, Malamat reports that in 1967 Albright had urged Israel not to return the Sinai to the Russians. Malamat expressed the view that for Albright the Suez canal represented the border between the Western world and the Communist East. Israel, in Albright's understanding, was the buffer between Western civilization and democracy and the undemocratic, uncivilized East. The authors also cite Yadin as complaining that Albright had been 'so free and open in supporting Israel politically, even in public press conferences, that I had to caution him a bit that he should perhaps be more careful on that' (Running and Freedman 1975: 378). He describes Albright as a champion of Israel but one who recognized the problem that the creation of the modern state caused for the Arabs. '*But on balance*, as he always used to say, be that if there were two just causes here, the justification for Israel to have a state was the greater one' (Running and Freedman 1975: 380). It is clear from these reported views and the statement in *New Palestine* that Albright's construction of the past, as a mirror of the present, was informed by his political views.

9 Wright's use of mutation to describe the uniqueness of Israel needs to be contrasted with the standard biological understanding of mutation as a change in the chemical structure of a gene which is rarely beneficial. Mutational changes in genes are random, and a random change in such a delicate mechanism is more likely to be harmful than beneficial (Keeton 1967: 541–2). Wright tries to counter this by arguing, like Albright, that evolution is divinely controlled and so the Israelite mutation is not a matter of chance but part of the divinely guided evolutionary scheme.

10 Elsewhere, he denies the uniqueness of Israelite historical experience. However, interestingly, the comparison is with the history of the USA. Ancient Israel's experience mirrors that of the USA:

Yet other peoples have had events in their background which are

249

not dissimilar. We in the U.S.A. have our founding fathers, our exodus from European oppression, our covenant in the Constitution and Bill of Rights, our conquest of America, and a succession of great men who have been the fathers of our country, beginning obviously with George Washington. In other words, the biblical event as an event of history is not overly impressive as to its uniqueness.

(Wright 1960: 10–11)

The uniqueness comes not in the event itself, but in the event as revelation of the divine plan. It can be seen how the past informs his understanding of the present and vice versa.

11 Bright (1981: 137–43) revised his understanding of the Israelite conquest in later editions by incorporating aspects of Mendenhall's revolt hypothesis.

12 He states explicitly in the foreword to the first edition that it was 'prepared with the particular needs of the undergraduate theological student in mind' (1960: 10). The epilogue to his work is a discussion of the theological implications of the history of Israel or, as he puts it, 'the *theological* destination of this history' (1960: 447). These are not questions for the historian to answer by the examination of data but for 'each man according to the faith that is in him' (1960: 447). This 'salvation history' (*Heilsgeshchichte*) points to the future promise of 'the ultimate triumph of God's rule in the world' (1960: 448). Bright proposes that there are two legitimate answers to the question of 'whither the history of Israel?' The first is the Jewish answer that it continues in Judaism; while the second, and more importantly for Bright, is the Christian answer which finds its theological fulfilment in Christ and the gospel:

So, two opposing answers to the same question: Whither Israel's history? It is on this question, fundamentally, that the Christian and his Jewish friend divide. Let us pray that they do so in love and mutual concern, as heirs of the same heritage of faith who worship the same God, who is Father of us all.

(Bright 1960: 452–3)

It is clear from this that the historical enterprise of Bright was motivated primarily by his theological convictions while assuring the reader throughout of the 'objectivity' of scholarship. Israel is the theological root of Bright's conception of his Christian present, and so the origins of Israel, this 'peculiar people', are crucial to his faith. Little wonder, then, that the silencing of Palestinian history is a question that is not raised in this account or others of the Baltimore school.

13 His critique has been extended by Gottwald (1979), Lemche (1985), and Coote (1990), among others, in questioning the conceptualization of nomadic societies and its application in the understanding of ancient Israel. Mendenhall (1973: 165) claims that there is not an adequate or well-documented model for understanding ancient Israelite tribes.

14 See further Mendenhall (1973: 175). However, note his statement (1973: 183) that although studies were still in their infancy 'such an approach

demonstrates the usefulness of the new evolutionary study, now several decades old, in anthropology'. Mendenhall, in appealing to the work of Service, recognized that the move from tribal organization to chiefdom was reversible.

15 His theological premise, underpinning his historical analysis, is stated as 'the rejection of God is the rejection of love and certainly, of life' (1973: 164).

16 Mendenhall's insistence on the social construction of ethnicity provides an important corrective to the usual assumptions in biblical studies:

> There was no such thing as an ethnic group of 'Israelites' in this early period. Throughout history, a feeling of ethnic identity has been the product of a very long and complex process of continuity and contiguity. The basis of solidarity changes as the nature of the social organization changed. What was at first a religious and ethical unity created from a very diverse population that did not even speak the same dialect of West Semitic gave way to an uneasy political unity that soon divided into two. Not until the political and religious institutionalism was destroyed did the basis again shift to a concept of ethnic unity, long after the Babylonian Exile, and that was thoroughly rejected and challenged by the reform movement that we now call Christianity.
>
> (Mendenhall 1973: 27–8)

Once again, however, he has drawn a direct connection between Israelite religion and Christianity implying that it is the latter which is the true expression of the biblical revolution.

17 Lemche (1985: 433) pointed out that such a caricature fails to recognize the central importance of social justice, the protection of the poor, the widow, the orphan, and the importance of the harmony of society in such religious systems. Instead they are dismissed as concerned only with sexual orgies and social abominations.

18 Gottwald, in answering various objections to the revolt model, particularly the claim that it lacks biblical evidence and retrojects Marxist ideology on to the past, is well aware of the subjective influences on constructing history:

> Such an invocation of sociology of knowledge contains an important caution which, of course, applies equally to all theoretical modelling. One must similarly consider whether the conquest model has not been motivated oftentimes by a desire to confirm the truthfulness of the Bible, and it may also be asked if the immigration model has not been stimulated by modish but mistaken ways of reconstructing history and social evolution which did not first occur to the critic from reading the biblical data. Moreover, it could easily be retorted that those who cavalierly dismiss the revolt model may be so influenced by their fear of or distaste for contemporary social unrest that they refuse to look at the historical evidence concerning Israel's origins. But to point out the predisposing effects of the interpreter's social and cultural

matrix toward one or another outlook on the material is not to
settle matters; it is merely to call for more careful controls on these
predispositions which will allow for close scrutiny of methods
and conclusions. Theoretical adequacy – namely, the ability to
account for the data over the widest range in the most coherent
manner – is the only answer to the suspicion of contaminating
presuppositions. While it is true that a current mood may lead
to distorting reconstructions of the past, it is also true that a
current temper of mind may be just the catalyst needed in order
to see analogous tempers and forces at work in other times and
other places. Like may indeed fabricate like, but like may also
discover like.

(Gottwald 1979: 218–19)

19 He offers (1979: 45–187) an extensive but very traditional source analysis
of the biblical traditions which acknowledges the influence of Alt, Noth,
and von Rad.

20 This presentation mirrors the conception of Israel as an egalitarian lower-
class society central to the left-wing, largely secular ideology of
European Zionism and the kibbutz movement.

21 He says this in relation to the incursion of the Philistines and the
imposition of a strong military aristocracy on the Canaanite city-states.
However, he implies, like Alt, that the Philistines failed to achieve the
ultimate move to statehood because they 'fell heir to the old internal
Canaanite subdivisions by city-states and incorporated those city-state
entities as a mode of their hegemony, just as the Egyptians before them
had done' (1979: 411).

22 He draws distinctions between what he terms 'Canaanite feudalism' and
'medieval European feudalism' (1979: 391–4). It is the nature of the
analogy which he draws which is important. He also emphasizes the
interrelationships between Canaanite feudalism and Egyptian imperialism within the exploitative system as a whole (1979: 391–4). Again it
is interesting to note the parallels with the period of Zionist immigration
as a period of first Turkish and then European imperialism in the region.
Elon (1983: 41–56) describes the brutal conditions of Jews living in
Eastern Europe in the latter half of the nineteenth century, emphasizing
the extreme form of egalitarianism of the *shtetl* which grew out of it:

In the *shtetl*, 'life was with people'. Simple human solidarity was
the *shtetl's* source of strength to survive as an island culture
surrounded by hostility. A ghost of the *shtetl* lingers on in modern
living institutions in Israel.

(Elon 1983: 47)

4 THE CREATION OF AN ISRAELITE STATE

1 Even in the post-First World War period, an influential time in the
development of biblical studies, the idea of a continuum between past
and present is evident. Sidebotham (1918) refers to the defeat of the Turks

in Mesopotamia and the need to secure a defensive frontier in Egypt which may lead to the 're-establishment of a Jewish State in Palestine'. The devaluation of the indigenous population and its culture is spelled out in the strongest terms:

> Nor is there any indigenous civilization in Palestine that could take the place of the Turkish empire except that of the Jews, who already numbering one-seventh of the population, have given to Palestine everything that it has ever had of value to the world.
>
> (cited in Khalidi 1971: 126)

2 Weinstein (1981) has demonstrated that Egyptian power was more dogged and lasted in the region much longer than previously thought.

3 Bright (1976) expands on his view of the Israelite empire confirming the shared assumptions with Alt and Noth on the construction of the monarchy.

4 This period is dominant in narrative terms as well. In Bright's account of some 444 pages of text, approximately 123 are devoted to the emergence of Israel ('the period of the Judges') and the formation of an Israelite state culminating in the reigns of David and Solomon: approximately a third of the narrative. By comparison, his account covers the period c. 2000–164 BCE, some 1800 years, of which the emergence of Israel to the death of Solomon (c. 1200–922 BCE) spans roughly two and a half centuries: a mere 13–15 per cent of the time span.

5 See Khalidi (1971: xxi–lxxxiii) for a discussion of the political manoeuvrings by the British and American governments from the beginning of the century to the creation of the state of Israel in 1948.

6 This presupposes that the Aegean groups were also a tribal organization. However, it is not clear what evidence he has to support such an assertion.

7 He refers later to the Philistines as commanding an 'extensive empire' (1966: 182).

8 There is a voluminous literature on state formation: see Cohen and Service 1978; Claessen and Skalnik 1978; 1981; Jones and Kautz 1981; Haas 1982.

9 Chomsky (1983: 99–103; 181–328) exposes the reality of the claims of the 'defensive' wars of modern Israel, particularly the 1978 invasion of Lebanon and the 1982 'Operation Peace for Galilee'.

10 1 Samuel 8 and 12, among other traditions, stress a negative assessment of the formation of the monarchy as a rejection of the theocracy of Yahweh. Eslinger (1985), by contrast, offers an alternative literary analysis which examines the different voices in the text.

11 Noth (1960: 238) notes that the Philistines tried to take advantage of the break-up of what he erroneously terms 'the empire of David and Solomon' and even though 'the earlier power of the Philistines had been broken by David once and for all' what ensued were border skirmishes with no far-reaching effects. Mazar (1984: 53) outlines the importance of Philistine settlement in the tenth century BCE. The most comprehensive treatment of Philistine culture is by T. Dothan (1982). For more

recent findings and assessments, see M. Dothan (1989), T. Dothan (1989), and M. and T. Dothan (1992).

12 Recent archaeological work, which undermines such constructions, will be considered later in the chapter.

13 The period after the Arab conquest is represented typically as a period of decline: 'Jerusalem simply declined to the status of a provincial town. Its only importance stemmed from its religious significance to Islam, focusing upon the mosque and shrine built in the Temple Enclosure' (1983: 260). The implication here appears to be that Islam is of marginal importance.

14 This is equivalent to Ben-Gurion's 'vision' of the borders of Israel as described on p. 126.

15 Noth tries to distinguish, unsuccessfully, between Oriental ideas of divine kingship and Israelite royal ideology. He claims that the use of the adoption formula in Psalm 2 verse 7 shows that 'whilst the Davidic monarchy made just as great claims in Israel as the monarchy did elsewhere in the ancient Orient, it was different in quality' (1960: 224). His view that the conception of Israel's god acting within history was different to conceptions of the divine nature of kingship in the ancient Near East has been undermined by Albrektson's study (1967) and subsequent work.

16 J. van Seters (1983) offers a radically different understanding of the development of Israelite historiography, while Harris's (1989) study on literacy in Greece and Rome throws serious doubt on the blithe assumption that the production of major historiographical works was developed before the Hellenistic period.

17 Interestingly, Herrmann (1975: 141) refers to 'Saul and his central Palestinian followers'.

18 Herrmann (1975: 171 n. 38) acknowledges that the description is taken from Alt's earlier study 'Das Grossreich Davids'.

19 His justification (1984: 42) for this is that the economic and political information seems so relevant that it is hard to believe that it could have been invented. However, this is an argument for proof based on verisimilitude alone.

20 She does not use the term 'Palestine' but a careful circumlocution to describe the area: 'the narrow strip of land between the Jordan River and the Mediterranean Sea'. Her careful avoidance of the term 'Palestine' in the context of arguing for the defensive nature of the Israelite empire suggests very strongly that she is aware of the political implications and context of her work but refuses to articulate this.

21 It is interesting to note that Ahlström (1993: 438), who rightly criticizes other scholars for interpreting archaeological evidence on the basis of the biblical text, interprets Khirbet ed-Duwwara with the rise of Saul even though there is nothing to point to such an understanding.

22 Ahlström (1993: 449 n. 2; 1986: 96) notes that Engnell designated Saul as the first empire-builder.

23 The fact that he uses the term 'empire' in quotation marks in a subheading (1993: 480; 488 n. 1) suggests that he does not accept this general description.

24 These narratives are described as 'folk legends. Certainly they are not to
    be read as historical record' (1986: 152). They admit that any attempt to
    reconstruct the 'historical' David will necessarily be 'highly speculative'
    (1986: 159). But, despite their description of the narratives as folk legends,
    they believe that they are based 'ultimately on actual historical persons
    and events' (1986: 159). Miller and Hayes are aware that their pre-
    supposition cannot be proved; their construction represents only a 'best
    guess' (1986: 160).

25 Miller (1991b) outlines some of the methodological problems involved
    in trying to assess the historical reliability of the biblical traditions for
    constructing the reign of Solomon. This is part of an exchange with
    Millard (1991) who argues for a positive appraisal of the historicity of
    the biblical traditions. Wightman (1990) questions the network of
    assumptions which has sustained the idea of 'Solomonic archaeology'.
    He is extremely critical of Aharoni's (1972: 302) claim that six-
    chambered gateways constituted a fixed chronological datum point for
    the archaeology of the tenth century BCE as one of the rare cases where
    it is possible to date a building exactly without inscriptional evidence.
    Wightman (1990: 9), by contrast, describes it as 'one of the not-so-rare
    examples in biblical archaeology where the exact date of a building is
    determined through circular reasoning'. Miller and Hayes (1986: 210)
    give a sober appraisal of the major archaeological material relating to the
    Solomonic period both in terms of the difficulties of interpretation and
    the 'impressiveness' of the building projects.

26 Miller (1991a: 95) points out that there is no evidence for a Davidic–
    Solomonic monarchy independent of the biblical traditions. Historians
    who refer to this entity are presupposing information which is drawn
    from the Hebrew Bible.

27 This is also true of the collection of essays edited by Gottwald (1986),
    despite the fact that they challenge many standard assumptions about
    the formation of an Israelite state. Coote and Whitelam (1987: 113) argue
    that this process should be studied as part of a continuum in the context
    of a wider Palestinian history. However, it is noticeable that this is still
    a history of the region which is dominated by Israel and which in effect
    is little more than a history of ancient Israel and not ancient Palestine.

28 Flanagan (1988) cites four reasons for the 'lapse of confidence regarding
    David and the monarchy' (1988: 18); Mendenhall and Gottwald showed
    the monarchy to be alien; Davidic stories came under attack after half a
    century of relative certainty contributing to a loss of confidence in
    biblical history; archaeology failed to yield signs of centralization that
    could be firmly dated to the tenth century BCE. Flanagan does, however,
    appreciate the importance of this period in shaping the past and that
    there are alternative constructions of this past:

> The common assumption that Israelite monarchy began with
> David, or possibly Saul, controlled the way that long- and short-
> term history were interpreted. If the sources were approached
> without presupposing a monarchical ethos, many details, I believe,

would be interpreted differently, and a substantially different picture would emerge.

(Flanagan 1988: 21)

Flanagan (1988: 75–6) tries to define what he terms 'social world studies' to take into account the many different sources available for exploring the Iron Age. He moves away from a narrow focus on a biblically inspired history of Israel but does not go so far as to refer to Palestinian history.

29 Garbini (1988: 16–19) highlights the startling fact of the lack of Israelite and Judaean epigraphy for the period of the monarchy. Garbini's statement has to be tempered now by the discovery of the Tel Dan inscription (see pp. 166–8), but it does not alter the fact that this so-called glorious empire of David and Solomon has left little or no archaeological trace, particularly in terms of the output of its supposed bureaucracy.

30 He cites (1993: 541 n. 3), seemingly with approval, the words of Herrmann (1984: 268) that David's state 'would not have been possible without David'. This is the history of great men *par excellence*.

31 Arnold (1990) provides a detailed description and critique of the history of the search for the identification of Gibeah with its manifold textual and archaeological problems.

32 See Noth (1960: 168) or Bright (1972: 186) who says that Saul's 'seat at Gibeah was a fortress rather than a palace'.

33 This would be accepted by many as an uncontroversial statement until very recently. He goes on to argue (1984: 55–6) that the burial and water systems were uniquely Israelite, along with the design of certain fortifications, such as casemate walls and six-chambered gates from the tenth century BCE. But the walls and gates of the ninth century resemble Syrian fortifications.

34 Avi Ofer is conducting the Judaean Highland Project survey. The results of his work, which are as yet unpublished, will need to be compared with Jamieson-Drake's conclusions. The data he has collected and alluded to in conference addresses will, like the data provided by Finkelstein, Zertal, Gal, and others involved in major surveys, provide the basis for future investigations of the history of the region. It still remains to examine the interpretation of this data and the interests and motivations which have determined the design of research strategies.

35 The inscription was originally published by Biran and Naveh (1993). It immediately attracted considerable attention, generating heated debate as to its date and interpretation (Davies 1994; Rainey 1994; Lemaire 1994; Cryer 1994; Shanks 1994). The article attributed to Shanks is said to be based upon Biran and Naveh (1993) supplemented by other material supplied by Biran.

36 It is admitted that there are major difficulties in excavating Jerusalem given the fact that it has been occupied constantly, coupled with religious sensibilities which have often hindered archaeological exploration. Mazar (1984) points to these difficulties and the problems with 'Davidic archaeology'. However, these circumstances should have led to greater caution and not less in terms of the construction of the past.

37 McEvedy and Jones (1978: 228) provide the basis for a broad comparison. The data from regional surveys will form the basis for a more detailed study of the demography of Palestine.

38 The fact that the modern state, as a world ranking power, appears to be an exception to this is to be explained by the massive subsidization of its military economy by the USA. Chomsky (1983) provides detailed figures. The modern period can be compared with the material prosperity of the Roman and Byzantine periods which was the result of massive external investment.

5 THE CONTINUING SEARCH

1 H. and M. Weippert (1991) have provided a detailed review of recent literature which can be supplemented by Coote's (1990) extensive bibliography. The collections of essays in Edelman (1991) and in *Scandinavian Journal of the Old Testament* (1991) illustrate the direction of the debate along with the growing differences between the various positions.

2 The impact of newer literary studies has been more extensive and is made more explicit in the work of Davies, Thompson, and Whitelam. It has had far less impact on the studies of Ahlström, Lemche, and Coote.

3 Alt (1959), in an article first published in 1944, also refers to the rhythms of Syrian and Palestinian history.

4 See Coote and Whitelam (1987) for a review of the settlement history of Palestine from the Early Bronze Age to the present. Whitelam (1994) sets out proposals for the pursuit of Palestinian history through the study of settlement history (cf. Dever 1992).

5 He put forward a similar view in 1985b: 80. However, as noted on p. 241 n.9, he has more recently acknowledged that a survey of the whole region, including the lowlands, for the Middle Bronze II to the Iron II is a pressing problem that needs to be carried out (1991: 48). It should be acknowledged that Finkelstein provides valuable data for other periods and that his reports are invariably a model of clarity allowing the historian to utilize the data in historical reconstruction. However, the point at issue here is the way in which the search for 'ancient Israel' has been a major obstacle in recognizing the potential and importance of the data for a regional Palestinian history.

6 The irony of these surveys is that they illustrate Viceroy Curzon's comment, at the turn of the century, about the British in India: 'It is . . . equally our duty to dig and discover, to classify, reproduce and describe, to copy and decipher, to cherish and conserve' (cited by Anderson 1991: 179). Detailed mapping allows the classification and control of the past. The mapping of Iron I sites, presented as Israelite, exposes the roots of modern Israel deep in the past. It is this particular segment of the past which is cherished and preserved. It is designed to provide an 'objective' illustration of the continuity between past and present.

7 The data tend to be scattered in specialist publications and journals. What

is needed is a comprehensive synthesis of the latest survey findings organized by period and area in order to allow comparisons to be made.

8 Elon goes on to describe the outbreak of enthusiasm for archaeology as a means of discovering and confirming Zionist claims to the land. He cites the recollections of Eliezer Sukenik, the excavator, which illustrate the motivations at the time:

> Suddenly people could see things that had never been so tangible before. . . . There was a feeling that this piece of ground, for which people had suffered so much, wasn't just any plot of land but a piece of earth where their forefathers had lived fifteen hundred to two thousand years ago. Their work in the present was cast in a different light. Their history was revealed to them and they saw it with their own eyes.
>
> (Elon 1994: 14)

9 See, for example, the debate between Aharoni and Yadin (1979) on the dating of these settlements and their relationship to the destruction of Hazor.

10 Miller (1991a: 97–9) similarly draws attention to Finkelstein's use of biblical traditions, such as the so-called Ark Narrative (1 Samuel 4–6; 2 Samuel 6), for controlling the interpretation of archaeological data (see also Dever 1991: 79).

11 This expectation informs a great deal of archaeological work on the early Iron Age. Gal (1992: 88), for instance, believes 'that the tribes of Zebulun and Naphtali, whose inheritances were within this subregion, were settled one or two generations after the destruction of these Canaanite cities'. This biblically inspired reasoning is taken to its extreme in Dar's publication of the Survey of Samaria for 800 BCE to 63 CE in which he conjectures that the early Iron Age farmhouse was a 'characteristic model of settlement by kinships (extended families) of the Joseph tribe' (1986: 2). He argues not only that the four-room house was an Israelite invention but also that the rural farmhouse was improved and developed by families of the tribes of Ephraim and Manassah. Similarly, the acceptance of the tribal allotments is evident in the reading of the archaeological data in Garsiel and Finkelstein's (1978) discussion of the Western expansion of the 'house of Joseph'. Surprisingly, it can also be found in Silberman's (1992: 192–8) review of recent scholarship on Israelite origins. Despite his attention to the political aspects of archaeology and biblical studies, he is still able to claim that Zertal's work on the territory of Manassah had been complemented by major new surveys in Galilee and 'the territories of the tribes of Ephraim and Judah'.

12 Callaway (1969; 1970; Callaway and Cooley 1971) is much more circumspect in terms of the identity of the inhabitants of Ai and Raddanah.

13 Shiloh's (1970) belief that the four-room house was an Israelite invention has been undermined by its discovery in a wide variety of locations throughout Palestine.

14 He bases his conclusions on data drawn from the earlier survey undertaken by Kochavi (1972).

15 Skjeggestad (1992: 159–65) has provided a detailed critique of Finkelstein's understanding of ethnicity.

16 This is a response in the *Biblical Archaeologist Review* to the SBL/ASOR session, the papers of which are contained in *Scandinavian Journal of the Old Testament* (1991).

17 This point is illustrated in reviews of these works by Bimson (1989; 1991) and Miller (1991a) which focus on their use of biblical traditions and their relevance for constructing early Israelite history. They do not pick up on the issue of Palestinian history and its relationship to biblical studies.

18 Carroll (1991) has been very forthright in arguing for the Hebrew Bible as the product of the second Temple period. He is also scathing of attempts to construct history from such texts: 'the gap between texts and the real world remains as unbridgeable as ever' (1991: 124). Coote, by contrast, regards many biblical texts as products of the Davidic bureaucracy in the tenth century BCE (Coote and Coote 1990; Coote and Ord 1991).

19 He reiterated his view of the texts as late and therefore of little value for constructing the early history of Israel at the Chicago symposium (Lemche 1991a: 14), adding that he did not believe that the Old Testament historians wrote history. He has added to this in numerous articles and later publications (1991b; 1994).

20 The growing unease with attempts to write biblical histories of ancient Israel is encapsulated in the methodological crisis represented by the works of Soggin and Miller and Hayes (cf. Davies 1985).

21 Whitelam (1986: 47) was able to state that 'it is important to address and refute claims that the study of the history of Israel cannot or should not be undertaken and to state clearly that it remains a fundamental task of research and teaching' (*contra* Davies, 1985: 172).

22 Rogerson (1986) and Martin (1989) raise important questions about the standard assumption that Israel was a tribal confederation.

23 See Whitelam (1994) for a discussion of some of the problems in trying to interpret the stele. Shanks (1991: 16) has dismissed as a passing fad the questioning of constructions of Israel in the pre-monarchic period. He asserts, astoundingly, that these 'negative historians' would like to 'send someone to the Cairo Museum to blow up the Merneptah stele' so that 'all their problems in connection with early Israel would be solved' (1991: 16).

24 He bases much of his analysis on Finkelstein's understanding of the chronological development of 'Israelite Settlement'.

25 Emerton (1988) has drawn attention to the inconsistencies and problems involved in trying to identify a ring structure in the inscription.

26 He cites (1991a: 24 n. 14) the final report from Hazor by Yadin *et al.* (1989: 25, 29) which claims that stratum XII, with its numerous pits but no buildings, was occupied by invading semi-nomadic Israelites. There is nothing in the archaeological record to support such an interpretation. Ahlström (1993) argues that it could just as easily have been due to the survivors from Hazor who lacked the tools or skills for rebuilding.

27 Ahlström (1991a: 19) claimed that the works of Lemche and Finkelstein

supported his proposals. He accepted that the archaeological evidence pointed to some non-Palestinian groups from the north in accordance with the demographic traditions of the country. He questions Mazar's use of the term 'Israelite' to describe the inhabitants of Giloh (1986: 29) and describes the material culture as Canaanite (1986: 35–6).

28 The subtle ways in which the contemporary context, or use of language, can shape perceptions of the past is brought out by his attempt to challenge the use of the ethnic label 'Israelite' to describe the inhabitants of these new settlements:

> An accurate label for the new settlers of the hills would be 'pioneers'. The lack of any specific 'Israelite' (meaning non-Canaanite) material culture at the excavated sites in the hills for the 12th century B.C. may be due to the lack of expertise and knowledge of advanced techniques practised by specialists who remained in the urban centres.
>
> (Ahlström 1986: 19)

The term 'pioneers', although widespread in terms of settlement in different parts of the world, has particular connotations, of course, in the contemporary contest for land. It is frequently used to describe Zionist settlers in the *kibbutzim* and agricultural settlements during the early immigrations into the area.

29 He appeals (1985: 387) to Snodgrass's description of post-Mycenaean Greece as an example.

30 Whitelam (1991), in discussing the problems of history and literature, frequently refers to 'Israel', encoded in such a way, and talks of a regional history of Palestine. The power of the discourse is still evident but the development of the current argument is already present:

> The growing body of archaeological evidence from the region supports the view that the Iron I highland villages, usually identified as 'Israel', emerged in Palestine as a result of a complex combination of indigenous processes and external pressures, culminating in the realignment of Palestine society. The fact that we are unable to identify, in ethnic terms, the inhabitants of these villages means that we have to resign ourselves to the study of the realignment of Palestinian society and the reasons for the settlement shift rather than an explanation *per se* of the emergence of Israel.
>
> (Coote and Whitelam 1987: 62–3)

The implications of this are more fully realized in Whitelam (1994).

31 For a response to Thompson's critique of Coote and Whitelam (1987), see Whitelam (1995a).

6 RECLAIMING PALESTINIAN HISTORY

1 I have been unable to obtain a copy of his new book on the career of Yadin. Clearly from the reviews (for example, Elon 1994), it addresses directly the issue of the politics of Yadin's archaeology.

2 The interconnections throughout the eastern Mediterranean during this and many other periods are well documented in archaeological deposits, although the precise connections, their regulation, and control are not nearly so clearly understood. The exploration of the economy of ancient Palestine is one of the key areas for future research.

3 Coote and Whitelam (1987: 49–71) explore some of the possible factors involved, placing particular emphasis on the effects of fluctuations in trade on the variability of settlement. Thompson (1992a: 180) doubts that the breakdown of international trade at the end of the Early Bronze and Late Bronze Ages could have had such an effect upon the Palestinian economy as to result in 'wholesale dislocations throughout the region, and especially in so many sub-regions (such as the hill country and the Northern Negev)' since such regions were only marginally affected by trade routes. He believes (1992a: 215) that the evidence points to major climatic change resulting in widespread drought and famine from c. 1200–1000 BCE. Climate is obviously an important factor given the marginal nature of the subregions of Palestine where dramatic variations in rainfall over two or more years can have devastating effects. Famine, however, is not always a direct result of periods of drought but is frequently the result of socio-political factors as the tragic events in parts of modern-day Africa all too vividly illustrate (cf. Thompson 1992a: 219–20). It is also the case that Palestine has witnessed important shifts in settlement during more modern periods when the climate in the region has remained stable. Thompson (1992a: 261) points out that the Phoenician cities survived the drought without widespread collapse, attributing their political and economic autonomy to their relative geographical isolation. This would suggest that it is socio-political factors which are of greater importance in understanding the settlement shifts rather than climatic change. Geographical isolation is no protection against catastrophic climatic change.

4 Dever (1991: 78) believes that the absence of collared-rim ware at large sites such as Gezer compared with its proliferation at smaller rural sites points to a socio-economic rather than ethnic dichotomy. Finkelstein (1991: 51) points out that Aphek and Qasile, usually described as urban centres, were no larger than 'Izbet Sartah.

5 Mazar's (1990) recent survey of the archaeology of the region is a good case in point of the way in which any female figurine is represented as part of a fertility cult.

BIBLIOGRAPHY

Abu-Lughob, I. (1987) *The Transformation of Palestine: Essays on the Origin and Development of the Arab–Israeli Conflict*, Evanston: Northwestern University Press.

Ackroyd, P. (1987) *Studies in the Religious Tradition of the Old Testament*, London: SCM.

—— (1984) 'The Jewish community in the Persian period', in W.D. Davies and L. Finkelstein (eds) *The Cambridge History of Judaism*. Vol. 1: *Introduction: The Persian Period*, Cambridge: Cambridge University Press.

Aharoni, Y. (1957) 'Problems of the Israelite conquest in light of archaeological discoveries', *Antiquity and Survival* 2: 131–50.

—— (1962) *The Land of the Bible. A Historical Geography*, London: Burns & Oates.

—— (1972) 'The stratification of Israelite Megiddo', *Journal of Near Eastern Studies* 31: 302–11.

—— (1982) *The Archaeology of the Land of Israel: From the Prehistoric Beginnings to the End of the First Temple Period*, London: SCM.

Ahlström, G.W. (1986) *Who Were the Israelites?*, Winona Lake: Eisenbrauns.

—— (1991a) 'The origin of Israel in Palestine', *Scandinavian Journal of the Old Testament* 2: 19–34.

—— (1991b) 'The role of archaeological and literary remains in reconstructing Israel's history', in D. Edelman (ed.) *The Fabric of History: Text, Artifact and Israel's Past*, Sheffield: Sheffield Academic Press.

—— (1993) *The History of Ancient Palestine from the Palaeolithic Period to Alexander's Conquest*, Sheffield: JSOT.

Ahlström, G.W. and Edelman, D. (1985) 'Merneptah's Israel', *JNES* 44: 59–61.

Albrektson, B. (1967) *History and the Gods: An Essay on the Idea of Historical Events as Divine Manifestations*, Lund: C.W.K. Gleerup.

Albright, W.F. (1942) 'Why the Near East needs the Jews', *New Palestine* 32 (9): 12–13.

—— (1949) *The Archaeology of Palestine*, Harmondsworth: Penguin Books.

—— (1957) *From the Stone Age to Christianity: Monotheism and the Historical Process*, New York: Doubleday.

—— (1966) *Archaeology, Historical Analogy, and Early Biblical Tradition*, Baton Rouge: Louisiana State University.

Alcalay, A. (1993) *After Jews and Arabs: Remaking Levantine Culture*, Minneapolis: University of Minnesota Press.

Alt, A. (1959) 'Der Rhythmus der Geschichte Syriens und Pälastinas im Alterum', in *Kleine Schriften zur Geschichte des Volkes Israel*, Vol. 3, München: C.H. Beck'sche Verlagsbuchhandlung.

—— (1966) *Essays on Old Testament History and Religion*, Blackwell: Oxford.

Alter, R. (1973) 'The Masada complex', *Commentary* 56: 19–24.

—— (1982) *The Art of Biblical Narrative*, London: Allen & Unwin.

Anderson, B. (1991) *Imagined Communities: Reflections on the Origin and Spread of Nationalism*, London: Verso.

Antonius, G. (1969) *The Arab Awakening: The Story of the Arab National Movement*, Beirut: Lebanon Bookshop.

Arnold, P.M. (1990) *Gibeah: The Search for a Biblical City*, Sheffield: JSOT.

Asad, Talal (ed.) (1973) *Anthropology and the Colonial Encounter*, London: Ithaca.

—— (1975) 'Anthropological text and ideological problems: an analysis of Cohen on Arab villages in Israel', *Economy and Society* 4: 251–82.

—— (1993) *Geneaologies of Religion: Discipline and Reasons of Power in Christianity and Islam*, Baltimore: Johns Hopkins University Press.

Ash, M. (1990) 'William Wallace and Robert the Bruce. The life and death of a national myth', in R. Samuel and P. Thomson (eds) *The Myths We Live By*, London: Routledge.

Avigad, N. (1980) *Discovering Jerusalem*, New York: Thomas Nelson.

Baly, D. (1974) *The Geography of the Bible*, Guildford: Lutterworth Press.

—— (1984) 'The geography of Palestine and the Levant in relation to its history', in W.D. Davies and L. Finkelstein (eds) *The Cambridge History of Judaism*. Vol. 1: *Introduction: The Persian Period*, Cambridge: Cambridge University Press.

Bellah, R.N. (1976) 'New religious consciousness and the crisis in modernity', in C.Y. Glock and R.N. Bellah (eds) *The New Religious Consciousness*, Berkeley: University of California Press.

Bernal, M. (1987) *Black Athena: The Afroasiatic Roots of Classical Civilization*, New Brunswick: Rutgers University Press.

Berofsky, R. (1987) *Making History. Pukapuka and Anthropological Constructions of Knowledge*, Cambridge: Cambridge University Press.

Bhabha, H. (ed.) (1990) *Nation and Narration*, London: Routledge.

Bimson, J. (1989) 'The origins of Israel in Canaan: an examination of recent theories', *Themelios* 15: 4–15.

—— (1991) 'Merenptah's Israel and recent theories of Israelite origins', *Journal for the Study of the Old Testament* 49: 3–29.

Biran, A. (ed.) (1985) *Biblical Archaeology Today. Proceedings of the International Congress on Biblical Archaeology*, Jerusalem, April 1984, Jerusalem: Israel Exploration Society.

Biran, A. and Naveh, J. (1993) 'An Aramaic stele fragment from Tel Dan', *Israel Exploration Journal* 43: 81–98.

Bloch, M. (1954) *The Historian's Craft*, Manchester: Manchester University Press.

Bohannan, P. (1967) 'Concepts of time among the Tiv of Nigeria', in J. Middleton (ed.) *Myths and Cosmos. Readings in Mythology and Symbolism*, Austin: University of Texas Press.

Bond, G.C. and Gilliam, A. (1994) *Social Construction of the Past. Representation as Power*, London: Routledge.

Bowerstock, G.W. (1988) 'Palestine: ancient history and modern politics', in E. Said (ed.) *Blaming the Victims: Spurious Scholarship and the Palestinian Question*, London: Verso.

Braudel, F. (1972) *The Mediterranean and the Mediterranean World in the Age of Philip II*, Vol. 1, London: Collins.

—— (1980) *On History*, London: Weidenfeld & Nicolson.

—— (1984) *Civilisation and Capitalism 15th–18th Century*. Vol. III: *The Perspective of the World*, London: Collins.

—— (1989) *The Identity of France*. Vol. 1: *History and Environment*, London: Fontana.

—— (1990) *The Identity of France*. Vol. 2: *People and Production*, London: Collins.

Bright, J. (1960) *A History of Israel*, London: SCM.

—— (1972) *A History of Israel*, 2nd edn, London: SCM.

—— (1976) 'The organization and administration of the Israelite empire', in F.M. Cross (ed.) *Magnalia Dei. The Mighty Acts of God*, New York: Doubleday.

—— (1981) *A History of Israel*, 3rd rev. edn, London: SCM.

Callaway, J.A. (1969) 'The 1966 'Ai (et-Tell) excavations', *BASOR* 196: 2–16.

—— (1970) 'The 1968–1969 'Ai (et-Tel) excavations', *BASOR* 198: 7–31.

Callaway, J.A. and Cooley, R.E. (1971) 'A salvage excavation at Raddana, in Bireh', *BASOR*, 201: 9–19.

Campbell, J. (1962) *Oriental Mythology (The Masks of God)*, New York: Viking.

Carneiro, R.L. (1970) 'A theory of the origins of the state', *Science* 169: 733–8.

Carroll, R.P. (1991) 'Textual strategies and ideology in the second Temple period', in P.R. Davies (ed.) *Second Temple Studies 1. Persian Period*, Sheffield: Sheffield Academic Press.

Césaire, A. (1972) *Discourse on Colonialism*, New York: Monthly Review Press.

Chakrabarty, D. (1992) 'Postcoloniality and the artifice of history: who speaks for "Indian" pasts?', *Representations* 37: 1–26.

Chaney, M. (1983), 'Ancient Palestinian peasant movements and the formation of premonarchic Israel', in D.N. Freedman and D.F. Graf (eds) *Palestine in Transition. The Emergence of Ancient Israel*, Sheffield: Almond Press.

Chomsky, N. (1983) *The Fateful Triangle. The United States, Israel and the Palestinians*, Boston: South End Press.

Cipolla, C.M. (1969) *Literacy and Development in the West*, Harmondsworth: Penguin.

Claessen, H.J.M. and Skalnik, P. (1978) *The Early State*, The Hague: Mouton.

—— (1981) *The Study of the State*, The Hague: Mouton.

Clarke, D. (1973) 'Archaeology: the loss of innocence', *Antiquity* 48: 6–18.

Clements, R.E. (1983) *A Century of Old Testament Study*, Guildford: Lutterworth Press.

—— (1989) 'Israel in its historical and cultural setting', in R.E. Clements (ed.) *The World of Ancient Israel. Sociological, Anthropological and Political Perspectives*, Cambridge: Cambridge University Press.

Cohen, A. (1965) *Arab Border-Villages in Israel: A Study of Continuity and Change in Social Organization*, Manchester: Manchester University Press.

Cohen, R. and Service, E.R. (1978) *Origins of the State*, Philadelphia: Institute for the Study of Human Issues.

Cohen, S.D. (1982) 'Masada: literary tradition, archaeological remains, and the credibility of Josephus', *Journal of Jewish Studies* 33: 385–405.

Coogan, M.D. (1987) 'Canaanite origins and lineage: reflections on the religion of ancient Israel', in P.D. Miller, P.D. Hanson, and S.D. McBride (eds) *Ancient Israelite Religion*, Philadelphia: Fortress Press.

Coote, R.B. (1990) *Early Israel: A New Horizon*, Minneapolis: Fortress Press.

—— (1991) 'Early Israel', *Scandinavian Journal of the Old Testament* 2: 35–46.

Coote, R.B. and Coote, M.P. (1990) *Power, Politics and the Making of the Bible. An Introduction*, Minneapolis: Fortress Press.

Coote, R.B. and Ord, D.R. (1989) *The Bible's First History*, Philadelphia: Fortress Press.

—— (1991) *In the Beginning. Creation and the Priestly Writer*, Minneapolis: Fortress Press.

Coote, R.B. and Whitelam, K.W. (1987) *The Emergence of Early Israel in Historical Perspective*, Sheffield: Almond Press/Sheffield Academic Press.

Cross, F.M. (1973) *Canaanite Myth and Hebrew Epic: Essays in the History of the Religion of Israel*, Cambridge: Harvard University Press.

Cryer, F. (1994) 'On the recently-discovered "House of David" inscription', *Scandinavian Journal of the Old Testament* 8: 3–19.

Dar, S. (1986) *Landscape and Pattern. An Archaeological Survey of Samaria 800 BCE–636 CE, with a Historical Commentary by Shimon Applebaum*, Part 1, Oxford: BAR.

Davies, P.R. (1985) 'Review of H. Jagersma, A History of Israel in the Old Testament Period', *Journal of Theological Studies* 36: 168–72.

—— (1987) 'The history of ancient Judah and Israel', *Journal for the Study of the Old Testament* 39: 3–4.

—— (1991) 'Sociology and the Second Temple', in P.R. Davies (ed.) *Second Temple Studies 1. Persian Period*, Sheffield: Sheffield Academic Press.

—— (1992) *In Search of 'Ancient Israel'*, Sheffield: JSOT.

—— (1994) '"House of David" built on sand: the sin of the biblical maximizers', *Biblical Archaeology Review* 20: 54–5.

Desborough, V.R. (1972) *The Greek Dark Ages*, London: Benn.

Dever, W.G. (1985) 'Syro–Palestinian and biblical archaeology', in D.A. Knight and G.M. Tucker (eds) *The Hebrew Bible and its Modern Interpreters*, Philadelphia: Fortress Press.

—— (1987) 'The contribution of archaeology to the study of Canaanite and early Israelite religion', in P.D. Miller, P.D. Hanson, and S.D. McBride (eds) *Ancient Israelite Religion*, Philadelphia: Fortress Press.

—— (1991) 'Archaeological data on the Israelite settlement: a review of two recent works', *BASOR* 284: 77–90.

—— (1992) 'Archaeology and the Israelite "Conquest"', *The Anchor Bible Dictionary*, New York: Doubleday.

—— (1993) 'Syro–Palestinian archaeology "comes of age": the inaugural volume of the Heshban series. A review article', *BASOR* 290–1: 127–130.

Dharwadker, V. (1993) 'Orientalism and the study of Indian literatures', in C.A. Breckenridge and P. van der Veer (eds) *Orientalism and the Postcolonial Predicament*, Philadelphia: University of Pennsylvania.

Dietrich, W. (1972) *Prophetie und Geschichte*, Göttingen: Vandenhoeck & Ruprecht.

Dothan, M. (1985) 'Terminology for the archaeology of the biblical periods', in A. Biran (ed.) *Biblical Archaeology Today. Proceedings of the International Congress on Biblical Archaeology*, Jerusalem, April 1984, Jerusalem: Israel Exploration Society.

—— (1989) 'Archaeological evidence for movements of the early "Sea Peoples" in Canaan', in S. Gitin and W.G. Dever (eds) *Recent Excavations in Israel: Studies in Iron Age Archaeology*, Winona Lake: ASOR/Eisenbrauns.

Dothan, T. (1982) *The Philistines and their Material Culture*, New Haven: Yale University Press.

—— (1989) 'The arrival of the Sea Peoples: cultural diversity in early Iron Age Canaan', in S. Gitin and W.G. Dever (eds) *Recent Excavations in Israel: Studies in Iron Age Archaeology*, Winona Lake: ASOR/Eisenbrauns.

Dothan, T. and Dothan, M. (1992) *People of the Sea. The Search for the Philistines*, New York: Macmillan.

Eberhard, W. (1965) *Conquerors and Rulers. Social Forces in Medieval China*, Leiden: Brill.

Edelman, D. (ed.) (1991) *The Fabric of History: Text, Artifact and Israel's Past*, Sheffield: JSOT.

Eden, C. (1989) 'Review of *The Emergence of Early Israel in Historical Perspective* by R.B. Coote and K.W. Whitelam and *The Archaeology of the Israelite Settlement* by I. Finkelstein', *American Journal of Archaeology* 93: 289–92.

Elon, A. (1983) *The Israelis: Founders and Sons*, Harmondsworth: Penguin.

—— (1994) 'Politics and archaeology', *The New York Review* 2 September 14–18.

Elton, G.R. (1983) 'Two kinds of history', in R.W. Fogel and G.R. Elton (eds) *Which Road to the Past? Two Views of History*, New Haven: Yale University Press.

Emerton, J.A. (1988) 'Review of G.W. Ahlström, *Who Were the Israelites?*', *Vetus Testamentum* XXXVIII: 372–3.

Eslinger, L. (1985) *Kingship of God in Crisis: A Close Reading of 1 Samuel 1–12*, Sheffield: Almond Press.

—— (1989) *Into the Hands of the Living God*, Sheffield: Almond Press.

Esse, D.L. (1991) 'The collared store jar: scholarly ideology and ceramic typology', *Scandinavian Journal of the Old Testament* 2: 99–116.

Fabian, J. (1983) *Time and the Other. How Anthropology Makes its Object*, New York: Columbia University Press.

Febvre, L. (1973) *A New Kind of History and Other Essays*, New York: Harper Torch Books.

Finkelstein, I. (1985a) 'Excavations at Shiloh 1981–1984: preliminary report', *Tel Aviv* 12: 123–80.

—— (1985b) 'Response', in A. Biran (ed.) *Biblical Archaeology Today. Proceedings of the International Congress on Biblical Archaeology*, Jerusalem, April 1984, Jerusalem: Israel Exploration Society.

—— (1988) *The Archaeology of the Israelite Settlement*, Jerusalem: Israel Exploration Society.

—— (1989) 'The emergence of the Israelite monarchy: the environmental and socio-economic aspects', *Journal for the Study of the Old Testament* 44: 43–74.

—— (1991) 'The emergence of Israel in Canaan: consensus, mainstream and dispute', *Scandinavian Journal of the Old Testament* 2: 47–59.

Flanagan, J. (1988) *David's Social Drama. A Hologram of Israel's Early Iron Age*, Sheffield: Almond Press.

Fogel, R.W. (1983) '"Scientific" history and traditional history', in R.W. Fogel and G.R. Elton (eds) *Which Road to the Past? Two Views of History*, New Haven: Yale University Press.

Fokkelmann, J.P. (1981) *Narrative Art and Poetry in the Books of Samuel: A Full Interpretation Based on Stylistic and Structural Analysis*. Vol. 1: *King David (2 Samuel 9–20 and 1 Kings 1–2)*, Assen: Van Gorcum.

—— (1986) *Narrative Art and Poetry in the Books of Samuel: A Full Interpretation Based on Stylistic and Structural Analysis*, Vol. 2: *The Crossing Fates*, Assen: Van Gorcum.

Foucault, M. (1984) 'Nietzsche, genealogy and history', in P. Rabinow (ed.) *The Foucault Reader*, Harmondsworth: Penguin.

Freedman, D.N. (1989) 'W.F. Albright as historian', in G. van Beek (ed.) *The Scholarship of William Foxwell Albright: An Appraisal*, Atlanta: Scholars Press.

Frick, F.S. (1985) *The Formation of the State in Ancient Israel. A Survey of Models and Theories*, Sheffield: Almond Press.

Fritz, V. (1987) 'Conquest or settlement? The early Iron Age in Palestine', *Biblical Archaeologist* 50: 84–100.

Gal, Z. (1982) 'The settlement of Issachar: some new observations', *Tel Aviv* 9: 79–86.

—— (1992) *Lower Galilee during the Iron Age*, Winona Lake: Eisenbrauns.

Garbini, G. (1988) *History and Ideology in Ancient Israel*, London: SCM.

Garsiel, M. and Finkelstein, I. (1978) 'The westward expansion of the house of Joseph in the light of 'Izbet Sartah excavations', *Tel Aviv* 5: 192–8.

Gellner, E. (1964) *Thought and Change*, London: Weidenfeld & Nicolson.

—— (1992) *Postmodernism, Reason and Religion*, London: Routledge.

Goody, J. (1968) *Literacy in Traditional Societies*, London: Cambridge University Press.

Gottwald (1979) *The Tribes of Yahweh. A Sociology of the Religion of Liberated Israel, 1250–1050 B.C.E*, London: SCM.

—— (ed.) (1986) *Social Scientific Criticism of the Hebrew Bible and its Social World: The Israelite Monarchy, Semeia* 37, Crico: Scholars Press.

Gould, S.J. (1987) *Time's Arrow, Time's Cycle: Myth and Metaphor in the Discovery of Geological Time*, Harmondsworth: Penguin.

Guha, R. (ed.) (1982–) *Subaltern Studies: Writings on South Asian History and Society*, Oxford: Oxford University Press.

Guha, R. and Spivak, G.C. (eds) (1988) *Selected Subaltern Studies*, Oxford: Oxford University Press.

Gunn, D.M. (1978) *The Story of King David: Genre and Interpretation*, Sheffield: JSOT.

—— (1987) 'New directions in the study of biblical narrative', *Journal for the Study of the Old Testament* 39: 65–75 .

—— (1980) *The Fate of King Saul: An Interpretation of a Biblical Story* Sheffield: JSOT.

Haas, J. (1982) *The Evolution of the Prehistoric State*, New York: Columbia University Press.

Halpern, B. (1988) *The First Historians. The Hebrew Bible and History*, San Francisco: Harper & Row.

Harris, W.V. (1989) *Ancient Literacy*, Cambridge: Harvard University Press.

Hauer, C. (1986) 'From Alt to anthropology: the rise of the Israelite state' *Journal for the Study of the Old Testament* 36: 3–15.

Hayes, J. (1987) 'On reconstructing Israelite history', *Journal for the Study of the Old Testament* 39: 5–9.

Hayes, J. and Miller, J.M. (1977) *Israelite and Judaean History*, London: SCM.

Herrmann, S. (1975) *A History of Israel in Old Testament Times*, London: SCM.

—— (1984) 'King David's state', in W.B. Barrick and J.R. Spencer (eds) *In the Shelter of Elyon. Essays on Ancient Palestinian Life and Literature in Honor of G.W. Ahlström*, Sheffield: JSOT.

Hobsbawm, E.J. (1990) *Nations and Nationalism since 1780: Programme, Myth, Reality*, Cambridge: Cambridge University Press.

Hughes, J. (1990) *Secrets of the Times: Myth and History in Biblical Chronology*, Sheffield: Sheffield Academic Press.

Hutteröth, W.D. and Abdulfattah, K. (1977) *Historical Geography of Palestine, Transjordan and Southern Syria in the Late 16th Century*, Erlangen: Fränkische Geographische Gesellschaft.

Iggers, G. (1980) 'Introduction: the transformation of historical studies in historical perspective', in G. Iggers and H.T. Parke (eds) *International Handbook of Historical Studies. Contemporary Research and Theory*, London: Methuen.

Inden, R. (1986) 'Orientalist constructions of India', *Modern Asian Studies* 20: 401–46.

—— (1990) *Imagining India*, Oxford: Blackwell.

Jamieson-Duke, D.W. (1991) *Scribes and Schools in Monarchic Judah. A Socio-archaeological Approach*, Sheffield: Almond Press.

Johnson, R. (1982) *Making History*, London: Hutchinson.

BIBLIOGRAPHY

Jones, G.D. and Kautz, R.R. (1981) *The Transition to Statehood in the New World*, Cambridge: Cambridge University Press.

Keeton, W.T. (1967) *Biological Science*, New York: W.W. Norton.

Kennedy, P. (1988) *The Rise and Fall of the Great Powers. Economic Change and Military Conflict from 1500 to 2000*, London: Fontana.

Kenyon, K. (1979) *Archaeology in the Holy Land*, London: Benn.

Khalidi, W. (1971) *From Haven to Conquest. Readings in Zionism and the Palestinian Problem until 1948*, Beirut: Institute of Palestine Studies.

—— (1984) *Before their Diaspora*, Washington: Institute of Palestine Studies.

Knauf, E.A. (1988) *Midian: Untersuchungen zur Geschichte Palästins und Nordarabiens am Ende des 2ten Jahrtausends*, Wiesbaden: O. Harrassowitz.

—— (1989) *Ishmael: Untersuchungen zur Geschichte Palästins und Nordarabiens im des 1sten Jahrtausends vChr*, Wiesbaden: O. Harrassowitz.

Knight, D.A. (ed.) (1982) *Julius Wellhausen and his Prolegomena to the History of Israel*, *Semeia*, 25 Chico: Scholars Press.

Kochavi, M. (1972) *Judea, Samaria, and the Golan: Archaeological Survey 1967–1968*, Jerusalem: Carta.

Kray, H. (1991) 'Gott und Krieg, Nation und Geschichte. Zeitgeschichtliche Einflüsse auf die Rekonstruktion der Geschichte Israels in der deutsche alttestamentliche Forschungsgeschichte von 1870–1971 von Julius Wellhausen bis Gerhard von Rad', unpublished thesis, University of Heidelberg

Kuper, A. (1973) *Anthropology and Anthropologist: The Modern British School*, London: Routledge & Kegan Paul

Lapp, P. (1965) 'Tell el-Ful', *Biblical Archaeologist* 28: 2–10.

Laqueur, W. (1972) *A History of Zionism*, New York: Schocken Books.

Laqueur, W. and Rubin, B. (eds) (1984) *The Israel and Arab Reader: A Documentary History of the Middle East Conflict*, New York: Penguin.

Leach, E. (1983) 'Anthropological approaches to the study of the Bible during the twentieth century', in E. Leach and D.A. Laycock (eds) *Structuralist Interpretation of Biblical Myth*, Cambridge: Cambridge University Press.

Lemaire, A (1994) '"House of David" restored in Moabite inscription', *Biblical Archaeologist Review* 20: 30–7.

Lemche, N.P. (1984) 'On the problem of studying Israelite history: apropos Abraham Malamat's view of historical research', *Biblische Notizen* 24: 94–124.

—— (1985) *Early Israel. Anthropological and Historical Studies in the Israelite Society before the Monarchy*, Leiden: Brill.

—— (1988) *Ancient Israel. A New History of Israelite Society*, Sheffield: JSOT.

—— (1991a) 'Sociology, text and religion as key factors in understanding the emergence of Israel in Canaan', *Scandinavian Journal of the Old Testament* 2: 7–18.

—— (1991b) *The Canaanites and their Land: The Tradition of the Canaanites*, Sheffield: JSOT.

—— (1994) 'Is it still possible to write a history of ancient Israel?', *Scandinavian Journal of the Old Testament* 8: 165–90.

Lestocquoy, J. (1968) *Histoire du patriotisme français des origines à nos jours*, Paris: A. Michel.

Levinson, M. (1989) 'Introduction' in M. Levinson, M. Butler, J. McGann, and P. Hamilton (eds) *Rethinking Historicism: Critical Readings in Romantic History*, Oxford: Blackwell.

London, G. (1989) 'A comparison of two contemporary lifestyles of the late second Millennium B.C.', *BASOR* 273: 37–55.

Long, B.A. (n.d.) 'Response to Van Seters', Society of Biblical Literature Annual Meeting, San Francisco, November 1992.

—— (1987) 'On finding the hidden premises', *Journal for the Study of the Old Testament* 39: 10–14.

Lord, A.B. (1965) *The Singer of Tales*, New York: Atheneum.

Lowenthal, D. (1985) *The Past as Foreign Country*, Cambridge: Cambridge University Press.

McEvedy, C. and Jones, R. (1978) *Atlas of World Population History*, London: Allen & Unwin.

McNeill, W. (1961) 'Some basic assumptions of Toynbee's *A Study of History*', in E.T. Gargan (ed.) *The Intention of Toynbee's History: A Cooperative Appraisal*, Chicago: Loyola University Press.

—— (1982) 'A defence of world history (the Prothero lecture)', *Transactions of the Royal Historical Society* 32: 75–89.

McPhee, J. (1980) *Basin and Range*, New York: Farrar, Straus & Giroux.

Malamat, A. (1983) 'The proto-history of Israel: a study in method', in C. Meyers and M. O' Connor (eds) *The Word of the Lord Shall Go Forth. Essays in Honor of David Noel Freedman in Celebration of His Sixtieth Birthday*, Winona Lake: Eisenbrauns.

Mannheim, K. (1985) *Ideology and Utopia: An Introduction to the Sociology of Knowledge*, London: Routledge.

Martin, J.D. (1989) 'Israel as a tribal society', in R.E. Clements (ed.) *The World of Ancient Israel. Sociological, Anthropological and Political Perspectives*, Cambridge: Cambridge University Press.

Mayes, A.D.H. (1983) *The Story of Israel between Settlement and Exile: A Redactional Study of the Deuteronomistic History*, London: SCM.

Mazar, A. (1981) 'Giloh: an early Israelite settlement site near Jerusalem', *Israel Exploration Journal* 31: (1–36).

—— (1982) 'Three Israelite sites in the hills of Judah and Israel', *Biblical Archaeologist* 45: 167–78.

—— (1984) 'The "Bull Site" – an Iron Age I open cult site', *BASOR* 247: 27–42.

—— (1990) *Archaeology of the Land of the Bible: 10,000–586 B.C.E.*, London: Doubleday.

Mazar, B. (1984) 'Archaeological research on the period of the monarchy (Iron Age II)', in H. Shanks and B. Mazar (eds) *Recent Archaeology in the Land of Israel*, Washington, DC: Biblical Archaeology Society.

Mendenhall, G.E. (1962) 'The Hebrew conquest of Palestine', *Biblical Archaeologist* 25: 66–87.

—— (1973) *The Tenth Generation: The Origins of the Biblical Tradition*, Baltimore: Johns Hopkins University Press.

—— (1975) 'The monarchy', *Interpretation* 29: 155–70.

—— (1983) 'Ancient Israel's hyphenated history', in D.N. Freedman and D.F. Graf (eds) *Palestine in Transition. The Emergence of Ancient Israel*, Sheffield: Almond Press.

Meyers, C. (1987) 'The Israelite empire: in defense of King Solomon', in M.P. O' Connor and D.N. Freedman (eds) *Backgrounds for the Bible*, Winona Lake: Eisenbrauns.

Millard, A.R. (1991) 'Texts and archaeology: weighing the evidence. The case for King Solomon', *PEQ* Jan.–Dec.: 19–27.

Miller, J.M. (1977) 'The Israelite occupation of Canaan', in J. Hayes and J.M. Miller (eds) *Israelite and Judaean History*, London: SCM.

—— (1987) 'In defense of writing a history of Israel', *Journal for the Study of the Old Testament* 39: 53–7.

—— (1991a) 'Is it possible to write a history of Israel without relying on the Hebrew Bible?', in D. Edelman (ed.) *The Fabric of History: Text, Artifact and Israel's Past*, Sheffield: JSOT.

—— (1991b) 'Solomon: International Potentate or Local King?,' *PEQ* Jan.–Dec.: 28–31.

Miller, J.M. and Hayes, J. (1986) *A History of Ancient Israel and Judah*, London: SCM.

Miller, P.D., Hanson, P.D., and McBride, S.D. (eds) (1987) *Ancient Israelite Religion*, Philadelphia: Fortress Press.

Momigliano, A. (1990) *The Classical Foundations of Modern Historiography*, Berkeley: University of California Press.

Muslih, M.Y. (1988) *The Origins of Palestinian Nationalism*, New York: Columbia University Press.

Nar-Zohar, M. (1978) *Ben-Gurion: A Biography*, New York: Delacourt.

Nelson, R.D. (1981) *The Double Redaction of the Deuteronomistic History*, Sheffield: JSOT.

Noth, M. (1960) *The History of Israel*, London: Adam & Charles Black.

—— (1981) *The Deuteronomistic History*, Sheffield: JSOT.

O'Gorman, E. (1961) *The Invention of America*, Bloomington: Indiana University Press.

Olmstead, A.T.E. (1931) *History of Palestine and Syria to the Macedonian Conquest*, New York: Charles Scribner & Sons.

Ong, W. (1982) *Orality and Literacy: The Technologizing of the Word*, London: Methuen.

Paterson, L. (1991) *Change and the Subject of History*, London: Routledge.

Paton, L.B. (1901) *The Early History of Syria and Palestine*, New York: Charles Scribner & Sons

Peters, J. (1984) *From Time Immemorial*, San Francisco: Harper & Row.

Pocock, D.F. (1967) 'The anthropology of time-reckoning', in J. Middleton (ed.) *Myth and Cosmos. Readings in Mythology and Symbolism*, Austin: University of Texas Press.

Pollock, S. (1992) 'Deep Orientalism? Notes on Sanskrit and power beyond the Raj', in C.A. Breckenridge and P. van der Veer (eds) *Orientalism and the Postcolonial Predicament*, Philadelphia: University of Pennsylvania.

Polzin, R. (1980) *Moses and the Deuteronomist: A Literary Study of the Deuteronomistic History*. Part 1: *Deuteronomy, Joshua, Judges*, New York: Seabury Press.

—— (1989) *Samuel and the Deuteronomist: A Literary Study of the Deuteronomistic History*. Part 2: *1 Samuel*, San Francisco: Harper & Row.

Prakash, G. (1990) 'Writing post-orientalist histories of the Third World: perspectives from Indian historiography', *Comparative Studies in Society and History* 32: 383–408.

Rainey (1982) 'Translator's Preface', in Y. Aharoni, *The Archaeology of the Land of Israel: From the Prehistoric Beginnings to the End of the First Temple Period*, London: SCM.

—— (1988) 'Historical geography', in J. Drinkard, G. Mattingly, and J.M. Miller (eds) *Benchmarks in Time and Culture: Essays in Honor of Joseph A. Callaway*, Atlanta: Scholars Press.

—— (1994) 'The "House of David" and the house of the deconstructionists', *Biblical Archaeology Review* 20: 47.

Ramsey, G.W. (1982) *The Quest for the Historical Israel: Reconstructing Israel's Early History*, London: SCM.

Redford, D.B. (1985) 'The relations between Egypt and Israel from El-Amarna to the Babylonian conquest', in A. Biran (ed.) *Biblical Archaeology Today. Proceedings of the International Congress on Biblical Archaeology*, Jerusalem, April 1984, Jerusalem: Israel Exploration Society.

Reifenberg, A. (1955) *The Struggle between the Desert and the Sown. Rise and Fall of Agriculture in the Levant*, Jerusalem: Government Press.

Renfrew, C. and Wagstaff, M. (1982) *An Island Polity: The Archaeology of Exploitation in Melos*, Cambridge: Cambridge University Press.

Rogerson, J.R. (1974) *Myth in Old Testament Interpretation*, Berlin: De Gruyter.

—— (1986) 'Was early Israel a segmentary society', *Journal for the Study of the Old Testament* 36: 17–26.

—— (1989) 'Anthropology and the Old Testament', in R.E. Clements (ed.) *The World of Ancient Israel. Sociological, Anthropological and Political Perspectives*, Cambridge: Cambridge University Press.

Rosen, Miriam 'The Last Crusade: British Archaeology in Palestine', unpublished dissertation.

Rowlands, M. (1994) 'The politics of identity in archaeology', in G.C. Bond and A. Gilliam (eds) *Social Construction of the Past. Representation as Power*, London: Routledge.

Running, L.G. and Freedman, D.N. (1975) *William Foxwell Albright: A Twentieth Century Genius*, New York: Morgan Press.

Said, E.W. (1984) 'Orientalism reconsidered', in F. Barker (ed.) *Europe and its Others: Proceedings of the Essex Conference on the Sociology of Literature, July 1984*, Vol. 1, Colchester: University of Essex.

—— (1985) *Orientalism*, Harmondsworth: Penguin.

—— (1986) 'The burdens of interpretation and the question of Palestine', *Journal of Palestine Studies* 61: 29–37.

—— (ed.) (1988) *Blaming the Victims: Spurious Scholarship and the Palestinian Question*, London: Verso.

—— (1991) 'Reflections on twenty years of Palestinian history', *Journal of Palestine Studies* 80: 5–22.

—— (1992) *The Question of Palestine*, London: Vintage.

—— (1993) *Culture and Imperialism*, London: Chatto & Windus.

—— (1994a) *The Politics of Dispossession. The Struggle for Palestinian Self-determination 1969–1994*, London: Chatto & Windus.

—— (1994b) *Representations of the Intellectual. The 1993 Reith Lectures*, London: Vintage.

—— (1995) 'East isn't East', *Times Literary Supplement* 3 February: 3–6.

Said, E.W., Abu-Lughob, I. and J., Hallaj, M., Zureik, E., *et al.* (1988) 'A profile of the Palestinian people', in E.W. Said (ed.) *Blaming the Victims: Spurious Scholarship and the Palestinian Question*, London: Verso.

Samuel, R. (1989) *Patriotism. The Making and Unmaking of British National Identity*, 3 vols, London: Routledge.

Samuel, R. and Thompson, P. (1990) *The Myths We Live By*, London: Routledge.

Sasson, J. (1981) 'On choosing models for recreating Israelite pre-monarchic history', *Journal for the Study of the Old Testament* 21: 3–24.

Schwartz, B., Zerubavel, Y., and Barnett, B. (1986) 'The recovery of Masada: a study in collective memory', *Sociological Quarterly* 27: 147–64.

Seger, J.D. (1985) *Biblical Archaeology Today. Proceedings of the International Congress on Biblical Archaeology*, Jerusalem, April 1984, Jerusalem: Israel Exploration Society.

Shanks, H. (1991) 'When 5613 scholars get together in one place: the annual meeting, 1990', *Biblical Archaeology Review* 17: 62–8.

—— (1994) 'David found at Dan', *Biblical Archaeology Review* 20: 26–39.

Shiloh, Y. (1970) 'The four-room house: its situation and function in the Israelite city', *Israel Exploration Journal* 20: 180–90.

Shohat, E. (1992) 'Antimonies of exile: Said and the frontiers of national narratives', in M. Sprinkler (ed.) *Edward Said: A Critical Reader*, Oxford: Blackwell.

Sidebotham, H. (1918) *England and Palestine: Essays towards the Restoration of the Jewish State*, London: Constable.

Silberman, N.A. (1982) *Digging for God and Country. Exploration in the Holy Land, 1799–1917*, New York: Doubleday.

—— (1989) *Between Past and Present. Archaeology, Ideology, and Nationalism in the Modern Middle East*, New York: Doubleday.

—— (1992) 'Who were the Israelites?', *Archaeology* 45, (2): 22–30.

—— (1993) 'Vision of the future: Albright in Jerusalem, 1919–1929', *Biblical Archaeologist* 56: 8–16.

Skjeggestad, M. (1992) 'Ethnic groups in early Iron Age Palestine', *Scandinavian Journal of the Old Testament* 6: 159–86.

Smend, R. (1971) 'Das Gesetz und die Völker: ein Beitrag zur deuteronomistischen Redaktionsgeschichte', in H.W. Wolff (ed.) *Probleme biblischer Theologie: Gerhard von Rad zum 70. Geburtstag*, München: Chr. Kaiser Verlag.

—— (1982) 'Julius Wellhausen and his prolegomena to the history of Israel', in D.A. Knight (ed.) *Julius Wellhausen and his Prolegomena to the History of Israel Semeia* 25: 1–20, Chico: Scholars Press.

Smith, G.A. (1894) *The Historical Geography of the Holy Land Especially in Relation to the History of Israel and of the Early Church*, London: Hodder & Stoughton.

Snodgrass, A. (1971) *The Dark Ages of Greece. An Archaeological Survey of the Eleventh to the Eighth century B.C.*, Edinburgh: Edinburgh University Press.

—— (1987) *The Archaeology of Greece. The Present State and Future Scope of a Discipline*, Berkeley: University of California Press.

Soggin, J.A. (1977) 'The Davidic–Solomonic kingdom', in J.H. Hayes and J.M. Miller (eds) *Israelite and Judaean History*, London: SCM.

—— (1984) *A History of Israel: From the Beginnings to the Bar Kochba Revolt, AD 135*, London: SCM.

Spivak, G.C. (1988) 'Subaltern studies: deconstructing historiography', in R. Guha and G.C. Spivak (eds) *Selected Subaltern Studies*, Oxford: Oxford University Press.

Swendenburg, T. (1989) 'Occupational hazards: Palestine ethnography', *Cultural Anthropology* 4: 265–72.

Taylor P.J. (1985) *Political Geography. World Economy, Nation State and Locality*, London: Longman.

Thompson, T.L. (1974) *The Historicity of the Patriarchal Narratives: The Quest for the Historical Abraham*, Berlin: De Gruyter.

—— (1987) *The Origin Tradition of Ancient Israel*. Vol. 1, *The Literary Formation of Genesis and Exodus 1–23*, Sheffield: JSOT.

—— (1991) 'Text, context, and referent in Israelite historiography', in D. Edelman (ed.) *The Fabric of History: Text, Artifact and Israel's Past* Sheffield: JSOT.

—— (1992a) *The Early History of the Israelite People: From the Written and Archaeological Sources*, Leiden: Brill.

—— (1992b) 'Palestinian pastoralism and Israel's origins', *Scandinavian Journal of the Old Testament* 6: 1–13.

Tibawi, A.L. (1969a) *British Interests in Palestine*, London: Oxford University Press.

—— (1969b) *A Modern History of Syria: Including Lebanon and Palestine*, London: Macmillan.

Tonkin, E. (1990) 'History and the myth of realism', in R. Samuel and P. Thomson (eds) *The Myths We Live By*, London: Routledge.

—— (1992) *Narrating Our Past: The Social Construction of Oral History*, Cambridge: Cambridge University Press.

Trigger, B. (1984) 'Alternative archaeologies: nationalist, colonialist, imperialist', *Man* 19: 355–70.

van Beek, G. (1989) *The Scholarship of William Foxwell Albright: An Appraisal*, Atlanta: Scholars Press.

van der Veer, P. (1993) 'The foreign hand: orientalist discourse in Sociology and communalism', in C.A. Breckenridge and P. van der Veer (eds) *Orientalism and the Post-colonial Predicament*, Philadelphia: University of Pennsylvania.

van Seters, J. (1975) *Abraham in History and Tradition*, New Haven: Yale University Press.

—— (1983) *In Search of History. Historiography in the Ancient World and the Origins of Biblical History*, New Haven: Yale University Press.

—— (1992) *Prologue to History. The Yahwist as Historian in Genesis*, Louisville: Westminster/John Knox Press.

von Rad, G. (1965) *The Problem of the Hexateuch and Other Essays*, Edinburgh: Black.

Webb, B.G. (1987) *The Book of Judges. An Integrated Reading*, Sheffield: JSOT.

Weinstein, J.M. (1981) 'The Egyptian empire in Palestine: a reassessment', *BASOR* 241: 1–28.

Weippert, H. (1988) *Palästina in vorhellenistischer Zeit. Hanbuch der Archäologie: Vorderasian II/Band I*, München: C.H. Beck'sche Verlagsbuchhandlung.

Weippert, H. and Weippert, M. (1991) 'Die Vorgeschichte Israels in neuem Licht', *Theologische Rundschau* 56: 341–90.

Weippert, M. (1971) *The Settlement of the Israelite Tribes in Palestine. A Critical Survey of Recent Scholarly Debate*, London: SCM.

Wellhausen, J. (1885) *Prolegomena to the History of Israel*, Edinburgh: Black.

Whitelam, K.W. (1986) 'Recreating the history of Israel', *Journal for the Study of the Old Testament* 35: 45–70.

—— (1989) 'Israel's traditions of origin: reclaiming the land', *Journal for the Study of the Old Testament* 44: 19–42.

—— (1991) 'Between history and literature: the social production of Israel's traditions of origin', *Scandinavian Journal of the Old Testament* 2: 60–74.

—— (1994) 'The identity of early Israel: the realignment and transformation of Late Bronze–Iron Age Palestine', *Journal for the Study of the Old Testament* 63: 57–87.

—— (1995a) 'New Deuteronomistic heroes and villains: a response to T.L. Thompson', *Scandinavian Journal of the Old Testament* 9: 97–118.

—— (1995b) 'Sociology or history: toward a (human) history of Palestine', in J. Davies, G. Harvey, and G. Watson (eds) *Words Remembered, Texts Renewed: Essays in Honour of John F.A. Sawyer*, Sheffield: Sheffield Academic Press: 149–66.

Wickham, G. (1990) 'The currency of history for sociology', in S. Kendrick, P. Straw, and D. McCrane (eds) *Interpreting the Past, Understanding the Present*, London: Macmillan.

Wightman, G.J. (1990) 'The myth of Solomon', *BASOR* 228: 5–22.

Wright, G.E. (1950) *The Old Testament against its Environment*, London: SCM.

—— (1960) 'The Old Testament', in G.E. Wright and R.H. Fuller (eds) *The Book of the Acts of God: Christian Scholarship Interprets the Bible*, London: Duckworth.

—— (1962) *Biblical Archaeology*, Philadelphia: Westminster Press.

Yadin, Y. (1966) *Masada: Herod's Fortress and the Zealots' Last Stand*, London: Weidenfeld & Nicolson.

—— (1979) 'Shechem: problems of the early Israelite era', in F.M. Cross (ed.) *Symposia*, Cambridge: ASOR.

—— Yadin, Y., Beck, P., and Ben-Tor, A. (1989) *Hazor III–IV. An Account of the Third and Fourth Seasons of Excavations, 1957–1958*, Jerusalem: Israel Exploration Society.

Young, R. (1990) *White Mythologies: Writing History and the West*, London: Routledge.

Zerubavel, Y. (1994) 'The death of memory and the memory of death: Masada and the holocaust as historical metaphors', *Representations* 45: 72–100.

INDEX